2022/04/04

Dear Nelson

let's tokenize the world

[signature]

Thomas Nägele

THE LEGAL NATURE OF TOKENS

UNDER LIECHTENSTEIN'S TVTG

WITH SPECIAL CONSIDERATION OF THE

TOKEN-CONTAINER-MODEL

{ T }

Dissertation for the Faculty of Law at the Private University in the Principality of Liechtenstein

This dissertation takes into account publications available until 29 April 2021 and was originally published in the German language.

Publisher:	DLT media LLC, Vaduz
Printer:	SuperPromo GmbH, Vaduz
Cover design:	PINK LEMON Anstalt, Vaduz
ISBN:	978-3-9525557-2-9

Foreword

This book considers, in particular, at the legal definition of the “token” in the Token and TT Service Provider Act (TVTG). Liechtenstein’s TVTG was the first framework law to comprehensively govern developments related to blockchain technology under civil law. Technological developments have time and again revolutionised and altered the world throughout history. In most cases, the legal classification of the associated problems represents a major challenge. For this reason, and where required for the sake of better understanding, the necessary technical aspects associated with block-chain and distributed ledger technology (DLT) will be examined.

I would like to thank everyone who helped to make my book a success. The greatest thanks goes to my doctoral supervisor, Univ.-Prof. Mag. Dr Alexander Schopper, who advised me on this piece.

Special thanks goes to Dr Barbara Gant, Rector of the Private University in the Principality of Liechtenstein. She constantly pushed me to finish this book and showed great understanding of the fact that I was writing it whilst also working as a lawyer.

I would also like to thank my friends and colleagues for their extremely valuable conversations, lively academic discussions and critical feedback.

In addition, I would like to thank Dr Thomas Dünser and Philipp Büchel for their critical review of my book.

Enormous thanks to Pablo Coirolo and Elisabeth Frommelt for their corrections.

My final thanks goes to my wife, Jeannine Nägele, and my parents, Thilde Nägele and Johann Potetz-Nägele, who have supported me throughout and whom I was often unable to spend time with.

For this reason, I dedicate this book, with enormous gratitude, to my wife,
Jeannine Nägele.

Overview of contents

Table of contents

List of Figures

Abbreviations

ABGB	Allgemeines Bürgerliches Gesetzbuch (General Civil Code)
Abbrev.	Abbreviation
Para.	Paragraph
AE	Aeternity
AJU	Amt für Justiz des Fürstentums Liechtenstein (Office of Justice of the Principality of Liechtenstein)
AML	Anti-money laundering
App	Application software
Art.	Article
ATH	All-time high
e.g.	for example
BTC	bitcoin
BuA	Bericht und Antrag der Regierung des Fürstentums Liechtenstein (Report and Application of the Government to the Parliament of the Principality of Liechtenstein)
CAP	Consistency, availability and partition
CBDC	Central bank digital currency
CHF	Swiss franc
SCO	Swiss Code of Obligations
SCC	Swiss Civil Code
DAO	Decentralised autonomous organisation
dApp	Decentralised application
DBMS	Database management system
DesG	Designgesetz (Design Act)
DesV	Designverordnung (Design Ordinance)
i.e.	that is

DLT	Distributed ledger technology
DNS	Domain name system
EAN	European Article Number
EIP	Ethereum Improvement Proposal
ENS	Ethereum Name Service
EOA	Externally owned accounts
ERC	Ethereum Request for Comments
EU	European Union
EVM	Ethereum Virtual Machine
EEA	European Economic Area
f.	following page
ff.	following pages
FMA	Liechtenstein Financial Market Authority
Footnote	Footnote
FrWG	Gesetz betreffend die Einführung der Frankenwährung (Act on the introduction of the Swiss franc)
FTS	Follow the Satoshi
GTIN	Global Trade Item Number
GUI	Graphical user interface
P.V.	Prevailing view
Ed.	Editor
ICO	Initial coin offering
a.a.	as amended
in gen.	in general
in part.	in particular
p.t.	pursuant to

ITO	Initial token offerings
KYC	Know your customer
leg. cit.	legis citatae (the cited legal provision)
LJZ	Liechtensteinische Juristenzeitung (Liechtenstein Legal Journal)
MiCA	Markets in Crypto-Assets
m	millions
MGGAF	Ministry of General Government Affairs and Finance
bn	billions
MSchG	Markenschutzgesetz (Trademark Protection Act)
MTF	Multilateral trading facility
NFT	Non-fungible token
No.	Number
OGH	Oberster Gerichtshof des Fürstentums Liechtenstein (Supreme Court of the Principality of Liechtenstein)
öABGB	(österreichisches) Allgemeines Bürgerliches Gesetzbuch ((Austrian) General Civil Code)
OTC	Over-the-counter
P2PKH	Pay-to-public key hash
P2SH	Pay-to-script hash
PIN	Personal identification number
PGR	Personen- und Gesellschaftsrecht (Persons and Companies Act)
PoS	Proof-of-Stake algorithm
PoW	Proof-of-Work algorithm
Dir.	Directive
p.	page(s)
SchlT PGR	Final section of the Persons and Companies Act
SEC	US Securities and Exchange Commission

SPG	Sorgfaltspflichtgesetz (Due Diligence Act)
SPV	Simplified payment verification
PL	Property law
StGB	Strafgesetzbuch (Criminal Code)
StGH	Staatsgerichtshof des Fürstentums Liechtenstein (Constitutional Court of the Principality of Liechtenstein)
STO	Security token offering
TCM	Token-Container-Model
TGE	Token Generating Event
ToG	Topographies Act
TVTG	Token and TT Service Provider Act
i.a.	inter alia
URG	Urheberrechtsgesetz (Copyright Act)
URL	Uniform resource locator
USB	Universal serial bus
USD	US dollar
UTXO	Unspent transaction output
Ord.	Ordinance
TT	Trustworthy technology
e.g.	for example
Cl.	Clause
XBT	bitcoin

PART 1 EXECUTIVE SUMMARY

§ 1 Background

Technological developments have time and again revolutionised and altered the world throughout history. In most cases, the legal classification of the problems associated therewith represents a major challenge.

IT law requires the legal practitioner to have not only an understanding of the law, but also broad knowledge in the field of information technologies. Sometimes, what appear to be complicated IT matters can be classified quite easily from a legal perspective. However, sometimes this is not the case.

In recent years, Liechtenstein has become an even more attractive location for companies in the **financial technology sector** (so-called **FinTechs**). Companies appreciate, in particular, access to the European Economic Area (EEA), the regulatory framework conditions and the often-cited "short distances" in Liechtenstein. FinTechs use new or existing technologies to offer services in the financial sector in a different, frequently more efficient manner. For several years, these new technologies have also increasingly included "**blockchain**" and "**distributed ledger technologies**". Of course, these new technological innovations also result in many legal challenges.

Liechtenstein legislators addressed many of these questions with a framework law, the Token and TT Service Provider Act (TVTG), and other modifications, in particular, the final section of the Liechtenstein Persons and Companies Act. In doing so, they had in mind the digital economy, called the "token economy". The objective of the legislative approach is to create the legal framework for what in some cases are new digital processes. The focus here was on those transactions involving a transfer of assets. The users of these technologies must be able to trust the enforceability of the transactions (transfer protection). Initially, it was assumed that the interesting applications, alongside the cryptocurrencies, were in the financial sector. Soon, however, it became clear that a suitable legal basis was feasible, one that would be capable of a much broader application. In essence, this involved the introduction of a new legal object as a result of the legal definition of the term "token" in the TVTG. It was necessary to introduce a new legal object in order to be able to transfer assets in the same way as securities - but in this case, digitally. For this reason, the token is defined as a sort of "container" that can represent rights and creates the conditions for establishing the connection to the legal subjects. Thus, the TVTG was ground-breaking in that it defined the token for the first time.

§ 2 Subject and purpose

This book focuses on the new legal object introduced by the TVTG, the token and the definition of its features (with the aim of classifying it legally). Only after the legal classification has been completed will it be possible to identify the resulting legal consequences and legal questions.

Firstly, the technological foundations will be explained, mainly using bitcoin, and the three core technologies behind the term "blockchain" will be examined. The legal definition of the token will then be broken down into its individual elements and analysed. The book distinguishes between tokens that do not represent any rights (intrinsic tokens) and those that represent rights (extrinsic tokens) and therefore derive their value from external assets. The "Token-Container-Model" referred to in the title of the book serves to illustrate the representation of rights in tokens. When representing rights in tokens, special attention will be paid to the connection between tokens and the represented right. The proposal of a "tokenisation-clause"[1], in particular, with respect to the representation of rights to property, is intended to answer questions that were only briefly touched upon in the legislative materials. The aim is to ensure adherence to the coordination requirement stipulated in Art. 7 TVTG. The so-called "relationship model" between tokens, TT-identifiers and TT-keys will also be examined in depth. In general, the terms in the TVTG that are necessary to understand the legal definition of the token will be discussed.

The new service providers introduced as a result of the TVTG will only be discussed if they are relevant. For example, the token generator will be discussed when the different ways in which tokens are created are brought up. The physical validator will only be broached when discussing the representation of rights to property.

As a starting point, the question of what the TVTG means by "information" in relation to tokens will be analyzed. Rather than relying predominantly on legal literature, internet sources will be primarily drawn upon. While existing legal literature considers some of the technological foundations, it only scratches the surface of these foundations. This is insufficient for including terms used in practice, such as "private key",

1 The term arose as a result of the analysis and is based on the certificate clause in the Securities Act.

"address", "pay-to-script hash", etc., under the term "TT-identifier". In addition, the approach by Liechtenstein is so far unknown and it is therefore necessary to more precisely analyse the two technological implementations (Bitcoin and Ethereum), which also served as examples for the Government. For this reason, software-related websites, such as github.com, and information technology literature are also used as sources.

The aim of this book is to provide a comprehensive classification of tokens pursuant to the TVTG and - where necessary - other legal foundations.

"The key to identifying and resolving legal problems in modern financial market transactions is [...] precisely determining the factual basis, i.e. the facts that need to be assessed from a legal perspective."[2]

This applies not only in the area of modern financial market transactions, but also, in particular, in the case of the use of "**trustworthy-technologies**" ("**TT**") and the entire TVTG.

Please note that this book relies on the definitions in Art. 2 and the wording of the TVTG. For example, the term "trustworthy-technologies" or the abbreviation "TT" is usually used for blockchain and/or distributed ledger technologies. The term "TT-key" is used instead of "private key".

---

2 SCHWARZ, Globaler Effektenhandel. Eine rechtstatsächliche und rechtsvergleichende Studie zu Risiken, Dogmatik und Einzelfragen des Trading, Clearing und Settlement bei nationalen und internationalen Wertpapiertransaktionen (2016), p. 27.

PART 2 INTRODUCTION

§ 1 Terms and selected technologies

I The three core technologies behind blockchain technology

In order to understand trustworthy-technologies, it is first necessary to understand "blockchain" and the individual technical principles behind it. The three key technological principles for blockchain systems – which will be further explained below – are:

1. peer-to-peer-networks;
2. asymmetric encryption; and
3. hashing.[3]

1 Peer-to-peer network

For application in "trustworthy-technologies", the transactions are not processed via a central entity – such as the server of a financial intermediary (such as a bank) – but rather directly between the connected computers.[4] Here, the type of computer network used plays a crucial role in whether or not the technology can be viewed as trustworthy pursuant to the TVTG.

Computer networks can be classified according to various criteria. One key criterion is the classification according to the method of dividing the work between the network participants. A distinction is made between "client-server networks" and "peer-to-peer networks". Client-server networks are highly centralised networks in which the server provides resources and functions centrally, and clients (the workstations) use them. The central server is the "single point of truth". For this reason, during a bank transaction bank clients effectively have no control over the data statuses for the systems involved.

With peer-to-peer networks, in contrast, the network participants ("clients" or "workstations") generally have equal rights ("peer" may be interpreted as "colleague" or "equivalent body"). Thus, all network participants provide the resources from their

---

3 VAN HIJFTE, Blockchain Platforms. A Look at the Underbelly of Distributed Platforms (2020), p. 33.

4 BUCHLEITNER/RABL, Blockchain und Smart Contracts, ecolex 2017, p. 4.

own computer to the other participants.[5] As a result, each participant is simultaneously a "server" and a "client" and control is exercised by all participants.[6] When information is transferred between the various nodes (participants), the different nodes may have different information statuses (e.g. out-of-date information or consciously modified information). There is no single point of truth.[7] It is therefore essential to know which participants – if any – can be trusted. If there is no central server, there are two ways to create trust. The first way is to ensure that all network participants have the same information (application of a so-called "gossip-protocol") and the second is through concepts based on "local" reputation.[8]

2 Asymmetric encryption

The core element of asymmetric[9] encryption (also known as a "public key process") is a **pair of keys** comprised of a public key and a private key. One key is used for encryption ("public key"), and another one is used for decryption ("private key"). The public key can and should – as the name implies – be known to everyone. In contrast, the private key must be kept secure and can, in simple terms, be viewed as a password. If the recipient's public key is known, any information or message can be encrypted using the public key. This encryption can only be decrypted by the person who has the right private key for the public key with which the message was encrypted. These asymmetric encryption technologies are used in addition to trustworthy-technologies such as blockchain/DLT systems, for example, on the internet (SSL) and for emails (PGP, S/MIME).[10]

3 Hash function

The "hash function" or "**hashing**" refers to the use of certain algorithms to change an input of an arbitrary length or size into an output of a certain length. This output is also referred to as the "hash". It is a **one-way function**, i.e. it should not be possible to determine the original input using the output (the hash). The input is always of an

---

5 KERSKEN, IT-Handbuch für Fachinformatiker[6] (2013), p. 194.

6 VAN HIJFTE, Blockchain Platforms, p. 7.

7 There is no central authority that determines which information status is correct.

8 VAN HIJFTE, Blockchain Platforms, p. 8 f.

9 In contrast to symmetrical encryption, in which the encryption and decryption use the same key. The key must therefore be exchanged securely, which makes it impossible to use as an application, for example, on the internet; see KERSKEN, IT-Handbuch für Fachinformatiker[6], p. 1129.

10 On asymmetric encryption, see KERSKEN, IT-Handbuch für Fachinformatiker[6], p. 1129.

arbitrary length. It may therefore be smaller than the output. The input used could be the length of this entire book and the output would in turn have a character string of at least the same length. Using the same input with the same hash function will yield the same result, the same hash. While defining a certain hash as the target output, and then adding, modifying or deleting characters to adjust the input until an input that yields the desired output is achieved, is possible, it should be as difficult to do as possible.[11] The algorithm used in the following examples to illustrate hashing was SHA-256, which results in an output with a character string of 64 characters:[12]

Using, for example, the input "TVTG" will result in the hash:

24ff016aa0c7112eb726b9bafd3284ba5c4c295e671f95346355fca80dac089e

Entering a space after "TVTG" (i.e. "TVTG ") will result in an entirely different output:

6125f0a50ec78fda456ac0b566913ef4f14f4ad5039525a909c21260fb81bb88

Another example of a relatively short text is the legal definition of token in the original German version in Art. 2, para. 1(c) TVTG.[13] This results in the following hash:

23d602fcbb3bec2200c89039f630e038ae31466e994381f837c54b67d32fab45

Thus, it is clear that hashing is very well suited to reviewing the integrity of data. For this reason, hashing has – as is hardly surprising – been used in IT for some time. If the user knows the input – for example, the entire legislative text of the TVTG – and wants to make sure that it has not changed, the user simply reviews whether the hash function leads to the same result. Therefore, the hash value at the start is compared with the information that is now available.[14] If the hash is the same, then the information has not been changed. The legislative text has therefore not been altered. This makes it possible to compare results (of any size) extremely quickly.[15]

---

11 VAN HIJFTE, Blockchain Platforms, p. 1 f.

12 Anyone can go to, for example, https://emn178.github.io/online-tools/sha256.html and select SHA256 as a hash and enter "TVTG" and achieve the same result.

13 The input used here is a "'token', the information on a TT system that: 1. can represent claims or rights of membership against a person, rights to property or other absolute or relative rights; and 2. are allocated to one or more TT-identifiers."

14 For example, software that is distributed via the internet can be checked to make sure that it has not been modified by a third party, for example, to insert malware into it. Software producers provide the hash values for the files for this purpose.

15 VAN HIJFTE, Blockchain Platforms, p. 33.

A practical example should make the benefits of hashing clear: The amount of data that is being exchanged is constantly growing, and emails usually cannot be sent with relatively large attachments. If a client would for example want to send a lawyer a number of documents electronically as PDF files, often a cloud service such as Google Docs or Dropbox.com is used. But how can the lawyer verify that the data was sent by the client? With email attachments, this is relatively simple. All the lawyer has to do is to look at the original message with the attachments. However, if the client sends an email with no attachments, but instead includes download links, the lawyer may occasionally have trouble verifying that the documents were sent by the client. In many cases, the download links are dynamic links. This means that the client can change the files referenced by the links and the lawyer will be unable to tell that something has been changed. In the worst case, the files can be changed or new files added without the lawyer knowing. One option would be to have the lawyer download the files. The list with the file names and the respective hash values would then be sent by email to the client, who would provide a brief confirmation of receipt. The lawyer can verify each individual file using the hash procedure before providing confirmation. The lawyer can thus be sure that they are using the correct basis for their legal work and, if necessary, that they can provide proof of this.

II Blockchain – how a chain of blocks is created

1 About the terms "blockchain" and "distributed ledger technologies"

Blockchain: The term "blockchain" was developed in connection with the first cryptocurrency, Bitcoin. It has many meanings. Amongst other things, "blockchain" refers to the technology that serves as the basis for various cryptocurrencies, such as bitcoin, ether, dash, aeternity and Litecoin. These cryptocurrencies are structured in different ways technologically, but "blockchain" is used as an overarching term for the technologies behind them.[16] The term "blockchain" is comprised of the words "block" and "chain". The blocks contain the transaction data and are arranged in chronological order and connected, or chained, to one another using a hash (a checksum): This results in a **chain of blocks.**[17]

---

[16] The 2008 white paper on Bitcoin does not refer to a "blockchain", but rather describes the system's operating principle as a "chain of blocks"; see NAKAMOTO (PSEUDONYM), Bitcoin: A Peer-to-Peer Electronic Cash System, https://bitcoin.org/bitcoin.pdf (accessed on 11 April 2020); see also NÄGELE, Sekundärmarkt für Security Tokens, p. 7.

[17] With further references. NÄGELE, Sekundärmarkt für Security Token, p. 7; and, in particular, LANGER/NÄGELE, IWB 2018, p. 1.

The transaction data that is stored in the blocks together forms the (distributed) **ledger (the distributed database),** which in turn provides an overview of the transactions and "account balances". This ledger is saved in a decentralised manner by as many users ("nodes") as possible in order to prevent it from being manipulated by small groups of users. Because the ledger is distributed across as many nodes as possible, some blockchain technologies are also referred to as "distributed ledger technologies".[18]

Distributed ledger technology (DLT): The term "**distributed ledger technology**" – as the name implies – refers to the technology behind distributed ledgers.[19] These are databases that provide data in a decentralised manner – usually distributed throughout the entire world. As a result, there is no central operator or someone with control over the network. However, it is not necessary for the data to be arranged in the form of blocks (blockchain) in order to fall under the term "DLT". For this reason, not all DLT systems are blockchains and not all blockchains are DLT systems. Both DLT systems and blockchain systems use consensus algorithms in order to achieve agreement. The main difference between the terms blockchain and DLT is the way the data is added. [20]

Measured in terms of trading volume, the most used[21] blockchains are the Bitcoin and Ethereum (**ETH – ether/Ethereum**) blockchain. A blockchain developed in Liechtenstein is the Aeternity blockchain.[22]

1.1 Transaction confirmation and the creation of chained blocks

The blockchain, as a chain of blocks, is – in simple terms – created as follows:

1. A participant **signs a transaction** using his private key.
2. Using a **gossip protocol**, the signed **transaction** is **distributed** to other network nodes (peers), who **validate** the transaction based on certain criteria.

[18] On distributed databases, see "Distributed Database" SUNYAEV, Internet Computing. Principles of Distributed Systems and Emerging Internet-Based Technologies[1] (2020), p. 267.

[19] With further references. NÄGELE, Sekundärmarkt für Security Token, p. 7; and, in particular, BuA No. 54/2019, p. 55.

[20] VAN HIJFTE, Blockchain Platforms, p. 37.

[21] Measured in terms of trading volume; COINMARKETCAP, 24-hour volume rankings (currency), https://coinmarketcap.com/currencies/volume/24-hour (accessed on 14 April 2020).

[22] NÄGELE, Sekundärmarkt für Security Token, p. 7 f.

3. Once the transaction is validated, it is **added to a block**, which is then **distributed to the network**. The transaction is then considered to be validated.
4. The new block becomes part of the database (ledger) and the next **block** is **connected** to the previous block **using hashing**. The transaction is thus **confirmed** for a second time, while the block is confirmed for the first time.
5. Every time a new block is confirmed, the previous blocks are confirmed again as well.[23]

One might now ask why blocks are only confirmed once. This is associated with the question of whether transactions using TT-systems are final.

1.2 The question of the finality of transactions

In the financial world, **finality** is an extremely central function and refers to the **time** or the status from which a **transaction** can – both legally and de facto – **be viewed as valid**. Only then is the consideration often paid. In modern transaction systems, fiat money or securities that are received are immediately used again or transferred. Without the status of finality this would not be possible.[24] Vitalik Buterin, the founder of Ethereum, provides a response to critics who state that true finality can never be achieved in blockchain systems, by positing that there is no 100% processing finality in any system, not even in a centralised system. Centralised systems can be attacked and the database altered, central banks can be subject to corruption and securities can be stolen.[25] This is a valid argument, in my opinion, which then means that it is only possible to say with a certain degree of certainty that a transaction can no longer be altered (that it is final). Depending on the TT-system used, from a technical perspective **finality is never achieved**.[26] In my view, this problem, in the case of both traditional and TT-based transaction systems, can only be resolved through a **legal fiction of finality**. The Government of the Principality of Liechtenstein (the

---

23 BASHIR, Mastering Blockchain. Distributed Ledgers, Decentralization and Smart Contracts Explained (2017), p. 24.

24 DEUTSCHE BUNDESBANK, Distributed-Ledger-Technologien im Zahlungsverkehr und in der Wertpapierabwicklung, https://www.bundesbank.de/resource/blob/665446/cfd6e8fbe0f2563b9fc1f48fabda8ca2/mL/2017-09-distributed-ledger-technologien-data.pdf (accessed on 19 January 2021), p. 43.

25 With further references on the blog of the Ethereum Foundation BUTERIN, On Settlement Finality, https://blog.ethereum.org/2016/05/09on-settlement-finality (accessed on 19 January 2021); and VAN HIJFTE, Blockchain Platforms, p. 30.

26 VAN HIJFTE, Blockchain Platforms, p. 30.

"Government") defines the finality of transactions on TT-systems in the legislative materials concerning the TVTG.[27]

For six confirmations of a transaction, the probability of an attacker with less than 25 percent of the hash power in the network successfully "overtaking" the transaction is 0.00137. For 13 confirmations, this probability falls to 0.000001. In practice, the sufficient number of confirmations for Bitcoin, for example, is between 7 and 10 confirmations. The reasoning for this is that a subsequent change – while theoretically possible – would be uneconomical because of the enormous costs involved.[28] One confirmation is viewed as sufficient for small transactions.

There have already been a couple of "reverse settlements" by so-called "forks", for example, in the case of "**the DAO**". The DAO was a decentralised autonomous organisation. This decentralised organisation had no management and no operators in the traditional sense. Financed by an ICO, the DAO token was published. Consequently, security gaps were exploited and assets worth around USD 50 million were withdrawn (known as the "DAO hack").[29] In order to undo this hack, the Ethereum community was polled in July 2016 and 85 percent voted in favour of a fork. The continued use of the old version of the protocol by some miners resulted in "Ethereum Classic". The transactions were thus – to put it in non-technical terms – reversed.[30]

2 Consensus algorithms

An "algorithm" is a step-by-step set of instructions for solving a mathematical problem. The word comes from Arabic mathematician Muhammad Ibn Musa Al-Khwarizmi. All computers understand one or more languages that can be used to program algorithms. If the computer knows an algorithm, the algorithm can be carried out repeatedly on the basis of input and the computer will carry out the step-by-

---

[27] See, in particular, Recital 14, Art. 3, para. 1 and 3; Directive 98/26/EC of the European Parliament and of the Council of 19 May 1998 on settlement finality in payment and securities settlement systems (Finality Directive), OJ EC 1998/166, p. 45.

[28] With further references. NÄGELE, Sekundärmarkt für Security Token, p. 10; and, in particular, BuA No. 54/2019, p. 126; and "Why is it expensive to manipulate the Blockchain" VOSHMGIR, Token Economy. How Blockchains and Smart Contracts Revolutionize the Economy[1] (2019), p. 59.

[29] Details on the DAO hack and the various proposed solutions (hard fork and soft fork) can be found at Coindesk, SIEGEL, The DAO Attack: Understanding What Happened, CoinDesk; on the DAO, see also BÜCH, Die Blockchain und das Recht, LJZ 2018, p. 58.

[30] See also Wikipedia, The DAO (accessed on 19 January 2021, https://en.wikipedia.org/w/index.php?title=The_DAO_(organization)&oldid=991306039).

step instructions and come up with a result. A simple algorithm can, for example, calculate the cost of a book.[31]

- Book form or PDF?
  - Input: PDF -> cost is CHF 19.90, calculation ended.
  - Input: Book form ->
- Would you like a hardcover or softcover?
  - Input: Softcover – cost is CHF 24.90, calculation ended.
  - Input: Hardcover – cost is CHF 28.90, calculation ended.

A consensus algorithm uses processes ("step-by-step instructions") to reach agreement on a certain result or a selection within a group or a network. In the case of the decentralised storage of information, the participants must agree on which data is to be stored. This ensures that everyone has access to the same data and the same information. This also prevents individuals from carrying out a transaction twice and thus being able spend the digital currency (e.g. a cryptocurrency) twice.[32] Blockchain systems mainly use two types of consensus algorithms: the Proof of Work and the Proof of Stake consensus algorithms.

2.1 Proof of Work ("PoW")

The most important consensus algorithm to date, which was also used in the first blockchain – the Bitcoin blockchain – is the Proof of Work ("PoW") algorithm. Over time, PoW has been used in and, in some ways, modified by many other blockchains. PoW provides miners with[33] a **complicated mathematical problem** that they need to solve. The process for finding the solution is referred to as mining. Miners who are successful receive what is called a "**block reward**".[34] They look for the "target hash" set by the network for the next block in the blockchain. In order to ensure that all miners receive a different task, a unique string of characters (called a nonce)[35] is also

---

[31] KERSKEN, IT-Handbuch für Fachinformatiker[6]), p. 34 f.

[32] EIGELSHOVEN/ULLRICH/GRONAU, Konsens-Algorithmen von Blockchain, I40M 2020, p. 30.

[33] This term is taken from the Gold Rush era when miners dug for gold.

[34] EIGELSHOVEN/ULLRICH/GRONAU, I40M 2020, p. 30.

[35] This string of characters also varies for each participant and is only valid once in order to prevent the blocks from being calculated in advance.

provided. The miners use a lot of computing power to randomly test different combinations (also known as the "**brute force** method"[36]) until the solution is found.[37] Because computers are becoming increasingly faster, the system adjusts the problems' level of difficulty. The more computing power the system has ("**hash rate**"), the more difficult the problems become. For Bitcoin, for example, it takes an average of 10 minutes until the next block is "mined". In turn, it is very easy to check whether the hash that has been found is a[38] correct solution to the problem.[39] The first person to find a suitable result is rewarded with the "block reward"; in the case of Bitcoin, the reward is currently 6.25 BTC per block. In the case of Bitcoin, the block reward is halved every four years (known as "Bitcoin halving"), which – in connection with the **maximum number of Bitcoins of 21 million** – will lead to scarcity. The maximum number of 21 million BTC will be reached in the year 2140.[40]

Of course, all of the other miners get nothing for making their computing power available and the resulting (high) energy costs. High energy consumption is one of the key points of criticism of PoW algorithms. However, this (expensive) incentive model ensures the security of blockchain transactions. The miners have little reason to provide incorrect solutions as this will be easily detected and they will receive no reward. Only correct solutions will lead other miners to begin "mining" the next block on the basis (hash) of this blockchain.[41]

It is possible for several miners to find the right solution at the same time. In this case, there will be two blockchains (called a **fork**) for a short period of time. However, this is usually only the case temporarily, as generally **the longest blockchain always continues to be used**. Based on this design, the miners are rewarded for their use of significant computing power with cryptocurrency ("block reward") in order to find the right solution. The transactions in the blocks are irrelevant. This incentive system results in the desired behaviour – the provision of computing power for ensuring the

---

[36] Brute force refers to raw power.

[37] On nonce, see also VÖLKEL, Vertrauen in die Blockchain und das Sachenrecht, ZFR 2020/218, p. 493.

[38] Based on the nonce, each miner must solve a different problem, i.e. there are various solutions to the problem.

[39] See also the remarks on hash function.

[40] On bitcoin halving and the block reward, see HUBER, Bitcoin 2020 – die Halbierung der Blockprämie, https://www.bitcoinsuisse.com/de/outlook/bitcoin-in-2020-halving-the-block-reward-2 (accessed on 7 February 2021).

[41] VAN HIJFTE, Blockchain Platforms, p. 45.

operation of the system. During this process, the results are automatically checked multiple times.

2.2 Proof of Stake ("PoS")

The Proof of Stake ("PoS") algorithm was developed in order to correct several disadvantages of the PoW algorithm. In particular, it reduced the amount of energy consumed, which had led to repeated criticism of PoW. The first PoS algorithm was used for Peercoin in 2012.[42]

"Stake" refers to the idea of having a share or participation in something. As the name implies, the decision regarding who adds the next block to the blockchain is not based on work, as is the case with Proof of Work. Instead, with Proof of Stake it is based on the share that someone is willing to stake. The higher the share of all available protocol tokens (coins) staked by the **validator**, the greater their risk of losing the staked tokens. Thus, they are willing to risk the tokens in order to operate a validator node. While the person making the tokens available operates as a validator, the tokens cannot be used for any other purpose (i.e. they "stake" the tokens, a process known as "**staking**"). Improper behaviour is punished by confiscating tokens. Here, too, an **incentive model** is created in order to obtain the desired behaviour. The simplest form of PoS implementation is known as the "Follow the Satoshi" (FTS) algorithm. Here, a **random generator** is used to choose a token and the token holder is allowed to attach the next block to the blockchain. In return, the token holder receives the block reward.[43]

In the case of **Ethereum 2.0**, ETH 32[44] must be staked in order to operate as a validator. This may seem like a lot, but compared with the initial costs for PoW mining, it is actually fairly low.[45] Based on the number of tokens[46] a network participant is willing to stake, their chance of being selected by the random generator to edit (mine) the next block increases. Depending on the algorithm, there are other criteria used in the selection.[47]

---

42 PEERCOIN, The Pioneer of Proof of Stake, https://www.peercoin.net/ (accessed on 30 April 2021).

43 SALEH, Blockchain Without Waste: Proof-of-Stake (2018), p. 8.

44 On 7 February 2021, this corresponded to a little more than USD 50,000.

45 MUZZY, What Is Proof of Stake? https://consensys.net/blog/blockchain-explained/what-is-proof-of-stake (accessed on 6 February 2021).

46 Or the protocol-specific coins, such as ether for Ethereum.

47 EIGELSHOVEN/ULLRICH/GRONAU, I40M 2020, p. 31.

Consequently, the number of tokens someone is willing to risk (more on this point in a moment) is directly associated with the chance of being selected as the miner of the next block. This algorithm is, of course, much more efficient than PoW. No computing power is "wasted" in order to be selected as the validator and be able to propose the next block and thus receive a reward. With Ethereum 2.0, rewards are provided not only when a block is proposed, but also when "**attestations**" about newly created blocks are provided as well. The block is only added to the blockchain after a certain number of attestations are available. The PoS incentive model also includes a – fairly mild – punishment for validators who do not accept a task because, for example, they are offline. However, if validators attempt to "attack" the blockchain by, for example, proposing incorrect datasets, the PoS algorithm provides for severe punishments (up to the loss of all holdings provided as a stake). In addition, the perpetrator is excluded from the network. Comparing the incentive model, or punishment in the event of undesired behaviour, of PoS and PoW, miners lose the opportunity to receive a block reward in the event of dishonest behaviour. In contrast, for PoS, dishonest miners who attack the blockchain lose the cost of the energy for their (unsuccessful) attack and receive no block reward. The loss of the tokens that have been staked would be similar to the loss of the investment made in all of the mining equipment with the PoW approach. That would give cause for consideration.[48]

Although there is less experience with PoS than with PoW, it can be assumed that PoS is more secure than PoW. Of course, those validators with the most tokens at stake also have the greatest interest in the orderly operation of the network. If unauthorised transactions were to occur (51-per-cent attack), this would harm not only those directly affected, but also the reputation of the entire network and thus the value of all tokens.[49]

48 MUZZY, What Is Proof of Stake?

49 VAN HIJFTE, Blockchain Platforms, p. 46.

§ 2 The development of the first cryptocurrency (Bitcoin) culminating in the TVTG

I The origin of cryptocurrencies

1 The creation of Bitcoin – the birth of the "blockchain" phenomenon

On 31 October 2008 at 2.10 p.m.[50], an unknown cryptographer using the pseudonym **Satoshi Nakamoto** published a discussion paper titled "Bitcoin: A Peer-to-Peer Electronic Cash System".[51] This paper is known as the "Bitcoin white paper". On 3 January 2009, the first block of the Bitcoin blockchain (also called the "genesis block")[52] was "mined" by Satoshi Nakamoto. The first version of a Bitcoin client software was published two days before that. On 12 January, Satoshi Nakamoto transferred 10 bitcoin to software developer Hal Finney. Almost nine months later, bitcoin was exchanged for US dollars for the first time. Based on the amount of energy expended, the exchange rate was BTC 1,392.33 for 1 US dollar.[53] In July 2010, bitcoin was traded on an exchange, called "Mt. Gox", for the first time at an exchange rate of USD 0.06. In February 2011, it reached parity with the US dollar and on 5 June 2017, the average market price was USD 2,820.96[54]. The trading volume on 5 June 2017 was USD 116,503,749.16, with some 270,000 transactions carried out daily. By November 2013, the exchange rate had reached a then-high peak of USD 1,242 and Bitcoin had a market capitalisation of USD 13.5 billion. The first significant price collapse occurred in connection with the insolvency of what was then the largest bitcoin trading platform ("crypto exchange"), Mt. Gox, in February 2014.[55] On 17 December 2017, the exchange rate reached another record level of around USD 19,500, before tumbling back down to USD 3,000 in December of the following year. The exchange rate reached its most recent all-time high ("ATH") on 13 March 2021, at over USD 60,000.[56] Although Bitcoin was developed as a means of payment (hence the term "crypto<u>currency</u>"), the

---

50 Satoshi Nakamoto, Bitcoin P2P e-cash paper, http://www.metzdowd.com/pipermail/cryptography/2008-October/014810.html (accessed on 10 June 2017).

51 Sixt, Bitcoins und andere dezentrale Transaktionssysteme, p. 1.

52 Bitcoin wiki, genesis block, https://en.bitcoin.it/wiki/Genesis_block.

53 Sixt, Bitcoins und andere dezentrale Transaktionssysteme, p. 29.

54 Blockchain.info, Währungs Statistik, https://blockchain.info/de/stats.

55 Deutsche Presse Agentur, Bitcoin-Börse Mt.Gox insolvent, FAZ.

56 CoinMarketCap, Bitcoin (BTC) Kurs, Grafiken, Marktkapitalisierung, https://coinmarketcap.com/de/currencies/bitcoin (accessed on 13 March 2021).

question may be raised as to whether cryptocurrencies like Bitcoin can truly fulfil the function of **money** in practice.

The current forms of money have developed over millennia and must have certain characteristics in order to serve as a:

1. means of payment and exchange,
2. unit of account and
3. store of value.

These are the three key functions of money.[57]

In order to serve as a means of payment and exchange, the money must be accepted by parties.[58] **Legal tender** is defined by law and must be accepted in the jurisdiction. In other words, legal tender cannot be rejected as payment for purchase contracts. Pursuant to Art. 1 FrWG[59], the Swiss franc, as the "Liechtenstein franc", is the sole legal tender in Liechtenstein. The coins, banknotes and other means of payments that are recognised in Switzerland are considered legal tender in Liechtenstein.[60] Consequently, if Switzerland were to introduce a digital Swiss franc on the basis of trustworthy-technologies (known as a central bank digital currency or "CBDC"), this digital currency would also be legal tender in Liechtenstein. There have been multiple points of acceptance for cryptocurrencies, especially bitcoin and ether, in Liechtenstein for some time now. For example, cryptocurrencies can be used as a means of payment for hotels, restaurants and service providers (mainly lawyers and tax advisors).[61]

Money can be used to set the price of goods in relation to one another. Money thus fulfils the function of a unit of account. This makes it possible to objectively **quantify products** and services: A litre of milk costs twice as much as two bread rolls. This

57 See, in particular, FRANK/BERNANKE, Principles of Economics (2001), p. 616 f.; and KOLLER/SEIDEL, Geld war gestern. [wie Bitcoin, Regionalgeld, Zeitbanken und Sharing Economy unser Leben verändern werden][1] (2014), p. 25.

58 KOLLER/SEIDEL, Geld war gestern[1], p. 24 f.

59 Act of 26 May 1924 on the introduction of the Swiss franc (FrWG), Liechtenstein Law Gazette (1924).

60 See Art. 1, para. 2 FrWG.

61 ALBRICH, Unklare Rechtslage noch ein Hindernis für Bitcoin-Automaten, Liechtensteiner Volksblatt; NÄGELE RECHTSANWÄLTE GMBH, on Twitter, https://twitter.com/NaegeleLAW/status/873156452482940930?s=20 (accessed on 23 January 2021).

ability to quantify products and services gave rise to complex and highly collaborative societies.[62] This money function can also be fulfilled by Bitcoin, for example.

The third function of money is the store of value function. As a result of this function, buying and selling does not have to occur at the same time and goods do not have to be exchanged directly.[63]

As already stated, Bitcoin was conceived as a means of payment and is also accepted as a means of payment by some people. Bitcoin fulfils the store of value function and can be used as a unit of account. As Bitcoin does not have inherent value and fulfils all of the functions of money, Bitcoin could also be qualified as fiat money.[64] On the other hand, as of 2021 Bitcoin was not widely accepted as a means of payment. For this reason, bitcoin is currently more similar to gold than to legal currencies.

2 The creation of Ethereum – a smart-contract platform for decentralised applications

The development of Ethereum was a significant step. On 27 November 2013, BUTERIN published a white paper entitled *"Ethereum: A Next-Generation Smart Contract and Decentralized Application Platform"*.[65] He saw the need for what he called a *"public ownership database"* that could do more than function like money. He wanted Ethereum to be a modular system for almost any application in order to enable individual currencies, financial derivatives, identity systems and decentralised organisations and much more through simple programming based on the Ethereum protocol. He also referred to it as the *"Lego of cryptofinance"*.[66] The financing campaign for Ethereum (the Ethereum ICO) took place from 22 July to 2 September 2014. As part of this campaign, it was possible to purchase ethers for bitcoins. Doing so involved the purchase with bitcoins of a token that did not exist yet because the underlying Ethereum protocol had not even been developed.

---

62 KOLLER/SEIDEL, Geld war gestern[1], p. 25.

63 DEUTSCHE BUNDESBANK, Begriff und Aufgaben des Geldes, https://www.bundesbank.de/Redaktion/DE/Dossier/Service/schule_und_bildung_kapitel_1.html?notFirst=true&docId=153022#doc153022bodyText1.

64 BuA No. 54/2019, p. 13.

65 ETHEREUM, History of Ethereum, https://ethereum.org/en/history (accessed on 28 February 2021).

66 BUTERIN, Ethereum white paper, https://web.archive.org/web/20140206034718/http://www.ethereum.org/ethereum.html (accessed on 28 February 2021).

The first version of Ethereum, called Frontier, went live on 30 July 2015. The "DAO hack", which led to an Ethereum "fork", is another notable aspect in the history of Ethereum (see Part 2, Sect. 2, II, 1.2), which gave rise to Ethereum Classic. On 1 December 2020, the Beacon Chain produced the first block and thus took a major step towards Ethereum 2.0, which saw the shift from the Proof of Work algorithm to the Proof of Stake algorithm.[67]

3 The creation of Aeternity – a blockchain protocol that was developed in Liechtenstein

The AETERNITY ANSTALT was entered into the commercial register of the Principality of Liechtenstein on 11 November 2016.[68] Phase 1 of the contribution campaign (ICO) was carried out on 3 April 2017 and Aeternity collected 40,000 ether. Phase 2 then followed in May 2017, during which participants could use both ether and bitcoin.[69] At the end of the second phase on 9 June 2017, the combined value of the ether and bitcoin collected was about USD 62.5 million.[70] Subsequently, Liechtenstein's Aeternity Anstalt developed the Aeternity blockchain with a (crypto) market capitalisation on 8 May 2018 of over USD 1 billion, making it the first "blockchain unicorn" in Liechtenstein.[71] Aeternity made a significant contribution to the development of the Liechtenstein blockchain ecosystem and, in its role as a pioneer, presented many unanswered and new questions to the local authorities for the first time. In addition, Aeternity helped lead the Liechtenstein Government to look at the regulatory questions related to ICOs and other blockchain-related topics relatively early on.

---

67 See also ETHEREUM, History of Ethereum.

68 OFFICE OF JUSTICE OF THE PRINCIPALITY OF LIECHTENSTEIN, commercial register entry for ATERNITY ANSTALT, https://oera.li/cr-portal/auszug/auszug.xhtml?uid=FL-0002.528.358-1# (accessed on 28 February 2021).

70 In Wikipedia, list of highest-funded crowdfunding projects (accessed on 28 February 2021, https://en.wikipedia.org/w/index.php?title=List_of_highest-funded_crowdfunding_projects&oldid=1008322414).

71 NÄGELE/FELDKIRCHER/BERGT/ESNEAULT, National legal & regulatory frameworks in select European countries, in *thinkBLOCKtank* (ed.), Token Regulation Paper v1.0., p. 118.

II The creation of the Token and TT Service Provider Act

The Liechtenstein Government has looked closely at developments related to blockchain since 2016, quickly recognising the potential of these new technologies, which goes significantly beyond their application for the creation of an alternative, intermediary-free means of payment (cryptocurrencies such as Bitcoin).[72] In writing the TVTG, the Government had in mind the vision of a token economy arising on the basis of these new technologies with the concept of representing real value in the form of rights embodied in tokens.[73]

The newly created regulatory lab at the Liechtenstein Financial Market Authority (FMA) was in contact with more than 100 companies in 2017 alone. As a result of this activity, the FMA has dealt in depth with the essential questions arising for these companies. This increased its expertise in this area substantially.[74] As a result, Liechtenstein dealt with cryptocurrencies, exchange offices, Bitcoin ATMs and ICOs early on.[75]

The Ministry of General Government Affairs and Finance (MMGGAF) of Prime Minister Adrian Hasler considered early on how a state should handle blockchain technology.[76] For this reason, the Liechtenstein Government established a blockchain working group back in 2016.[77] At the beginning, in particular, the government working group looked at the question of whether the existing legal framework for innovation offers sufficient space for these new technologies. Taking account of new technological developments in the legal framework too early can result in limitations to the innovative power of such developments. There is also a risk that the law will address or describe the technology itself and that it will thus not be sufficiently abstract. On the other hand, it was also necessary to determine whether existing law provided users of such technologies with sufficient protection. Both questions were answered

---

[72] BuA No. 54/2019, p. 11.

[73] BuA No. 54/2019, p. 26 ff.

[74] HASLER, speech by Prime Minister Adrian Hasler on the occasion of the 4th Finance Forum Liechtenstein on 21 March 2018 in the Vaduzer Saal, https://www.regierung.li/media/medienarchiv/2018-03-21_Ansprache_Finance_Forum_2018_RC.pdf?t=637433298910799802 (accessed on 27 February 2021).

[75] HASLER, NZZ Neue Zürcher Zeitung AG.

[76] HASLER, NZZ Neue Zürcher Zeitung AG.

[77] On the working group, see the acknowledgements; the members of this working group were Thomas Dünser, Patrick Bont, Joahnn Gevers, Thomas Nigg and Peter Schnürer as well as the author of this dissertation, Thomas Nägele; DÜNSER, Legalize Blockchain. p. 14.

with the publication of the first draft law. It was decided that there was a need to act. Prime Minister Adrian Hasler presented the legislative proposal for the Liechtenstein Token and TT Service Provider Act (TVTG[78]) to the public for the first time on 21 March 2018:

"The act will therefore govern this shift from the real world to a digital blockchain trading system and the basic services based on it in a way that enables the creation of new business models and increases legal certainty for all participants."[79]

Prime Minister Hasler made it clear at the time that the creation of **legal certainty for companies and clients** was extremely important when drafting the legislative proposal. Blockchain covers more than just cryptocurrencies. However, in order for other assets, such as cars, music titles or securities to be traded using blockchain technology, it is necessary to have civil law regulations in addition to regulatory rules. The TVTG follows such a comprehensive approach and therefore also includes a civil law component.

Another milestone of the Blockchain country Liechtenstein is marked by the approval through the Financial Market Authority in August 2018 of the **first securities prospectus** on the **public offering of security tokens** in the European Economic Area (EEA) and the European Union (EU).[80] The public offering of security tokens is called a security token offering ("STO)"), similar to an ICO. That same month, on 28 August 2018, the Government approved the **consultation report on the "Blockchain Act"**. At the time, the draft was still titled: "Act on Trustworthy-Technologies (TT) based on Transaction Systems (Blockchain Act; TT Act, VTG) and the Amendment of Other Acts".[81] The consultation period ended on 16 November 2018, with statements from Liechtenstein and abroad. Consequently, there was significant interest in the Liechtenstein proposal. In particular, the statements involving civil law questions and the proposed registration and supervisory system stood out. This led the Government to

---

78 Act of 3 October 2019 on Token and TT Service Providers (TVTG), Liechtenstein Law Gazette (2019).

79 HASLER, speech by Prime Minister Adrian Hasler on the occasion of the 4th Finance Forum Liechtenstein on 21 March 2018 in the Vaduzer Saal.

80 LIECHTENSTEIN FINANCIAL MARKET AUTHORITY (FMA), list of approved prospectuses to 20 July 2019, register.fma-li.li/fileadmin/user_upload/dokumente/publikationen/Prospekte_nach_WPPG/Liste_geb_Prospekte_bis_20190720_6_20200103.pdf (accessed on 4 March 2020), p. 16.

81 GOVERNMENT OF THE PRINCIPALITY OF LIECHTENSTEIN, consultation on the Blockchain Act has commenced, https://www.regierung.li/de/mitteilungen/212312/?typ=news (accessed on 28 February 2021).

modify the structure of the draft by creating a clear **separation** between the **civil law section** and the **public law section**. In addition, the definitions were detailed and explained further, with some modified, in particular, the terms TT-identifier and the definition of a token.[82]

At its meeting on 7 May 2018, the Government approved the **report and application** on the creation of an act on tokens and TT-service providers (Token and TT Service Provider Act; TVTG) [83].[84] The first reading[85] in the Parliament of the Principality of Liechtenstein took place in June 2019, and the **legislative proposal was uncontested**. The questions that were raised were answered by the Government and at its meeting on 3 September 2019, the Government approved the statement[86] on the creation of an act on tokens and TT-service providers (Token and TT Service Provider Act; TVTG) as well as the amendment of other acts. The members of the Liechtenstein Parliament (Landtag) raised questions, in particular, about the risk, the term "trustworthy-technologies", "long-term storage" in blockchains, TT-service providers, the planned supervisory system and who would be entrusted with carrying it out. The Government then further clarified the provisions regarding the duties of care by deleting the term "payment token" and modifying the term TT exchange service provider. The fee model was also adjusted.[87] Finally, the second reading took place on 3 October 2019 and the **Landtag of the Principality of Liechtenstein approved the draft** after the second reading with 22 votes in favour, representing a **unanimous vote**.[88] Even before entering into force, the TVTG was presented at the UN in New

---

82 Government of the Principality of Liechtenstein, report and application on the "Blockchain Act" approved, https://www.regierung.li/de/mitteilungen/222667/?typ=news (accessed on 28 February 2021).

83 BuA 54/2019.

84 Government of the Principality of Liechtenstein, report and application for the "Blockchain Act" approved.

85 Parliament of the Principality of Liechtenstein, minutes of the parliament, 5-7., June 2019, Part 2, p. 1049 ff.

86 Government of the Principality of Liechtenstein, BuA No. 93/2019.

87 Government of the Principality of Liechtenstein, statement on the Token and TT Service Provider Act ("Blockchain Act") approved, https://www.regierung.li/de/mitteilungen/222882 (accessed on 28 February 2021).

88 Parliament of the Principality of Liechtenstein, minutes of the parliament for 2-3 October 2019, Part 2, p. 1911.

York on 25 October 2019 and attracted a significant amount of interest.[89] This shows that the draft law attracted interest beyond the country's borders and was viewed extremely positively.[90] The **TVTG entered into force on 1 January 2020**.

In 2020, Art. 14, 20, 25 and 40 TVTG had to be amended because of the revision of the Insolvency Act and the modification of the terms in it. This amendment entered into force on 1 January 2021. The revision of the introduction of a "TT-agent" entered into force on 1 April 2021. This amendment also extended the scope of application of the Due Diligence Act to include TT-agents in order to create the same framework conditions for TT-service providers based in Liechtenstein and foreign providers.[91]

89 In addition to Dr Thomas Dünser, Thomas Nägele also participated as a panellist; GOVERNMENT OF THE PRINCIPALITY OF LIECHTENSTEIN, Liechtensteins Blockchain-Gesetz stösst in der UNO auf grosses Interesse, https://www.regierung.li/de/mitteilungen/223020/?typ=news (accessed on 28 February 2021).

90 On the positive reception of the act, see WURZER, Practical Applications According to the Law on Tokens and TT Service Providers (Token and TT Service Provider Act; TVTG), SPWR 2019, p. 252.

91 GOVERNMENT OF THE PRINCIPALITY OF LIECHTENSTEIN, BuA No. 132/2020, p. 23 f.

PART 3 THE LEGAL DEFINITION OF TOKENS PURSUANT TO THE TVTG

§ 1 The creation of a new legal object, the Token

While there are some initial local approaches for legal definitions of the term "token", there is still no uniform civil law definition of tokens in Europe. The European Banking Authority and the European Securities and Markets Authority (ESMA) also draw a distinction in regulatory law between the categories established in practice in Liechtenstein, noting that it is often difficult to clearly assign a token to one category (so-called hybrid token). These agencies view as essential a clear distinction between those tokens to which **financial market law applies** and **other tokens**.[92] In Liechtenstein, tokens – depending on their (economic) function – are also divided in practice into the following three groups from a regulatory law perspective[93]: **Utility tokens, payment tokens** (currency coins/tokens) and **security tokens** (equity tokens). However, such an approach, which aims at introducing different classifications, was not taken by the TVTG.[94]

The Government had the "token economy" in mind when it created the TVTG. For this reason, the **regulatory concept** behind the TVTG also aims for **as broad an application of the legal principles as possible**. The legal definition creates a **new legal object**, the **token**. Tokens can have their own internal value ("**intrinsic tokens**") and function like, for example, a currency. Or they can represent external assets in the form of a right ("**extrinsic tokens**"), for example, "shareholders' rights".[95]

---

[92] NÄGELE/BONT, Tokenized structures and assets in Liechtenstein law, Trusts Trustees 2019, p. 635 f.

[93] BuA No. 54/2019, p. 141; see also LANGER/NÄGELE, IWB 2018, p. 6; see also SCHOPPER/RASCHNER, Die aufsichtsrechtliche Einordnung von Krypto-Börsen in Österreich, ÖBA 2019, p. 250; on the classification under European law, see NÄGELE/BONT, p. 635.

[94] BuA No. 54/2019, p. 142.

[95] BuA No. 54/2019, p. 58.

With the **Token and TT Service Provider Act (TVTG)**, Liechtenstein became one of the first countries in the world to introduce a legal definition for tokens.[96] The TVTG defines the term in Art. 2, para. 1(c):

"Token"as information on a TT-system that can represent claims or rights of membership against a person, rights to property, or other absolute or relative rights and that are assigned to one or more TT-identifiers.

Consequently, the TVTG defines the token as **information** using the relevant technology that can represent rights. As a result, a new legal object (sui generis) has been introduced into Liechtenstein law.[97]

This approach did not go unnoticed. Thus, on 24 September 2020, the European Commission, with the publication of the "digital finance package"[98], presented a proposal for a Regulation on "**Markets in Crypto-assets (MiCa)**)"[99] that contains the following definition of "crypto-asset" in Art. 3, para. 1, cl. 2:

"Crypto-asset" – a digital representation of assets or rights that can be transferred or stored electronically using distributed ledger technology or a similar technology.

It appears that the European Commission was inspired by the legal definition in the TVTG and that it used the notion of representation as the basis for its approach.[100] Therefore, the TVTG and MiCA complement one another very well.[101]

---

[96] It may even be the world's first legal definition; on this point, see *A.* FRICK, Zivilrechtliche Aspekte von Token im Zusammenhang mit dem liechtensteinischen Token- und VT-Dienstleister-Gesetz. Diplomarbeit Fakultät für Rechtswissenschaften der Universität Innsbruck, Schaan, Innsbruck (2020), p. 16.

[97] See NÄGELE, Sekundärmarkt für Security Token, p. 9; and, in particular, BuA No. 54/2019, p. 60 ff; *A.* FRICK, Zivilrechtliche Aspekte von Token im Zusammenhang mit dem liechtensteinischen Token- und VT-Dienstleister-Gesetz, p. 18.

[98] FINANCIAL STABILITY, FINANCIAL SERVICES AND CAPITAL MARKETS UNION, digital finance package, https://ec.europa.eu/info/publications/200924-digital-finance-proposals_en (accessed on 21 January 2021).

[99] EUROPEAN COMMISSION, proposal for a Regulation on Markets in Crypto-assets (MiCa).

[100] See the answers from Dr Joachim Schwerin of the European Commission to the question on the sources of inspiration in RUGAARD, Towards a European token economy – driven by the EU Commission! https://thetokenizer.io/2021/01/10/towards-a-european-token-economy-driven-by-the-eu-commission (accessed on 23 January 2021), p. 8.

[101] "The Liechtenstein TVTG and MiCA are milestones: they complement each other perfectly", said Joachim Schwerin; see NÄGELE, Why Liechtenstein is an attractive location for the token economy, https://thomas-naegele.medium.com/why-liechtenstein-is-an-attractive-location-

The TVTG thus focuses on the **legal definition** of the term "token", around which the TVTG was developed. It does so with the aim of creating an adequate legal basis for the token economy. "**Token economy**" refers to the digitalisation of the economy through the "tokenisation" of assets. "**Tokenisation**" is the **representation of rights by tokens**. The TVTG and the legislative materials on the TVTG refer to the token as a sort of "container to represent rights"[102]. The term "**Token-Container-Model**" has now become established.[103] The definition of token will be analysed in-depth below.

For this purpose, the individual elements have been rearranged and numbered and the representation of rights grouped as follows:

"Token":

> *(1) information on a*
>
> *(2) TT-system that*
>
> *(3) can represent rights, such as*
>
> > *(3a) claims or rights of membership against a person,*
> >
> > *(3b) rights to property, or*
> >
> > *(3c) other absolute or relative rights and*
>
> *(4) those that are assigned to one or more TT-identifiers.*

They will then be analysed more closely.

§ 2 (1) "Information"

The definition of token in Art. 2, para. 1(c) TVTG uses the term "**information**", without explaining it further in the legislative materials. For this reason, this chapter will consider the "information" element from a technical point of view, in order to be able to carry out a legal classification. In order to avoid drawing inaccurate conclusions,

---

for-the-token-economy-91d23c8ab1b0; on the MiCA and the TVTG, see, in particular, 2.5 MiCA and TVTG – These are the differences in NÄGELE, MiCA — Markets in Crypto-assets Regulation and the DLT Pilot Regime – What impact might these proposed EU regulations have on Liechtenstein and the TVTG (aka Blockchain Act)?

[102] BuA No. 54/2019, p. 58.

[103] Nägele first spoke publicly of the Token-Container-Model as a speaker at the seminar "Blockchain Meets Liechtenstein" on 6 September 2019: UNIVERSITY OF LIECHTENSTEIN, Blockchain Meets Liechtenstein, https://www.uni.li/de/universitaet/medienportal/medienmitteilungen/blockchain-meets-liechtenstein (accessed on 17 May 2021).

such as that the token is the information that enables access to the data, a corresponding detailed analysis of this term is required..[104] Where necessary, the individual technological applications will also be discussed, e.g. the various token standards.

A What are information and data in general?

I The term data from a technical perspective

From an IT perspective, there is a significant difference between information and data. **Data** is the **reinterpretable**[105] **representation of information** in a formalised manner suitable for communication, interpretation, or processing.[106] It represents information in analogue[107] or digital form and, in its digital form, is coded in a binary manner (with the status "on" or "off", represented symbolically by 0/1, power is flowing or not flowing).[108] **Information is digital** when it is represented in the form of numbers, can be **stored** more precisely **in a binary manner** and cannot be broken down any further (smallest information unit).[109] In other words, data is machine-readable (electronically editable) coded information.[110]

---

[104] Thus, the dataset does not represent the key, but rather – staying with this example – a closed container that enables certain interactions with the TT key (e.g. transactions), even though the token can, in turn, serve as a key; thus, the description by Raschauer/Silbernagl is too simplified; RASCHAUER/SILBERNAGL, Grundsatzfragen des liechtensteinischen „Blockchain-Gesetzes" – TVTG, ZFR 2020/3, p. 13.

[105] Without interpretation, data would not be able to represent the information in a useful manner, as the information only becomes available through interpretation in accordance with certain principles. Applying other principles will result in a different result. In my view, it is therefore more appropriate and easier to follow if we talk about "reinterpretabe" rather than "interpretable". See SONNTAG, Informationstechnologie: Grundlagen, in *Jahnel* (ed.), IT-Recht[3] (2012), p. 5 with further references.

[106] SONNTAG in *Jahnel*, p. 5; see also the entry on the term "data" in: INTERNATIONAL ORGANIZATION FOR STANDARDIZATION (ISO), (in ISO, Information technology), Information technology, https://www.iso.org/obp/ui/#iso:std:iso-iec:2382:ed-1:v1:en (accessed on 29 April 2021).

[107] Analogue information: Analogue information can be represented in a continuous wave form and is divided into ever smaller units; see KERSKEN, IT-Handbuch für Fachinformatiker[6], p. 54.

[108] SONNTAG in *Jahnel*, p. 4; KERSKEN, IT-Handbuch für Fachinformatiker[6], p. 53 f.

[109] KERSKEN, IT-Handbuch für Fachinformatiker[6], p. 53 ff.

[110] See ZECH, introductory remarks on Sections 87a ff., in *Schuster/Grützmacher* (ed.), IT-Recht[1] (2018), p. 1832.

If data must be **processed electronically**, it must be in **binary form** and, where necessary, translated in advance ("**digitalisation**"[111]).[112] The sequence of ones and zeroes can be stored on **data carriers** in various ways (magnetically, optically, magneto-optically or with semiconductors).[113] Obtaining the original data as it existed before the digitalisation requires a process of reverse digitalisation, so to speak. Doing so requires a corresponding interpretation of the data. Because data only becomes information (again), receiving meaning, within a concrete context.[114] In other words, **the sequence of ones and zeroes** becomes information **through interpretation.**[115] For example, "4711" may be a number, a postal code (a number with a special meaning), a date or a trade name (text).[116] Usually, though, only one interpretation of the data is sensible and desirable. For example, an image file can also be used as a piece of music. People will have a hard time understanding this interpretation of the data as music, and the representation of the information "image" as data can therefore only be reproduced when the data is interpreted "correctly" in order to obtain an image again.[117]

II The civil law classification of data

In recent years, digitalisation and digital data have become important topics in many areas of our economy. "Data is gold", according to many reports by various media outlets. Due to the European General Data Protection Regulation (GDPR)[118], in particular, many people have become aware of the importance of personal data. In addition to its classification as property according to property law (PL)[119] – and thus its

---

[111] Digitalisation: "Die Umwandlung der analogen Eindrücke aus der Realität in computergeeignete digitale Daten"; see: KERSKEN, IT-Handbuch für Fachinformatiker[6], p. 55.

[112] SCHNABEL, Computertechnik-Fibel, https://www.elektronik-kompendium.de/shop/buecher/computertechnik-fibel, p. 9.

[113] KERSKEN, IT-Handbuch für Fachinformatiker[6], p. 146; on semiconductor storage such as solid state disks (SSD), see data storage on Wikipedia (accessed on 27 December 2020, https://en.wikipedia.org/wiki/Data_storage).

[114] SONNTAG in *Jahnel*, p. 6.

[115] SCHNABEL, Computertechnik-Fibel[5], p. 9.

[116] SONNTAG in *Jahnel*, p. 5.

[117] SONNTAG in *Jahnel*, p. 6.

[118] Regulation (EU) 2016/679 of the European Parliament and of the Council of 27 April 2016 on the protection of natural persons with regard to the processing of personal data and on the free movement of such data, and repealing Directive 95/46/EC (General Data Protection Regulation) (text with EEA relevance) (GDPR), OJ EC 2016/119, p. 1.

[119] Property law of 31 December 1922 (PL), Liechtenstein Law Gazette (1923).

subjection to the rules on ownership and property[120] – the discussion also revolves around its classification as intellectual property and the question of which protective rights should be applicable.

However, there is a general consensus that data can be the subject of purchase and exchange agreements[121], gifts and – where data is considered work under copyright law[122] – licensing agreements.[123] Surprisingly, however, it has **not yet been definitively clarified** how **data is to be classified legally**. There is a question of whether data can be considered a legal object. It depends on the level at which data is delineated. Data can be delineated at:

- semantic (meaning)
- syntactic (linguistic) or
- structural (carrier) level.[124]

On a structural level (carrier level), it is fairly indisputable that physical data carriers represent an object under property law (e.g. a pen-drive).[125] Data is rarely found as the object of legal regulations at the syntactic level (linguistic level). Examples include protection under criminal law as specified in Section 126a of the Criminal Code[126]. This penalty provides protection against data corruption by modifying, deleting or making it unusable.[127] In contrast, at the semantic level (meaning level), personal data is protected, in particular, by data protection law.[128] With this distinction in mind, the question now is how the data can be classified under civil law.

[120] *A.* SCHMID/SCHMIDT/ZECH, Rechte an Daten – zum Stand der Diskussion, sic! 2018, p. 627.

[121] There is also the question of the subject of the contract. The data carrier (structural level) is usually the subject of the contract and not the dataset (syntactic level) itself; see below.

[122] Act of 19 May 1999 on Copyright and Related Rights (Copyright Act), Liechtenstein Law Gazette (1999).

[123] ECKERT, Digitale Daten als Wirtschaftsgut: digitale Daten als Sache, SJZ 2016, p. 245 f.

[124] On the German classification, see margin no. 22 ZECH in *Schuster/Grützmacher*, p. 1832; on the Swiss concept of data, see *A.* SCHMID/SCHMIDT/ZECH, sic! 2018, p. 628.

[125] For Germany, see margin no. 23 ZECH in *Schuster/Grützmacher*, p. 1832.

[126] Criminal Code, Liechtenstein Law Gazette (1988).

[127] For Germany, see margin no. 24 ZECH in *Schuster/Grützmacher*, p. 1833.

[128] For Germany, see margin no. 25 ZECH in *Schuster/Grützmacher*, p. 1833.

1 The question of the subjection of data to property law

The **subjection** of data **to property law** (PL) is frequently discussed. Liechtenstein property law is adopted from Swiss property law[129], and for this reason Swiss doctrine and case law applies. There is no legal definition of the term "property" to be found in Liechtenstein or Swiss property law, on which it is based.[130] For this reason, it is necessary to rely on customary doctrine and jurisprudence.[131] Swiss law defines property as "a physical object that is delineated from other objects and that is subject to actual and legal control[132]."[133]

A central element for the conceptual classification according to Swiss doctrine is **Corporeality**.[134] Physicality requires "a tangible object", thus limiting the concept to **material objects that have a mass**, delineating them from other rights and other non-physical objects used in commerce.[135]

1.1 Introductory remarks on Liechtenstein property law

In contrast to the view of Swiss doctrine, another **concept** that also **encompasses non-physical data** is also conceivable:[136] As in Section 285 of the Austrian General Civil Code (ABGB)[137], which is shaped by natural law, physicality is not a prerequisite

---

[129] In Switzerland, property law is covered in Art. 641 ff. of the Swiss Civil Code (SCC).

[130] For Switzerland, see WIEGAND in *Honsell/Vogt/Geiser*, Basler Kommentar[5] (2015), introductory remarks on Art. 641 ff., p. 847 N 5.

[131] *A.* SCHMID/SCHMIDT/ZECH, sic! 2018, p. 629.

[132] The controllability of data seems to be fairly uncontested. However, the terms data and information appear to be equal here; see also the remarks in B about what information is needed for a token; on controllability, see also ECKERT, SJZ 2016, p. 248; see also *A.* FRICK, Zivilrechtliche Aspekte von Token im Zusammenhang mit dem liechtensteinischen Token- und VT-Dienstleister-Gesetz, p. 18.

[133] WIEGAND in *Honsell/Vogt/Geiser*[5], introductory remarks on Art. 641 ff., p. 847 N 6; in particular, on the situation in Liechtenstein regarding the question of physicality as a constituent feature of the concept, see also RIETZLER/*M.* FRICK/CASELLINI, Liechtensteinisches Blockchain Gesetz, in *Piska/Völkel* (ed.), Blockchain rules (2019), p. 363 f.

[134] On physicality, see WIEGAND in *Honsell/Vogt/Geiser*[5], introductory remarks on Art. 641 ff., p. 847 N 5; based on the materials for the TVTG, it appears that the information's lack of physicality that comprises a token is the primary reason why property law cannot be applied; see BuA No. 54/2019, p. 62.

[135] WIEGAND in *Honsell/Vogt/Geiser*[5], introductory remarks on Art. 641 ff., p. 849 N 10.

[136] OPILIO, Liechtensteinisches Sachenrecht. SR; Arbeitskommentar (2010), p. 32 f.

[137] See the concept in Section 285 of the Austrian General Civil Code: "Everything that is distinct from a person and that can be used by people is classified in the legal sense as property"; Austrian General Civil Code for All the German Hereditary Provinces of the Austrian Monarchy (öABGB), Judicial Law Collection (1811).

for the concept.[138] Liechtenstein property law, like the country's other civil laws, was originally adopted from Austria and was also based on the ABGB. For this reason, physicality was also not a prerequisite in Liechtenstein. Property law was only later adopted from Switzerland.

However, it is still possible to argue that **physicality** is not a prerequisite in Liechtenstein, even after property law was adopted from Switzerland. This is because Liechtenstein has laws based on natural law, such as the ABGB[139] adopted from Austria, and laws such as the PGR, which is based on legal positivism. The codification based on natural law does not make a sharp distinction between property law and the laws of obligations. In contrast, Liechtenstein property law, like the original law that now serves as its basis, the Swiss Civil Code (SCC), distinguishes between property law and the laws of obligations. Swiss property law and the Swiss Civil Code are largely based on Roman law and view property law and the laws of obligations as being relatively distinct from one another. It can be argued that property law has the same legal positivist background as other civil laws. This would result in a legal positivist interpretation of property law, which would lead to a broad concept with no physicality criterion. This interpretation would then make it easier to explain why property law equates certain non-physical property (rights) with physical objects (see Art. 34 PL)[140]. These include, for example, condominium ownership in Art. 170a ff. PL, which grants condominium owners a share of co-ownership of a property, together with special rights to the exclusive use of certain parts of a building, or natural forces in Art. 171 PL.[141] If natural forces can be subjected to legal control, they become the object of chattel ownership, even though they do not have the qualities of property. Consequently, the rules of property law can be applied to energy and other natural forces, albeit only analogously.[142]

For the aforementioned reasons, a **concept would be acceptable** if it also **encompassed non-physical objects.**[143] The question is whether the legal consequences of treating digital data as an economic good, a so-called "res digitalis", would result in

---

[138] Persons and Companies Act (PGR), Liechtenstein Law Gazette (1926).

[139] Austrian General Civil Code (ABGB), Liechtenstein Law Gazette (1811).

[140] See also margin no. 15 WIEGAND in *Honsell/Vogt/Geiser*[5], introductory remarks on Art. 641 ff., p. 851.

[141] OPILIO, Liechtensteinisches Sachenrecht, p. 34 f.

[142] WIEGAND in *Honsell/Vogt/Geiser*[5], introductory remarks on Art. 641 ff., p. 851.

[143] OPILIO, Liechtensteinisches Sachenrecht, p. 34.

adequate solutions. Subjecting it to this concept and thus applying the rules of property law has been hotly discussed in Switzerland, with many rejecting[144] this view.[145] However, it would be difficult to fully assess the consequences of doing so.[146]

1.2 Subjecting digital data to property law (res digitalis)

As outlined above, data is stored and processed in the form of ones and zeroes. A minority view in literature is that this technology-related activity (storing digital data on a data carrier) represents the "embodiment" of data and thus a bridge to property law. In such cases, the digital data would exist on its own, stored temporarily or permanently as property on a data carrier. The minority view concludes that, as a result, the data is physically accessible and real.[147] This argument is not particularly convincing. The data is not physically embodied on the data carrier; rather, the data carrier, i.e. the real property, is modified in order to store the data. Even if one wanted to view this modification as an object in and of itself, it is inextricably connected to the data carrier and thus cannot be viewed except in connection with the object.

This can be illustrated with optical data carriers, such as DVDs. As data carriers, DVDs have a reflective metal surface that "stores" a certain sequence of two conditions (pit/land ~ ones and zeroes) in the form of indentations ("pits") and smooth surfaces ("land"), i.e. digital data, in a binary form. A laser beam scans this metal surface and emits the sequence of conditions.[148] Three "exact copies" of DVDs are three objects under property law (structural level) that can be possessed by different people and have different owners. In contrast, the data stored on the DVDs (semantic level) is identical. It is not always clear which dataset is the original and which is the copy. In addition, it is possible to store digital data on the data carrier that can be assigned to a number of different legal subjects. If someone acquires derivative ownership of one of the three DVDs (structural level), this would represent a transfer of the rights to the stored digital data (semantic level), which would only be supported by the legal

---

144 For the current state of the discussion, see: *A.* SCHMID/SCHMIDT/ZECH, sic! 2018.

145 For an expansion of the concept to include digital data: ECKERT, SJZ 2016; for the opposite position, which proposes no expansion of the concept, see: *A.* SCHMID/SCHMIDT/ZECH, sic! 2018; for an affirmative view of an expansion in Liechtenstein, albeit one that equates data with information and argues for controllability through the blockchain, see: RIETZLER/*M.* FRICK/CASELLINI in *Piska/Völkel*, p. 363 ff.

146 See also the materials for the TVTG, which dealt with the question of the applicability of property law to tokens: BuA No. 54/2019, p. 62.

147 ECKERT, SJZ 2016, p. 248.

148 KERSKEN, IT-Handbuch für Fachinformatiker[6], p. 146.

system if the conditions for the transfer were met, especially if there were multiple "data owners".

In practice, property law also plays a subordinate role in the embodiment of rights in securities and the related physicality of the certificate. In Switzerland, these rights have long been represented in the form of book-entry and uncertified securities. In Liechtenstein, book-entry securities existed before the entry into force of the TVTG and the amendments to the PGR; claims and rights of membership have also appeared as tokens and TT-systems and thus as purely digital register rights since 1 January 2020.[149]

1.3 Non-subjection to property law

The subjection to property law described above is artificial and does not take into account the key advantages of digital data: In contrast to physical objects, data is:

- non-rivalrous,
- non-consumable and
- non-exclusive.

Digital data is non-rivalrous because its **use by one person does not affect its use by another person**, even if the data is used at the same time. The data cannot be entirely consumed because it can be **reproduced as many times as desired** and stored on a wide variety of storage media. Digital data is non-exclusive because its **use by a third party cannot be excluded**.[150] In my view, embodying data in real objects (data carriers) in order to make them subject to property law brings with it more disadvantages than advantages, and overlooks the advantages of the characteristics of digital data. Let us return to the previous example with the three DVDs and assume that the same PDF file is stored on each of them. Every owner of a DVD can, in turn, make as many copies of the information stored on it (as a PDF file) as they wish in the form of binary, digital data. The fate of digital data at a semantic level and the data carrier subject to property law at a structural level often diverge from one another. In this context, it is important to look at how data is stored nowadays. In a very small number of cases, data is still stored, shared and edited on optical data carriers such as DVDs. Largely the data is stored in data centres, whose geographical location users are usually unaware of ("cloud"). However, it should be obvious that in

[149] WIEGAND in *Honsell/Vogt/Geiser*[5], introductory remarks on Art. 641 ff., p. 849.

[150] On the concept of data, see: *A.* SCHMID/SCHMIDT/ZECH, sic! 2018, p. 628.

the very few cases of **legal responsibility under property law** in the form of possession and ownership of the data carrier (structural level), there should and can be the same legal fate as that of the digital data stored on it (semantic level), which in most cases is assigned to other legal subjects as a result of **(intellectual property) rights**.

The subjection of digital data to the concept and thus also to the transfer rules pursuant to property law often leads to a divergence of legal conditions and reality. Therefore, it seems more appropriate to separate the fate of physical objects (data carriers) from the data stored on them digitally. In contrast to natural forces, data is also non-consumable. As has already occurred with the TVTG for tokens, an autonomous regulation is an option – de lege ferenda – for digital data.[151] Ownership of intellectual property rights could serve as an example.[152]

2 Classification of data under intellectual property rights

In addition to the less promising subjection of data to property law, intellectual property rights, as already mentioned, would appear to be a more promising basis for a solution. What is interesting here is the doubling of the scope of intellectual property rights. The data carrier is a movable good pursuant to PL, while the ideas stored on it, in contrast, are subject to intellectual property law.[153] Here, too, the fate of the data carrier (structural level) is separated from the content (semantic level). For the purpose of the legal classification, it is therefore also worth taking a look at copyright law. In Liechtenstein, the Copyright Act (URG) was adopted from Switzerland and, because of its membership of the European Economic Area (EEA), modified by the Database Directive.[154] The discussion on rights to data has once again gained in importance as a result of big data analyses. The economic interest in these large datasets as well as database producer rights play a key role here.[155] Subjection to intellectual

[151] On the question of autonomous regulation and non-subjection to property law by the TVTG, see RASCHAUER/SILBERNAGL, Grundsatzfragen des liechtensteinischen „Blockchain-Gesetzes" – TVTG, ZFR 2020/3, p. 13.

[152] *A.* SCHMID/SCHMIDT/ZECH, sic! 2018, p. 638; Wiegand also speaks out in favour of the separation (or the "doubling of the legal scope"); see margin no. 10 on physicality: WIEGAND in *Honsell/Vogt/Geiser*[5], introductory remarks on Art. 641 ff., p. 849.

[153] WIEGAND in *Honsell/Vogt/Geiser*[5], introductory remarks on Art. 641 ff., p. 849 N 10.

[154] Directive 96/9/EC of the European Parliament and of the Council of 11 March 1996 on the legal protection of databases (Database Directive), OJ EC 1996/77, p. 20; the aforementioned directive was added to the EEA legal framework by means of Resolution No. 59/1996 of the EEA Joint Committee and entered into effect for Liechtenstein on 1 July 2000.

[155] ZECH in *Schuster/Grützmacher*, p. 1828; see also *A.* SCHMID/SCHMIDT/ZECH, sic! 2018, p. 627.

property rights, in particular, the copyright protection of databases, will be examined below.

3 Application of the Copyright Act to computer programs

According to Art. 2, para. 1 URG, works are intellectual creations of literature and art that have an individual character, regardless of their value or purpose. Various works are specified in para. 2 of the Copyright Act. At first glance, this does not include digital data. A work, such as a piece of music, is distinguished from its digital reproduction on an .mp3 file. Art. 2, para. 3 of the Copyright Act then includes **computer programs** among **works of literature and art**. However, they cannot be classified as literary or scientific works.[156] Computer programs are thus **not works, but they are treated as such**. There is no legal definition of computer programs in the Copyright Act. However, the legislators responsible for the original law noted that "computer programs in the traditional sense, understood as a sequence of commands that the computer executes to solve a task", would fall under the term, and that it would also include "purely formal descriptions of tasks".[157] If a computer program meets the usual protection requirements, it is subject to copyright. This is true as a general rule because the protection requirements are not strict.[158]

Art. 16 of the Copyright Act then specifies the activities that require authorisation for computer programs. In particular, these property rights include the duplication, adaptation or reworking and any form of distribution of the original version of a computer program. Art. 24 of the Copyright Act provides permission to decrypt computer programs to establish interoperability, provided certain conditions are met.

Digital data in the form of computer programs are not works pursuant to the Copyright Act, but, as has been shown, are treated as such and given special protection.

4 Subjection of data to database rights

The term "database" refers to the collection of data itself, on the one hand, and the program that manages the data on the other. In the first case, the term refers to a collection of information on various subjects structured in accordance with certain rules. The program (database management system, or DBMS), on the other hand,

---

[156] HANDLE, Der urheberrechtliche Schutz der Idee, SMI 2013, p. 241.

[157] For a detailed discussion, see HANDLE, SMI 2013, p. 233.

[158] HANDLE, SMI 2013, p. 245 f.

manages the data and provides functions for searching, sorting, filtering and formatting information.[159]

Creating the database structure, obtaining, reviewing and presenting the information (content) in a database sometimes requires substantial qualitative and quantitative investments. Creating a copy of a (published) database, on the other hand, is easy to do and the content easy to use.[160] Therefore, as far back as 1996, the European Union saw the need to better protect the producers of databases with a Database Directive[161] in order to promote investments in modern data storage and data processing systems within the Community.[162] It viewed copyright law as a suitable method for protecting databases.[163]

The Copyright Act (URG) implements the Database Directive in Liechtenstein and stipulates sui generis protection of investments in databases in Art. 45 URG. The subject of protection is not the database itself or the structure of the database, but rather the **investment by the producer** (manufacturer) in the content of the database.[164] The sui generis protection of databases does not affect existing database content rights.[165] Thus, an appropriate distinction is made between the carrier of the information, or its design and functions, and the investments in them. The database content is, in turn, subject to separate copyrights insofar as it is a protected work pursuant to Art. 2 URG or copies of such works.

III Conclusion on the civil law classification of data

A minority view allows for the subjection of digital data to the concept of property (within the realms of property law) in Liechtenstein. The prevailing opinion that it is not being subject to property law seems more convincing. This take into account the nature of digital data, which differs from the forces of nature, for example. A distinction must be made between the data carrier and the data stored on it. The data carrier is a movable good pursuant to property law, while the ideas stored on it, in contrast,

---

159 KERSKEN, IT-Handbuch für Fachinformatiker[6], p. 699.

160 See Art. 45, para. 1 URG; see also BLOCHER, Gewerblicher Rechtschutz und Urheberrecht, in *Jahnel* (ed.), IT-Recht[3] (2012), p. 242; see Recitals 7 and 8 of the Database Directive, OJ EC 1996/77, p. 20.

161 Database Directive, OJ EC 1996/77, p. 20.

162 Database Directive, OJ EC 1996/77, p. 20, Recital 12.

163 Database Directive, OJ EC 1996/77, p. 20, Recital 5.

164 BLOCHER in *Jahnel*, p. 245.

165 Database Directive, OJ EC 1996/77, p. 20, Recital 18.

are subject to and protected by intellectual property law. Digital data in the form of computer programs are not works pursuant to the Copyright Act, but as has been shown are treated as such and subject to special protection.

B The "information" that makes up a token

I Preliminary remark

As has been shown, information is generally digital data that has been interpreted. The information that makes up a token must therefore be distinguished from the data that stores and processes this information in digital form.[166] The information also lacks physicality[167], which is why, from the point of view of the government, when the TVTG was created, tokens were not to be subsumed within this concept: *"Since a token technically only represents information or an entry on a TT-system, i.e. it 'only' consists of digital strings of characters, it is clear that a token has no physicality."*[168] Therefore tokens are not property pursuant to property law. The Government also saw the need to make "deep cuts" to property law in order to enable adequate regulation and therefore created a separate regulation for tokens.[169]

Nor do the protective rights granted under copyright that were discussed take adequate account of the information (i.e. the interpreted, digital data) that makes up tokens, as protective rights such as property law do not allow for the digital

[166] Thus, the proposition that tokens are data "from a technical standpoint" is correct. However, for tokens as a new legal object pursuant to the TVTG, this does not go far enough. Thus, Nägele/Xander argue in favour of a separate definition even before entry into force of the TVTG; see NÄGELE/XANDER in *Piska/Völkel*, p. 376 f.

[167] On the question of physicality, see BuA No. 54/2019, p. 62.

[168] However, subordination under property law would have been possible. On this point, see the remarks in Part 3, Section 2, A, II, 1.2.

[169] On the question of why tokens are not subject to property law, see, in particular, the remarks by the Government in BuA No. 54/2019, p. 62.; on the question of whether the path of a separate regulation is more convincing, see the affirmative commentary in *A* FRICK, Zivilrechtliche Aspekte von Token im Zusammenhang mit dem liechtensteinischen Token- und VT-Dienstleister-Gesetz, p. 31; SILBERNAGL, Zivilrechtliche Regelungen des liechtensteinischen Blockchaingesetzes (TVTG) - Möglichkeiten für Österreich? Zak 2020/7, p. 10; on the condition of physicality for tokens, see also NÄGELE, Sekundärmarkt für Security Token, p. 14; LAYR/MARXER, Rechtsnatur und Übertragung von «Token» aus liechtensteinischer Perspektive, LJZ 2019, p. 12 f.

"transport" of rights.[170] For this reason, a detailed analysis of the "information" constituent feature is provided below.

For the sake of completeness, the debate in Swiss legal doctrine over whether to include Bitcoin under the term **subjective right** will also be discussed here.[171] This is understood as an individual right (Legal benefit) with certain aspects of a legal subject that is recognised by the legal system (objective right). Not everyone is automatically entitled to this right (exceptional nature of the right). Subjective rights can be further divided into rights with an absolute character (which apply erga omnes), and rights with a relative character (which only apply inter partes).[172] A corresponding discussion in Liechtenstein – at least since the entry into force of the TVTG – is moot, as the TVTG also covers intrinsic tokens such as bitcoin.

Thus, tokens and the information that makes up a token can be divided on the basis of how they are created and how they can be used. For this reason, two examples will be presented below using the Bitcoin and Ethereum blockchain system tokens (coins). Tokens created on the basis of an existing blockchain through smart-contracts (tokens in the proper sense) will then be looked at more closely. These will be illustrated using the example of tokens based on Ethereum and Aeternity. For the sake of better understanding, the most important token standards will be presented, which in turn define the minimum information tokens must contain.

II System tokens (coins)

1 Bitcoin tokens (bitcoin)

1.1 Bitcoin blockchain and the transaction model

When Bitcoin is presented as a large, decentralised database, people tend to think that this database is set up in the form of a table with account numbers (TT-identifiers) and corresponding values assigned to these account numbers. When there is a transaction, the amount is deducted from account A and credited to account B. This model is called the "account model" and we will see it again in the case of Ethereum.

---

170 On the classification under intellectual property rights for Switzerland, see THOUVENIN/FRÜH/LOMBARD, Eigentum an Sachdaten: Eine Standortbestimmung, SZW 2017, p. 28 f.

171 Subjective rights are hotly discussed; ZOGG, Bitcoin als Rechtsobjekt – eine zivilrechtliche Einordnung, recht 2019, p. 100.

172 ZOGG, recht SJZ 2019, p. 100.

However, Bitcoin does not maintain any accounts in its decentralised database. Although the typical user interfaces, such as wallets and Blockchain Explorer[173], provide the information in this way, the way transactions are processed differs from traditional models. The Bitcoin decentralised database – put simply – is comprised of all transactions that have ever been conducted and that are connected to one another. If one would want to know how many bitcoins a person[174] has, they need to check how many bitcoins have been transferred to the TT-identifier(s) for this person. Thus, they would need to go through every transaction ever conducted and add together all those received by a particular "person" that have not been paid out again – i.e. processed as part of another transaction. This yields the result in the number of bitcoins a person has. For this reason, in the case of Bitcoin it is said that the bitcoins "move from transaction to transaction". This is also called the "**transaction model**".

Thus, bitcoin are transferred from transaction to transaction by means of a transaction. Viewed more closely, a Bitcoin transaction is comprised of **inputs** and **outputs**. The transaction, comprised of inputs and outputs, is transferred to the Bitcoin network in order to combine it in blocks. A transaction always references the outputs of a previous transaction (**transaction output**), including it in the new created transaction input (**transaction input**). The **total value of bitcoins** for the output must always **be used** in the new entries (less the transaction fees)[175]. As noted, the bitcoins "move" from transaction to transaction. However, a transaction cannot be partially transferred. Instead, all of the bitcoin must be redistributed. If the last transaction involved BTC 1.2, all BTC 1.2 must be transferred. The transactions themselves are **not encrypted** and can be **searched by anyone.** [176] To better understand the transaction model and, in particular, the assignment to TT-identifiers, it is necessary to look at the way the inputs, outputs and scripts work:

As already mentioned, an <u>input</u> is always a reference to an output of a previous transaction. The input must meet the condition (**unlocking script**) defined in the output in the locking script. Only if this condition can be met is it possible to create an input

---

[173] See, for example, a transaction on blockchain.info; BLOCKCHAIN.INFO, Blockchain Explorer, https://www.blockchain.com/btc/tx/a5cbbb32c7f3e2508cd1edef8db817ee9c0fc94b46ee97d5e2f8dd981c4fef48 (accessed on 17 May 2021).

[174] A person who has the right of disposal over a certain TT-identifier.

[175] To be precise, all inputs are processed simultaneously ("congestion") and the fees are only deducted from the outputs.

[176] BITCOIN WIKI, Transaction, https://en.bitcoin.it/wiki/Transaction (accessed on 8 February 2021).

and transfer the bitcoins to a new output.[177] Multiple inputs can be combined into one transaction. Thus, it is possible to combine bitcoins from multiple outputs through the corresponding inputs in a single transaction. One would therefore have bitcoins from multiple outputs via a single transaction.

An output contains the instructions for sending bitcoin and is made up of two parts:

- value of bitcoin that can be transferred via this output in the form of satoshis (BTC 1 = 100,000,000 satoshi);
- a condition defined in the locking script, which "locks" the value of the bitcoin and can only be "opened" if the condition defined in the script is met.[178]

By default, a **locking script** requests an appropriate signature for the defined public key or a variation thereof (TT-identifier, public key, address). Sensibly, the public key that is defined is the one in the locking script to which the transaction recipient has access via the private key. However, there are locking scripts that request the signature of multiple TT-keys ("**multi-signature**"). There are even locking scripts for which no conditions need to be fulfilled or for which the conditions cannot be fulfilled. In the former case, anyone can transfer the bitcoin, while in the second, no one can transfer them. For example, the requirement can be set that 10 private keys must be used, or a password instead of a private key in order to transfer the bitcoin. Or even no authorisation or similar; the bitcoin can then be transferred by the first person who wishes to do so.[179]

As multiple inputs can be combined, multiple outputs can also be combined in a single transaction. In this case, however, there are not too few BTC in an output, but rather too many and it may not be necessary to transfer the entire amount to a third party. It is therefore possible to combine several outputs and transfer the entire value of an input. For example, a portion may be transferred back to the sender themselves. It is important to note that each output of a transaction can only be used once as an input for a subsequent transaction based on this output. This is the reason why all bitcoin must always be transferred.[180]

---

177 BITCOIN WIKI, Transaction.

178 ANTONOPOULOS, Mastering Bitcoin, p. 121.

179 BITCOIN WIKI, Transaction.

180 BITCOIN WIKI, Transaction.

An example will make this clear: If someone has BTC 50, but only wants to transfer BTC 25 to someone, two outputs with BTC 25[181] need to be created, with one payment going to the recipient and one back to the sender (also referred to as "change", as it is given back to the sender). The number of bitcoin that are not specified in an output are considered to be a transaction fee. The person creating the block (miner) can collect the transaction fee by including the transaction fees in the "coinbase" transaction for the respective blocks.[182]

1.2 Unspent transaction outputs (UTXO)

A transaction output that is not transferred is considered to be not spent ("unspent transaction output", or "UTXO").[183] Thus, there are two statuses for outputs:

- spent ("spent transaction outputs") and
- unspent ("unspent transaction outputs").[184]

The decentralised ledger – in other words, the Bitcoin database – does not store information about account balances, but rather about all transactions. Thus, the bitcoin over which a user has power of disposal can be distributed over thousands of unspent transaction outputs ("UTXO").

So the conception most people have of bitcoin being transferred from wallet to wallet or from address to address is, upon closer inspection, incorrect. Instead, bitcoin are transferred from transaction to transaction.[185] To avoid the need to carry out time-consuming calculations for each transaction, full nodes temporarily store all UTXOs in a local database. These databases are called a "UTXO set" or "**UTXO pool**". Wallet software can utilise this database by not downloading the entire Bitcoin blockchain database, but rather only the UTXO pool and then checking the relevant transactions and adding them to the database.[186]

---

181 No transaction fees were included in this example in order to make it easier to understand.

182 BITCOIN WIKI, Transaction.

183 ANTONOPOULOS, Mastering Bitcoin, p. 119 f.

184 MYCRYPTOPEDIA, Bitcoin's UTXO Set Explained - Mycryptopedia, https://www.mycryptopedia.com/bitcoin-utxo-unspent-transaction-output-set-explained (accessed on 8 February 2021).

185 VAN HIJFTE, Blockchain Platforms, p. 85.

186 ANTONOPOULOS, Mastering Bitcoin, p. 119 f.

1.3 The information that makes up a bitcoin(-token)

Now that we know how Bitcoin transactions work, we can turn to the **information** that **"makes up" a bitcoin**. Bitcoin can be divided, with one bitcoin equal to 100,000,000 satoshi. The number of bitcoin allocated to a person with the right of disposal is determined using a calculation based on the outputs for which they can fulfil the condition(s) (usually by signing with a private key) and that have not been transferred ("UTXO"). Thus, the information about who "has" how many bitcoins cannot be seen directly in the database stored in a decentralised manner in the form of a blockchain, but is instead calculated by each full node and stored temporarily in a local UTXO pool database.[187] However, this means that a bitcoin is not a string of characters (syntactic level), i.e. is not comprised of data itself, but rather information as interpreted data, specifically the calculation of the UTXO (semantic level). For this reason, it is appropriate that the TVTG, when it defines a token, **does not refer to a character string**.

In the case of Bitcoin, the person who has the power of disposal is the person who is able to fulfil the condition(s) that are defined in the relevant output (locking script). Usually, the required condition is knowledge of the private key (TT-key) in order to sign a transaction. As in the early days of Bitcoin, an IP address can also be used as a TT-identifier, or any other condition defined in the locking script. As already noted, it is also possible to define no condition. Thus, the tokens will not be allocated to any TT-identifier and – strictly speaking – no longer meet the criteria of the token definition in Art. 2, para. 1(c) TVTG. In this case, the bitcoins are considered to be "**abandoned**". The person who created the output apparently no longer wanted to keep them within their right of disposal and power of disposal. Pursuant to the principles of property law, the person has abandoned the bitcoin. If someone finds the abandoned bitcoins and allocates them to a TT-identifier again via a transaction (functionally adequate for appropriation pursuant to Art. 188 of the Property Law), the tokens in turn meet the requirement for assignment and thus for tokens pursuant to the TVTG. Thus, the person with the power of disposal is the person who allocates an "abandoned" token to a TT-identifier over which he has power of disposal with the "intention of appropriating" it.

[187] See also NÄGELE/XANDER in *Piska/Völkel*, p. 376.

2 Ethereum tokens (ether)

2.1 Ethereum Virtual Machine (EVM)

Bitcoin was developed as a digital currency. In contrast, Ethereum was developed as a decentralised computer. For this reason, Ethereum is more than a decentralised database. Ethereum is also referred to as a "**world computer**". This is an emulated computer that runs on all Ethereum nodes and carries out smart-contracts (computer programs). A copy of the EVM thus runs on all nodes and reviews the execution of the programs. In contrast, the **Ethereum blockchain**, i.e. the decentralised computer, stores the **status of the world computer** that carries out the transactions and smart-contracts. This emulated computer is called the "**Ethereum Virtual Machine**", or "**EVM**".[188]

2.2 The information that makes up an ether (-token)

In contrast to Bitcoin, Ethereum uses a model with account balances instead of a transaction model. As expected, the accounts have an account balance and – if someone wishes to carry out a transaction – the sender's account is checked to make sure there is a sufficient balance. If this is the case, the amount is credited to the recipient account and deducted from the sender account, which is called the **account model**.[189] Thus, the information that makes up the ether is the result of an inquiry to determine how many ethers are allocated to which TT-identifier.[190]

3 The creation of system tokens through mining

It is important to understand how a token is created when entering the information that makes up a token. The TVTG provides for a single role, the token generator, for creating tokens, and therefore refers to this process appropriately as the generation of tokens, not their creation. As some tokens have no generator in the proper sense, however, I will also use the term "creation" below. Tokens pursuant to the TVTG can be "created" in various ways. One way they can be created is based on **"mining" for new tokens**, or "mining" them. With Bitcoin's Proof of Work ("PoW") algorithm, which was explained above, miners receive a so-called "**block reward**" every time

---

[188] ANTONOPOULOS, Mastering Bitcoin, p. 26.

[189] VAN HIJFTE, Blockchain Platforms, p. 157.

[190] See also NÄGELE/XANDER in *Piska/Völkel*, p. 376.

they successfully solve a problem.[191] The first person to find a suitable result is given the reward, leaving the others with nothing. With Bitcoin, successful miners currently receive BTC 6.25 per block, with the block reward halved every four years (a process known as "**bitcoin halving**"). Thus, "new" bitcoin are created and allocated to the miners on their TT-identifiers, until the maximum number of bitcoins – 21 million – is "found". The maximum of 21 million bitcoins will be reached in the year 2140. In this sense, there are **no issuers** who allocate the tokens. The process is very similar to "digging for gold", as it takes some effort and whoever finds the gold becomes its original owner.[192] The draft of a Markets in Crypto-assets (MiCa)[193] Regulation issued by the European Commission also provides for exceptions to the obligations under MiCa for crypto-assets (tokens) that are **mined automatically** in Art. 4, para. 2(b)). These exceptions apply if the *"cryptoassets are mined automatically as payment for the maintenance of the DLT or the validation of transactions."*[194]. In other words, it would be possible under MiCA to publicly offer a new Bitcoin protocol without a licence. Trading on trading platforms would also not be subject to a licence.

Mining usually results in the creation of so-called system "protocol tokens" or "coins", such as bitcoin. Bitcoins can only be technically structured or modified to a limited extent. Conditions in the so-called "**locking script**" can be defined (for this reason, there are no smart-contracts in the proper sense). In practice, the relevant features include, for example, multi-signature requirements that can be implemented via the relevant condition. Multiple signatures would then be required to be able to initiate a transaction. Bitcoins are **intrinsic tokens** that are **created through mining**. They are Bitcoin blockchain "system tokens" ("coins"). Therefore, they do not have an actual generator and do not derive their value from the represented rights.

---

[191] On bitcoin halving and the block reward, see HUBER, Bitcoin 2020 – die Halbierung der Blockprämie.

[192] Some are of the legal opinion that the miners form a simple partnership for the purpose of issuing, for example, bitcoins. The primary aim here is to find a regulatory subject under regulatory law. A simple partnership has no legal personality and in any case recourse would have to be sought with the individual miners, which is not possible in practice, as the miners are generally anonymous. In my view, it would be necessary to understand TT-systems and their nature in order to adequately apply regulatory law. In any event, the subjection to existing law should be reconsidered since the publication of the MiCA draft by the European Commission.

[193] EUROPEAN COMMISSION, proposal for a Regulation on Markets in Crypto-assets (MiCa).

[194] Art. 4, para. 2(b) EUROPEAN COMMISSION, proposal for a Regulation on Markets in Crypto-assets (MiCa).

III Tokens in the proper sense

In addition to the aforementioned system tokens (coins) that can be created through mining, it has also become possible to create new tokens on the basis of existing blockchains. These tokens are technically structured by smart-contracts. Using the example of Ethereum and Aeternity, the content of smart-contracts used to create tokens, i.e. the information that makes up the token, will be presented below. It will be shown that the information makes no distinction between the individual tokens, or that each token has a clear identifier and is thus no longer fungible.

1.1 The creation of tokens through smart-contracts

Ethereum made the creation of tokens much easier. Rather than developing an entirely new TT-system from the ground up to mine protocol tokens, as is the case with Bitcoin, it is possible to create relatively simple proprietary tokens based on Ethereum or Aeternity, for example, in a **modular system**[195]. In particular, using the standard that has become known as "ERC-20", tokens can be "programmed" and "deployed" within minutes. In such cases, usually only the token name, an abbreviation and the desired number of tokens are defined. The tokens created through the smart-contract are then allocated to TT-identifiers upon technical creation.

These tokens are thus created not through mining, but rather through programming and **deployment** on an existing system. It only costs a couple of Swiss francs to create them. These tokens have no intrinsic value and have usually been used within the framework of initial coin offerings ("ICOs") to finance companies. What the purchaser can do with the token largely depends on the technical functions and options of the token and the rights that the token represents.

1.2 The creation of tokens through minting

Once a new token has been created through the deployment of a smart-contract and the number of tokens has been defined, there are other options for creating tokens. If provided for in the smart-contract, it is possible to increase the total number of available tokens, also known as "**minting**". There are virtually no costs associated with doing so. The value of all of the available tokens simply has to be increased and the new tokens allocated to a TT-identifier.

---

195 A number of offerings can be found online, such as: VITTORIO MINACORI, Create ERC20 Token for FREE, https://vittominacori.github.io/erc20-generator (accessed on 21 February 2021).

2 The various token standards

2.1 General information about the token standards based on Ethereum

Token standards describe a combination of functions that must be included in a smart-contract in order for them to be able to interact with other smart-contracts or software, such as crypto exchanges or wallets. There is no universal standard for all tokens. Depending on the technology used, a distinction must be made between different standards. However, the fact that tokens are usually not compatible with one another makes interoperability difficult. The most common token standard at present is the ERC-20 standard. ERC stands for "**Ethereum Request for Comments**". This term comes from software development and has the following background: In addition to the blockchain, Ethereum also refers to the software or the protocol for the Ethereum blockchain. The smart-contract-programming language for Ethereum is called "**Solidity**". The Ethereum software is continuously developed and developers must continuously agree on new functions and improvements. This is done by having developers publish a so-called **Ethereum Improvement Proposal** (EIP). An EIP is a design document that describes the proposed new functions or improvements.[196] Once an EIP achieves a certain status, the EIP becomes an ERC. ERC is therefore a sort of "label for some EIPs" that define a standard when using Ethereum.[197] Token standards such as ERC-20 and ERC-721 are examples of such standards. The number after ERC stands for the discussion or the discussed topic (EIP) and is an ongoing number. For example, EIP-16[198] involved a discussion of whether standards should be defined for certain EIPs, or ERCs. EIP-20 resulted in ERC-20, which is now the most common token standard.

2.2 ERC-20 tokens (fungible tokens)

ERC-20 tokens are intended to enable applications that are as broad as possible and can therefore represent almost everything on Ethereum, such as:

- reputation in an online game,
- skills of game pieces,

---

[196] ANTONOPOULOS/WOOD, Mastering Ethereum. Building smart contracts and DApps (2018), p. 32; ETHEREUM, ethereum/EIPs, https://github.com/ethereum/EIPs (accessed on 21 February 2021).

[197] ANTONOPOULOS/WOOD, Mastering Ethereum, p. 33 f.

[198] ETHEREUM, ethereum/EIPs Issue #16 ·, https://github.com/ethereum/EIPs/issues/16 (accessed on 21 February 2021).

- lottery tickets,
- financial instruments, such as shares in a company,
- legal currency, such as CHF or
- 1 g of gold.[199]

Thus, an ERC-20-compatible **token smart-contract** has one primary function: **to be transferable**. For this reason, it does need a lot of functions. These are the main functions:

- **Transferring tokens** from one TT-identifier to another ("**transfer**"),
- **querying the number of tokens allocated to a TT-identifier ("balanceOf") and**
- querying the **total number of available tokens** ("**totalSupply**").

It is therefore not only easy to transfer tokens from one address[200] to another, but also to query the number of tokens per address and the total number of tokens as well. In addition, it is possible, among other things, to give tokens a name ("**name**", e.g. "TetherToken"), a symbol ("**symbol**", e.g. "USDT"), define the number of decimals ("**decimals**", e.g. 8, after which the token can be divided by 100,000,000) and be given the option of being able to transfer tokens via a smart-contract ("**transferFrom**").[201] Changes to the smart-contract code can no longer be made after the smart-contract has been deployed. If the tokens are not programmed with the corresponding requirements, or if they contain security gaps, there may be significant consequences, including the complete functional failure of the tokens. This is also the rationale for including **token generation** as a service subject to registration under regulatory law in the TVTG.

By default, ERC-20 tokens are **freely transferable** and **cannot** be **distinguished** from one another (**fungible** -> **generic obligations**). However, if an ERC-20 token smart-contract is structured so it cannot be divided (totalSupply = 1 and decimals = 0), then there is only one, indivisible token. This token can be clearly identified by the token smart-contract address -> to this extent, the ERC-20-compatible token is a

---

199 ETHEREUM, ERC-20 Token Standard, https://ethereum.org/en/developers/docs/standards/tokens/erc-20 (accessed on 21 February 2021).

200 In the wording of the TVTG, addresses are TT-identifiers.

201 BUTERIN; VOGELSTELLER, ethereum/EIPs 20.

specific obligation.[202] This example shows how important it is to look at all of the specific issues in detail. Not all ERC-20-compatible tokens can simply be classified as generic obligations without a closer review of their technical structure.[203]

If no additional functions are used when creating an ERC-20 smart-contract, it will no longer be possible to use the tokens if the TT-key is lost (they **cannot be recovered**). Tokens cannot be "reclaimed" from other TT-keys, and it is also **not possible** to **change the number of available tokens** ("**totalSupply**"). However, the aforementioned functions are essential to many applications. For example, when issuing book-entry securities using TT-systems, measures must be taken to ensure that the last person with the right of disposal can be granted the power of disposal in the event of the loss of the TT-key following the **cancellation procedures** pursuant to Art. 10 TVTG. In addition, it must be specified that tokens can only be allocated to TT-identifiers for whom the person with the power of disposal has been identified in advance. In practice, this is done through a so-called "whitelisting function". As part of this function, the token smart-contract reviews whether the recipient address is on a **whitelist** (i.e. a list of authorised recipients) before the transaction is carried out. If this is the case, the transaction is carried out. If not, the transaction is not carried out. Without a corresponding review, legal entities only know the TT-identifiers (addresses) and not the identity of the shareholders.[204] However, the whitelist is not a function provided for in the ERC-20 standard. It has developed other standards. For more information, see the remarks on ERC-1400 in Part 3 , § 2, B, III, 2.4.

Nor does the standard allow, for example, a function to increase the total number of available tokens "**mint**"), also referred to as "minting". In contrast to mining, there is no effort ("PoW") or commitment ("PoS") involved to increase the **number of tokens**. Instead, all that is required is the authorisation to do so and the inclusion of the "mint" function in the programming of the token smart-contract. Supplementing an ERC-20 standard smart-contract to include a mint function does not cause it to

202 In practice, it may be sensible for compatibility reasons to use ERC-20-compatible programming instead of an ERC-721-compatible smart contract. On the other hand, the deployment of a smart contract always involves fees. For this reason, in practice the advantages of compatibility must be weighed against the disadvantage of the associated costs.

203 VOGELSTELLER/BUTERIN, ERC-20 Token Standard, https://github.com/ethereum/EIPs/blob/master/EIPS/eip-20.md (accessed on 21 February 2021).

204 Not least in order to meet the obligations for maintaining a register of beneficial owners; the Act of 6 December 2018 on the Register of Ultimate Beneficial Owners of Domestic Legal Entities (Gesestz über das Verzeichnis der wirtschaftlichen Eigentümer inländischer Rechtsträger (VwEG), Liechtenstein Law Gazette (2019).

lose its ERC-20 compatibility. However, this may be the case with other functions. Depending on the application, however, there may be a significant impact on whether the total number of available tokens (totalSupply) can be changed after the creation and deployment of the token. On the one hand, it may in some cases be necessary to increase or decrease the number of tokens. On the other hand, there are applications where this is not supposed to be possible (scarce goods, such as some cryptocurrencies). For example, if a token is used to represent co-ownership shares, it is important to make sure the number of tokens cannot be changed easily.

All of these smart-contract functions, just like smart-contracts themselves, are carried out on Ethereum by the Ethereum Virtual Machine (EVM). Thus, Ethereum, as stated in the introduction, is similar to a large decentralised computer, whose computing power is paid in the form of fees (called "gas") in ether or its subunit "gwei"[205]. Thus, each transaction costs an amount in ether or a fraction of ether, gwei.[206]

The respective token smart-contract must define whether a token is a **specific or generic obligation**, whether there is an unchangeable, fixed number or a variable number of total tokens and whether there are restrictions on transfers. Thus, the smart-contract must be read and understood in order to determine its legal classification. If new tokens are deployed, for example, on the basis of Ethereum, it has become standard practice to deploy the token smart-contract in plain language[207]. Each token has a so-called "**contract address**". The contract address makes it possible to **clearly identify** the smart-contract. The name of the smart-contract ("**name**") does not have to be unique. Any number of smart-contracts can have the same name.

For the sake of better understanding, an example of an ERC-20-compatible token smart-contract will be discussed in more detail below. A token used in an ICO, such as the Aeternity token, will serve as a good example. This token smart-contract can be publicly viewed on, for example, etherscan.io, like any other contract based on Ethereum. However, not all have been deployed in readable form. The AE ERC-20 token is a modified version of an ERC-20 standard **token smart-contract**. The smart-contract for the AE ERC-20 token from Aeternity and its "contract address" can be found at:

---

[205] 1 ether = 1,000,000,000 gweis.

[206] ANTONOPOULOS/WOOD, Mastering Ethereum, p. 85.

[207] By default, the source code of the token smart contract is not deployed.

https://etherscan.io/address/0x5ca9a71b1d01849c0a95490cc00559717fcf0d1d#code[208]

The more comments[209] there are in the source code, the easier the code is to understand. Thus, the following code can be read for the above example:

```
function AEToken() HumanStandardToken(0, "Aeternity", 18, "AE") { unit nYears = 2; transferableUntil = now + (60 * 60 * 24 * 365 * nYears); }
```

The comment below this reads: *"// Date when the tokens won't be transferable anymore"*. So the token expires and can no longer be transferred after about[210] two years. This is a token with a fixed term. After the end of the term, the token can no longer be transferred again and thus loses what is likely its most important function.

The Aeternity ERC-20 smart-contract also allows, for example, all tokens to be allocated at the beginning to the TT-identifier that deployed the smart-contract on the Ethereum blockchain ("creator")[211]:

"balances[msg.sender] = _initialAmount; // Give the creator all initial tokens"

Consequently, it is not so difficult to understand what the individual functions mean.

In summary, it can be said that the most common token standard, ERC-20, is used in practice as the basis for cryptocurrencies and will continue to do so and often to represent generic obligations. However, as has also been shown, it is important to consider the structure of the **token smart-contract** in detail in order to avoid surprises, such as unchangeable token expiry times. Nor is there a single answer to the question of whether an ERC-20 token is an **intrinsic** or an **extrinsic** token. Most ERC-20-based tokens were structured as cryptocurrencies, which is why they are intrinsic tokens and their value does not depend on an external value. If these tokens are used, for example, to function as book-entry securities or **stablecoins**[212], they would derive their value from the book-entry security or from some other asset. In turn, these tokens would be classified as extrinsic tokens.

---

208 ETHERSCAN.IO, Aeternity (AE) contract address, https://etherscan.io/address/0x5ca9a71b1d01849c0a95490cc00559717fcf0d1d#code (accessed on 8 February 2021).

209 In the case of the Ethereum programming language, called Solidity, comments are marked with a "/". Explanations can be included in the comments.

210 As Ethereum has no direct time system, the block height is used for this purpose, as it can be converted into an approximate time. The average time needed until the next block is mined is used.

211 This is also standard.

212 On stablecoins, see the explanatory definition in the introduction.

2.3 ERC-721 tokens (non-fungible tokens)

The major difference between the (fungible) ERC-20 standard token and the non-fungible token according to **ERC-721** is the ability to clearly distinguish or identify them. The ERC-721 standard for **non-fungible** tokens ("NFT") was published on github.com in September 2017. Under this new ERC-721 standard, every token can be identified on the basis of the same smart-contract through a unique "**tokenID**". It is important to understand the interplay of the smart-contract's contract address with the tokenID. It must be possible for other smart-contracts to provide the same tokenIDs. Otherwise, tokenIDs would become a scarce resource, like domain names on the internet. The combination of contract address and tokenID can be compared with the model number and the serial number of a product. The model number describes the version, while the serial number describes the individual unit in the model series (e.g. "12345678"). A camera can have the same model number or the same serial number as a luxury watch. The individual item is only clearly identified by the combination of the model number and the serial number. The same applies to the contract address and the tokenID. The contract address describes the token model, while the tokenID, as the serial number, describes the individual unit in the model series. Knowing the contract address and the tokenID makes a clear assignment possible.

The assignment of the respective token to a TT-identifier is carried out in the ERC-721 standard using a function called "**ownerOf**". This function restores the TT-identifier to the individual to whom the token with a specific tokenID has been allocated. In other words, the TT-system is asked to whom a token "belongs". In addition, it is possible for a "**tokenUri**" to be set for a specific token which may contain, for example, a link to a website with additional information.[213]

ERC-721 tokens can also be distinguished by their age, for example. They are uncommon to different degrees or have a different output, for example, an image, when used in decentralised applications (dApps). The information that results in the image may, some cases, be protected as a work under intellectual property law, and the creator as the author pursuant to copyright law. ERC-721-compatible tokens are a specific obligation because of their individual description, as they involve an identifiable token.[214]

---

[213] ETHEREUM, ERC-721 Non-Fungible Token Standard, https://ethereum.org/en/developers/docs/standards/tokens/erc-20 (accessed on 21 February 2021).

[214] ETHEREUM, ERC-721 Non-Fungible Token Standard.

2.4 ERC-1400 security tokens (share tokens)

As already stated, when using tokens as a cryptocurrency, the ability to transfer them freely is a key function. However, if, for example, book-entry securities (digital securities) are to be used in the form of tokens involving TT-systems, then free transferability would result in problems. ERC-1400 has tackled this – like other specific challenges when using tokens to represent member rights, such as shareholder rights. For this reason, tokens created according to this standard are also called share tokens.

The discussion originally started with EIP 1400 was split into EIP 1411 ("Security Token Standard") and EIP 1410 ("Partially Fungible Token Standard"). However, the number for the standard remained the same and the name was modified to ERC-1400. The standard description for ERC-1400 states that ERC-1400 tokens must be backwards compatible with ERC-20. In addition, the following compulsory functions, which are essential to the life cycle of book-entry securities, were defined:[215]

- **canTransfer**: To check whether a transfer will be successful (e.g. advance query of a whitelist);
- **controllerTransfer** ("force transfer"[216]): Enables, for example, the legal enforcement of token transfers without the involvement of the person with the right of disposal;[217]
- **events** on issue and redemption: When issuing and redeeming tokens, events[218] must be initiated that can then serve as the start for additional processing steps;

[215] ETHEREUM, ERC 1400: Security Token Standard · Issue #1411 · ethereum/EIPs, https://github.com/ethereum/eips/issues/1411 (accessed on 21 February 2021).

[216] Force transfer is discussed in more detail in ERC-1644, which is part of ERC-1400 and which enables a controller to carry out transfers, which is why it is also called the "Controller Token Operation Standard"; DOSSA/RUIZ/VOGELSTELLER/GOSSELIN, ERC-1644: Controller Token Operation Standard · Issue #1644 · ethereum/EIPs, https://github.com/ethereum/EIPs/issues/1644 (accessed on 22 February 2021).

[217] Because another TT-identifier is defined here that can initiate transactions; a corresponding transaction can be initiated either by the creator or a specific "controller", e.g. a court or a service provider; ETHEREUM, ERC 1400: Security Token Standard · Issue #1411 · ethereum/EIPs.

[218] These events can be used to initiate other actions. Without events (also referred to as transactions), the Ethereum blockchain would not be "active".

- **metadata**: There must be an option to add further information about, for example, special shareholder rights or transfer restrictions; it must be possible to modify this metadata during transfers to include both off-chain and on-chain data as well as the transfer parameters;
- **documentation**: It must be possible to query or subscribe to relevant documents related to the book-entry security (e.g. a white paper, securities prospectus).[219]

In addition, under the standard it is possible for **data signed** off-chain to be **included** in a **transfer transaction** in order to validate the **transaction on-chain**.[220]
Another important function is **destroying tokens** or making them unusable (also referred to as "**burning**" them). The simplest way of doing so is sending the tokens to an address no one can use, such as the address "oxo". Of course, controllers have this option as they can initiate transactions to any address.[221]
Identity plays a major role when applying tokens as book-entry securities. As already stated, legal entities must know the identity of their members (shareholders) in order to meet their obligations. This stems in part from the due diligence duties. In Liechtenstein, the free transferability of bearer instruments has been restricted (immobilisation of bearer shares).[222] The canTransfer-function can be used, for example, to query approval lists ("**whitelists**") prior to a transfer with all of the addresses which have undergone a KYC[223] and AML[224] process.

3 Tokens based on Aeternity

The Aeternity blockchain was developed by Aeternity Anstalt, based in Vaduz, Liechtenstein. The programming language for developing smart-contracts for the Aeternity blockchain is called "**Sophia**".[225] It is very similar to the Ethereum smart-contract programming language "Solidity". Examples of smart-contracts based on Sophia for fungible tokens, non-fungible tokens and other smart-contracts can be found on

[219] ETHEREUM, ERC 1400: Security Token Standard Issue #1411 ethereum/EIPs.

[220] ETHEREUM, ERC 1400: Security Token Standard Issue #1411 ethereum/EIPs.

[221] ANTONOPOULOS/WOOD, Mastering Ethereum, p. 223.

[222] GOVERNMENT OF THE PRINCIPALITY OF LIECHTENSTEIN, BuA No. 69/2012, p. 4.

[223] KYC: Know your customer. This involves determining the contractual partner's identity.

[224] AML: Anti-money laundering. This involves, for example, determining the source of funds.

[225] AETERNITY, The Sophia language, https://aeternity-sophia.readthedocs.io/en/latest (accessed on 22 February 2021).

github.com.[226] What etherscan.io is for Ethereum, aeternal.io is for Aeternity. While the technical implementations in this example are similar, they sometimes lead to significant differences as regards inclusion.

3.1 Aeternity fungible tokens

Fungible tokens based on Sophia are also exchangeable, divisible and identical, which is why they are suitable for use as cryptocurrencies and are classified as a generic obligation. In most cases, they are therefore intrinsic-tokens.[227] When they are created, the "**owner**" of the smart-contract who is receiving the right to "**mint**" tokens must be defined. In addition, there is a "**burn**" function that makes it possible to destroy the number of tokens that are allocated to an address. Thus, Sophia already includes a number of needed standard functions. Tokens are allocated to an "account" or an address that corresponds to the "TT-identifier", to use the language of the TVTG. Users with the power of disposal can transfer tokens, destroy tokens or give third parties the option of transferring tokens in their name. The token smart-contract also makes it possible to check the address to which a token has been allocated and how many tokens there are in total ("**total_supply**").[228]

3.2 Aeternity non-fungible tokens

Sophia can also be used as the basis for NFTs. Here, too, there is a clear ID, called a "**token_id**". This makes it possible to distinguish the token involved, which makes it a specific obligation. "**token_uri**" can be used to allocate metadata to the token, e.g. the URL of a website showing an authenticity certificate.[229]

Although no example of the application of book-entry securities has yet been published, the requirements that have been defined in, for example, ERC-1400, can also be implemented with Sophia. Aeternity speaks here of "**restricted fungible tokens**".[230]

---

[226] AETERNITY, aepp-sophia-examples, https://github.com/aeternity/aepp-sophia-examples (accessed on 22 February 2021).

[227] Like fungible tokens on Ethereum, there are also tokens that are extrinsic tokens, as their value is derived from external assets.

[228] GITHUB, Fungible token example, https://github.com/aeternity/aepp-sophia-examples/tree/master/libraries/FungibleToken (accessed on 22 February 2021).

[229] AETERNITY, Non-fungible token example, https://github.com/aeternity/aepp-sophia-examples/tree/master/libraries/NonFungibleToken (accessed on 22 February 2021).

[230] AETERNITY, æternity - a blockchain for scalable, secure and decentralized æpps, https://aeternity.com/#sophia (accessed on 22 February 2021).

IV The question of the controllability of data

As shown, data is not the same as information and thus a nuanced view is required. Some argue that trusted technologies (Blockchains) would make data controllable and that property law should therefore apply to tokens. RIETZLER/FRICK/CASELLINI[231] spoke in favour of the application of property law to tokens before entry into force of the TVTG. NÄGELE/XANDER took the opposite view in the same publication.[232] Their main argument involved the controllability of tokens by the TT-key. It only became possible to make data controllable with Bitcoin.[233] As already shown, however, a distinction is now made between data and information. The TVTG purposely does not use the term "data"; instead, it speaks of "information". Therefore, it is not data that becomes controllable through the use of blockchain, but rather tokens through the use of blockchain.. For the first time, blockchain **technology made it possible** to allocate **certain information that was protected against manipulation** to a TT-identifier with no central authority and that could only be disposed of via the TT-key. "No one can use my bitcoins but me, no one can copy them."[234] This information is then distributed, stored and processed by as large a number of network participants as possible in the form of data on a wide variety of data carriers. Thus, the **information** that makes up a token is – in most practical cases – specially classified, interpreted digital data that has been stored and processed by as large a number of network participants as possible. As a result, in contrast to what is stipulated by RIETZLER/FRICK/CASELLINI, the data is not more controllable than before as a result of the introduction of decentralised systems, but rather less controllable than before.[235]

V Conclusion on the information that makes up a token

When the TVTG speaks of "information", it means "interpreted data" stored on TT-systems. The distinction between data and information is important here. What data and information (interpreted data) have in common is that they are not property pursuant to property law. The key delineating feature here is the lack of physicality

---

231 RIETZLER/*M.* FRICK/CASELLINI in *Piska/Völkel,* p. 364 f.

232 NÄGELE/XANDER in *Piska/Völkel,* p. 367 ff.

233 RIETZLER/*M.* FRICK/CASELLINI in *Piska/Völkel,* p. 364.

234 A simplified example has been used here for illustration purposes. The features of Bitcoin will be explained in more detail below.

235 This is also clearly demonstrated by the discussion related to the non-compatibility of the General Data Protection Regulation (GDPR) with blockchain. The right to be forgotten de facto cannot be implemented because the data is stored by any number of network participants.

of both data and information. Tokens and the information that makes up a token are different from the data that stores and processes this information. For this reason, the TVTG uses the term "information", which requires further explanation, rather than data as a constituent feature in its definition of the term "token". The interpreted data that makes up the information in a token varies depending on the token. The information that makes up a bitcoin is somewhat elusive and starts with the question of how many bitcoins have been allocated to a person with the right of disposal. The information about who "has" how many bitcoins cannot be seen directly in the database stored in a decentralised manner in the form of a blockchain, but is instead calculated by each full node and stored temporarily in a local database. The information that makes up a bitcoin is thus not a simple character string (syntactic level), but rather the result of a calculation (transaction model). In contrast to Bitcoin, Ethereum uses a model with account balances. As expected, the accounts have an account balance and – if someone wishes to carry out a transaction – the sender's account is checked to make sure there is a sufficient balance. If this is the case, the amount is credited to the recipient account and deducted from the sender account, which is called the account model. Thus, the information that makes up the ether is the result of an inquiry to determine how many ethers are allocated to which TT-identifier. However, in order to understand the term fully, it is important to look not only at how system tokens (coins) are created through mining and allocated and transferred as part of transactions, but also how tokens in the proper sense are technically structured through the programming of smart-contracts. This is because, in addition to system tokens (coins), it has also become possible to create new tokens on the basis of existing TT. These tokens are technologically structured by smart-contracts. New tokens can be created relatively easily based on, for example, Ethereum or Aeternity in a modular system. These tokens are thus created not through mining, but rather through programming and deployment on an existing system. The information that makes up a token created in this way is therefore different than the information that makes up a system token. The token smart-contract defines the information that is available. Token standards describe a combination of functions that must be included in a smart-contract in order for them to be able to interact with other smart-contracts or software such as crypto-exchanges or wallets. In other words, they therefore describe a certain minimum content. These smart-contracts are highly relevant to the legal classification. The respective token smart-contract must define whether a token is classified as a specific or generic obligation, whether there is an unchangeable, fixed number or a variable number of total tokens and whether there are restrictions on transfers. The major difference between the (fungible) ERC-20 standard token and the non-fungible token according to ERC-721 ("NFT"), for example, is the ability to clearly distinguish or identify them. In addition, there are many other standards, including several for security tokens (e.g. ERC-1400). In summary, it can be said that the constituent feature of information is that it includes the flexibility needed to encompass a wide variety of tokens, both system tokens and tokens based on other TT-systems.

VI Side note on the token generator pursuant to the TVTG

The supervisory model and thus TT-service providers pursuant to the TVTG are not the focus of this book. As the delineation of the services provided by the token creator is closely connected to the creation of the token, a brief definition of a possible delineation will be provided here.

Art. 2, para. 1(l) TVTG defines the token generator as a service provider as follows:

"Token generator": a person who generates one or more Tokens".

The generation of tokens must be delineated from the activities before the generation and after the generation as well as other activities. The question is which activities the law aims to subject to the registration obligation pursuant to the TVTG. In this context, the remarks on token generators on p. 153 of BuA 54/2019[236] must be read, along with those on p. 38 of BuA 54/2019[237]. The "creation" of tokens and thus the delineating feature of processes not subject to the registration obligation are described on p. 38 as follows:

Token creation is the process of adding[238] information to a transaction system. Consequently, the token is a priori available to the generator (or creator on Ethereum). Thus, the person who has added a token on Ethereum, for example, is easy to determine by checking the **creator** value. The answer will be a TT-identifier. Technically, it is therefore easy to see which TT-identifier a smart-contract has deployed. Consequently, on Ethereum, the **creator** is the same as the **token generator pursuant to the TVTG**, as this person adds (deploys) the token smart-contract (which here refers to "information") to a transaction system (here, Ethereum). The token generator is

[236] BuA No. 54/2019, p. 153.

[237] BuA No. 54/2019, p. 38.

[238] Depending on the TT system, the process is called initialisation or deployment of the token (or "deployment of the smart contract").

usually the person with the power of disposal over a token, identified by the TT-identifier. In most cases, the technical structure is carried out by a service provider who has the power of disposal, but is not the person with the right of disposal.

Usually, the person who has programmed a token smart-contract is the one who deploys it. In some cases, however, the token generator may wish to assume **responsibility** and **control**, but may not want to carry out the technical structuring. In this case, the programmer is not the same as the token generator pursuant to the TVTG. For this reason, the TVTG views generation as the critical process that is subject to the registration obligation pursuant to the TVTG. In other words, the decisive factor for classification as the token generator pursuant to the TVTG is that the token is **generated by a service provider professionally**, i.e. added on the TT-system. Service providers that do not generate tokens on the TT-system do not need to be registered. The latter create the rules (software, protocol) regarding how the tokens behave, which interactions are possible and, in particular, under which circumstances they can be transferred[239]. In practice, these technical services are also provided by token generators in some cases, but this does not result in an obligation to register[240]. The addition of a token on a TT-system does not correspond to a public sale that is sometimes subject to registration as a token issuer and that regularly occurs after generation.[241]

Consequently, a token issuer can, for example, use a service provider to implement the token technically for a fee (the service provider programs the token smart-contract). As long as the issuer also carries out the generation itself, i.e. adds the token to the TT-system (deployment), it is acting pursuant to Art. 2, para. 1(l) TVTG, but there is no professional activity pursuant to Art. 12 TVTG.

§ 3 (2) "On a TT-system"

A Trustworthy-Technologies (TT) and TT-systems

The meaning of trustworthy-technologies and TT-systems is of utmost importance. The subject, purpose and scope of the general, civil law and regulatory law provisions

---

239 BuA No. 54/2019, p. 153.

240 This is comparable to a lawyer who has their administrative assistant prepare simple paperwork (e.g. for debt enforcement proceedings) and then simply signs it. In such cases, the administrative assistant does not need to be admitted to the bar.

241 In some cases, tokens are sold that are yet to be created. The time sequence is not a delineation criterion here; BuA No. 54/2019, p. 38 f.

always refer to trustworthy-technologies (see Art. 2, para. 1, Art. 3, para. 1, Art. 11, para. 1 TVTG). In Art. 7, para. 1 and para. 2 TVTG, in particular, the aim of the law is to connect the represented right and the token in a way that ensures that the right cannot be asserted or transferred to others without the token. The desired commercial security of transactions involving tokens makes it necessary for people to trust the apparent legality of the token. In other words, if the token represents the right to own a watch, then it is sufficient for the purpose of demonstrating ownership if the token holder demonstrates the right to dispose of the token (identification-function pursuant to Art. 8, para. 1 TVTG). A payment by the debtor to the person identified in such a way liberates the debt (liberation-function pursuant to Art. 8, para. 2 TVTG).[242]

If a service provider does not use TT or TT-systems, then the service provider is not a TT-service-provider and may not refer to itself as such (designation protection pursuant to Art. 24 TVTG). However, this also means that if no TT-system is used for the service provision, then the service provider cannot be registered as a TT-service-provider. It should not be possible to offer services such as TT-token-custody without the secure custody and transparency of TT-systems that enable this new regulatory approach with no intermediaries in the first place.

These wide-ranging legal consequences create the legal certainty that legislators intended when they drafted the TVTG. But why weren't these legal consequences assigned to digital transactions with no intermediaries before the development of TT and TT-systems, and what distinguishes a TT-system from a "normal" database application? Let's take the example of a mobile phone application that makes it possible to buy and sell securities. The IT system here is operated by a regulated intermediary. The user cannot see the IT system and needs to be able to trust that the displays in the application are correct. If a client buys a certain number of shares in a particular stock and these are displayed in the app, the clients trust that they have become shareholders in the company. Such securities services are reserved for regulated intermediaries that have been licensed and are monitored by a supervisory authority. The extensive regulation and supervision of the intermediary reduces the risk that the client will be harmed. They can trust the service provider. Of course, from a technical standpoint it would be easy for the intermediary to alter the information in the databases it operates. However, the supervision and the system in which the intermediary is integrated make this difficult or would make it obvious sooner or later, which would result in consequences under regulatory law. In the case of regulated

[242] See Part 3, Section 4(C).

intermediaries, it is irrelevant for the regulatory approach whether the records are in analogue or digital form. Because the intermediary manages them, it can influence them. The ease with which such manipulations can be carried out make the extensive regulation of intermediaries necessary to prevent misuse. In contrast, TT and TT-systems make it possible to almost totally rule out misuse, including on digital systems, with no regulated intermediaries:

> *"Blockchain technology is important because of its ability to represent 'information' digitally in a way that makes it practically impossible to copy or manipulate and allows it to be transferred securely between different people. This security is ensured solely by mathematical procedures (e.g. encryption technology, cryptography) and defined rules."*[243]

Because of the technical structure of the systems, it is almost impossible for individuals to change information in their favour and without authorisation. If this applies to a system, then the system enables a new regulatory approach with no intermediaries, but only where the technological structure of the systems can prevent misuse. The systems structured in this way are classified as TT and TT-systems and will be examined below.

The desire for a "list" of TT and TT-systems is understandable, but such a list does not exist. Neither the Government nor the FMA have published lists like this. The original intention of creating a list of criteria at regulatory level was rejected not only for constitutional reasons, but also in favour of **technological neutrality**.[244] The terms "TT-systems" and "trustworthy-technologies" are therefore deliberately broad. Assistance in interpreting these terms can be found, in particular, in BuA 54/2019 on p. 130 ff. The following paragraph on page 131 is especially relevant:

> *"In the case of the TT-systems that are currently known, the trustworthiness arises as a result of their decentralised nature and thus the number of operators of the technology itself, which ensures the integrity of the tokens and the transaction register through, for example, encryption technology, the principle of distributed ledger and pre-defined rules."*[245]

---

243 BuA No. 54/2019, p. 5.

244 On the reasons why no criteria were defined in the first legislative draft, see GOVERNMENT OF THE PRINCIPALITY OF LIECHTENSTEIN, consultation report on the Blockchain Act (accessed on 16 November 2018), p. 85 f., https://www.llv.li/files/srk/vnb-blockchain-gesetz.pdf; BuA No. 54/2019, 131, 134.

245 BuA No. 54/2019, p. 131.

On the one hand, the intent is to cover all possible forms of "secure" systems to the greatest extent possible. On the other hand, systems that do not justify the use of intermediaries should be prevented from benefiting from these legal consequences and the use of the protected terms. As already stated, the civil law provisions, the registration obligations and the designation protection are directly dependent on the technology used. Thus, it is up to the legal practitioner to determine in the individual situation whether or not the criteria have been met and a technology can be classified as "**trustworthy technology**" pursuant to the TVTG. In my view, however, such a review during the selection of the system would have to suffice and not be repeated continuously if, for example, there are only short-term security concerns, but these can be remedied in an appropriate amount of time. For example, even a short-term 51% attack on the classification as TT and a TT-system would not be harmful.[246]

In order to understand the legal definition of trustworthy-technologies and thus TT-systems, a basic understanding of the individual technologies that have led to this abstract, technology-neutral definition is required. Only such an understanding makes it possible to include these features within the delineation. Thus, it is always a question of delineation that must take account of the individual situation. This ranges from established systems such as Ethereum to simple centralised databases stored on a server with information about token holdings. As clearly as Ethereum is a TT and TT-system pursuant to the TVTG, this clearly does not apply to a database that can easily be changed by an individual. For this reason, the criteria that make Bitcoin and Ethereum a TT-system will be explained below. In the case of other systems, individual elements are replaced with others in order to classify them as TT and TT-systems.

I The definitions of TT and TT-systems

In practice and in the limited literature to date, the terms TT and TT-systems are often used as synonyms for "blockchain" and "DLT".[247] When looked at more closely, the latter two terms are not even synonymous with one another. **Blockchain** refers

[246] For more on this point, see the attack opportunities.

[247] See, for example, the remarks on TT-systems by FALKER/TEICHMANNLiechtenstein – Das TVTG und Risiken der Blockchain-Technologie, InTeR 2020, p. 62.

to both the technology and the "database" or "distributed ledger" itself, and can be divided into further subgroups. **DLT**, in contrast, refers to the technology.[248]

It is hardly surprising that the delineation in practice causes few problems at present, as most service providers use Ethereum as a TT-system. The Government also clearly used **Bitcoin** and **Ethereum** – i.e. "*known TT-systems*"[249] – as **models** of trustworthy-technologies.

The term "Bitcoin" appears a total of 60 times in BuA 54/2019; in contrast, "Ethereum" appears only four times. For the end users of technology, the way the technology works is in most cases less relevant. However, if the legal system **attaches legal consequences to the technology** and does not clearly state the specific forms that are necessary for this, then the situation changes. Viewed from the outside, it is not apparent whether an app[250] or a website serves as a GUI[251] for a blockchain application or for a central internet service. It is not clear to the user what will happen to the data that is entered. The data may be forwarded to the centrally managed database of an individual operator or a TT-system and processed there. This can best be demonstrated using two examples that occurred repeatedly in Liechtenstein from 2016 to 2019:

<u>Case 1 – Aeternity crowdfunding campaign (ICO)</u>: A group of (mostly younger) entrepreneurs has an idea that they cannot fund themselves. They intend to develop software that provides certain functions that users can only use with tokens. The entrepreneurs describe their project in a white paper, which they publish on their website, and start an initial coin offering (ICO), with which they will sell crowdsale tokens[252] that they created – relatively easily – on Ethereum as ERC-20 tokens. The crowdsale tokens will be transferred to the ICO participants' own TT-identifiers. However, these

[248] The Government views DLT as the distribution of the ledger (transaction register) between many computers connected via the internet – peer-to-peer; see BuA No. 54/2019, p. 17; Van Hijfte clearly distinguishes between blockchain and DLT, their concept and the goals that can be achieved with them; see VAN HIJFTE, Blockchain Platforms, p. 36 f.

[249] In this sense, tokens can be generated on existing TT-systems (e.g. ERC-20-compatible tokens on the Ethereum blockchain) or on proprietary TT-systems. BuA No. 54/2019, p. 153; on Bitcoin as a model, see also *A.* FRICK, Zivilrechtliche Aspekte von Token im Zusammenhang mit dem liechtensteinischen Token- und VT-Dienstleister-Gesetz, p. 13.

[250] Abbreviation for application; usually as a term for software on a smartphone.

[251] GUI stands for graphical user interface.

[252] For the sake of better understanding, tokens that were issued for crowdfunding campaigns are called "crowdsale" tokens; the corresponding token smart contract can be viewed on etherscan.io: ETHERSCAN.IO, Aeternity (AE) token tracker, https://etherscan.io/token/0x5ca9a71b1d01849c0a95490cc00559717fcf0d1d (accessed on 6 February 2021).

crowdsale tokens cannot be used to utilise the functions of the newly created blockchain. The software first needs to be developed.

All participants can review the transactions conducted with the crowdsale tokens themselves by looking at the Ethereum blockchain, for example, by going to www.etherscan.io. The participants can immediately transfer the ERC-20 crowdsale tokens to whomever they wish. Depending on the structure of the ERC-20, the number of tokens is fixed and can no longer be changed by the company after the token smart-contracts have been created. In other words, the ICO participants finance the development of the software through their purchase of crowdsale tokens. These tokens have no other use. The AE tokens, which are the tokens which are actually useful, are only received after the software is completed.

The entrepreneurs document the project progress on their blog, while the software development can be followed at github.com[253]. In the white paper, they describe what the new software will be able to do. As soon as the software is completed, the old crowdsale tokens will be converted (also referred to as "token migration") into new AE tokens on the new platform.[254] The old crowdsale tokens will have fulfilled their purpose and will no longer have any value. What is left unsaid, of course, is whether the company will be successful and the AE tokens can be used for the purposes described in the white paper.

Case 2 – "Fraudulent" ICO[255]:

"Tokens" were being publicly offered for sale on a website. But those offering the tokens had a criminal purpose in mind. Instead of using the funds they collected to

---

[253] GITHUB, æternity, https://github.com/aeternity (accessed on 6 February 2021).

[254] Anyone can see how many addresses have tokens and how many have sent their tokens to the "migration contract" address in order to receive new tokens. This amounted to about 89% as of 6 February 2021. ETHERSCAN.IO, Aeternity (AE) token tracker - balances, https://etherscan.io/token/0x5ca9a71b1d01849c0a95490cc00559717fcf0d1d#balances (accessed on 6 February 2021).

[255] One case stands out in my memory. We received a request at our law firm from a company that wanted to develop a new blockchain. Similar to Bitcoin and Ethereum, only "much better" and without "the known problems with transaction speeds". During the first meeting, we were told that tokens had already been sold. When I asked which blockchain had been used for the sale of the tokens (after all, they wanted to develop their own blockchain, which was not yet available), the "entrepreneurs" said that their blockchain already worked for this purpose. I was then shown a website with a www.*****.com/wp-admin address ("wp-admin" is usually used to access the administrative console of websites on certain systems). The website's back-end really did have a client database with users and token holdings. However, on a normal

carry out their business idea, they intended to use them to finance their excessive lifestyle. For this reason, the tokens were not created and transferred using a TT-system, but rather on a standard website. The criminals merely created the "tokens" using a web server database and then allocated these tokens to the purchasers. The token purchasers only saw the website, not the technology behind it. And the website could not be distinguished from the website in the first case. It was only possible to see the differences after looking "behind" the website. The fraudsters acting as the operator of the website and the database in case 2 had complete control over the data. They could modify the contents whenever they wanted. In particular, they could allocate "tokens" to whichever users they wanted without creating new "tokens", make "tokens" disappear or simply delete the website, including all of the information about the users and their supposed "tokens".

The entrepreneurs have complete control over the website data in case 1 as well. They control the deployment and transfer of the tokens, but no more. In other words, their ability to exert influence is limited. In addition, the transactions are public and can therefore be tracked and thus checked by anyone. If more tokens are created (than what is specified in the white paper), this can also be tracked (see tokenSupply). If the tokens are not allocated to different TT-identifiers, it can be assumed that not many participants have purchased tokens. This can be an indicator that the crowd-funding campaign is being artificially presented as more successful than it really is through fake transactions. This transparency makes it much more difficult to carry out fraud over the long run. Although the entrepreneurs in case 1 could delete the company's website, the tokens and transactions and other information on the TT-system are not under their control. Injured parties in case 2 would have a more difficult time proving what happened. Of course, in both cases the websites are not based on TT-systems. In case 1, however, the tokens were generated and transferred on TT-systems. This can be illustrated by the image of two icebergs that look to be the same size on the surface. Only after looking below the water-surface it becomes clear, how much mass one iceberg has in comparison to the other one.

This takes us to the crux of the term "**trustworthy-technologies**" – trustworthiness. We trust the technology, not the actors. However, this requires something from the technical structure, which will be further explained below.

---

website this is usually stored centrally in a MySQL database. Those without IT knowledge would not be aware of this.

1 The trustworthiness of trustworthy-technologies and TT-systems

The term "**trustworthy technology**" (or "TT") is an overarching term introduced by the TVTG for certain qualified technologies, such as certain blockchain or DLT systems. The term refers to trustworthiness as a result of technology and not as a result of a regulated intermediary, for example. The term "**trustless**"[256]technologies is also used in IT.[257] **Trustless** (or "trust-free") systems refers to systems that **operate without the trust of users** in order to provide certain functions. In the case of TT-systems, which by definition must be "trustless", it refers to systems that provide storage and **transaction systems** for which "trustworthy" intermediaries are usually used. But where does this trustworthiness stem from? This is precisely the question the creator of Bitcoin had to answer when he invented blockchain technology. He had found an answer to the problems that unleashed the financial crisis. He provided the answer, published in a white paper under the pseudonym SATOSHI NAKAMOTO, as follows:

> *"What is needed is an electronic payment system based on cryptographic proof instead of trust, allowing any two willing parties to transact directly with each other without the need for a trusted third party."*[258]

This whitepaper also presented **solutions for the problems** that had until then made it difficult to carry out transactions **digitally without intermediaries**. Several of the key challenges of digital transactions without intermediaries and the solution to these problems through Bitcoin will be presented below. These solutions are what make Bitcoin a trustworthy technology and a TT-system and help to make the terms more concrete. The main opportunities for attack and their likelihood of success will also be presented. The resulting findings will then be used as a general tool for interpreting whether a system can be included under the terms "TT" and "TT-system".

---

[256] Trustless.

[257] NÄGELE, Sekundärmarkt für Security Token, p. 8; and Prime Minister Adrian Hasler during the first reading of report and proposal no. 54/2014 on the TVTG in the Landtag of the Principality of Liechtenstein: minutes of the Parliament 5-7, June 2019, Part 2, p. 1071.

[258] NAKAMOTO, (PSEUDONYM), Bitcoin: A Peer-to-Peer Electronic Cash System, p. 1.

2 What enabled digital transactions without intermediaries?

2.1 The Byzantine Generals Problem

The **Byzantine fault** is a thought experiment in IT. It attempts to show the challenges and problems that occur when it is necessary to communicate via insecure and untrustworthy nodes and between multiple participants.

The Byzantine Generals are planning on capturing an extremely powerful city. This requires a coordinated and, above all, simultaneous attack from several sides. The generals and their troops therefore disperse in front of the city and attempt to determine the time of the attack. Because of the distance between them, they communicate via messenger. The generals assume there are traitors among them who want to prevent them from being able to agree on a coordinated attack. The problem is further complicated by the spatial separation that makes it necessary for the generals to send the messengers back and forth. The messengers may be killed, captured or bribed.[259] Before Satoshi Nakamoto presented his solution in 2008[260], various other solutions had been published dating back to 1982. However, these solutions will not be covered here.[261] Satoshi Nakamoto's solution creates an electronic means of payment without trustworthy intermediaries. Like the Generals, users can use messengers (nodes) to disclose their transactions to the entire network. In doing so, they do not have to trust anyone and can be sure that everyone has the same information. The participants agree between themselves and reach a consensus without the need for mutual trust (Byzantine Generals Problem). Because they can reach agreement in this way in a trustless manner, another key problem can be solved, the "double spend problem".

2.2 Double spend problem –the ability to copy digital information

The **double spend problem** refers to the problem that a digital currency can be spent multiple times. Obviously, this problem does not exist with banknotes and coins, but it is easy to copy information stored digitally. For this reason, digital currencies could lead to a growing money supply and a loss of confidence in money if

---

[259] See LAMPORT/SHOSTAK/PEASE, The Byzantine generals problem, ACM transactions on programming languages and systems 1982, p. 382 f.; and VAN HIJFTE, Blockchain Platforms, p. 24; as well as WIKIPEDIA, Byzantine fault, https://en.wikipedia.org/wiki/Byzantine_fault (accessed on 17 January 2021).

[260] VAN HIJFTE, Blockchain Platforms, p. 24.

[261] For details, see LAMPORT/SHOSTAK/PEASE, , ACM transactions on programming languages and systems 1982.

there is no adequate solution to the "double spend problem". This problem is traditionally solved by a central entity (**single source of truth**), an intermediary who confirms the transactions to the payment system participants. This intermediary also has the competence to create new money. Thus, it is possible to easily check whether the sender of a transaction has the corresponding amount of money by asking this central intermediary. Of course, this central entity has transaction information and can change the information it manages if it so wishes. It is therefore necessary to **be able to trust this intermediary**. Another problem presented by this central solution is its vulnerability (**single point of failure**). The Bitcoin cryptocurrency uses a technology (blockchain) for the first time that solves the double spend problem by **distributing the transaction information between all participants** and **automatically reaching consensus through algorithms** (PoW).

2.3 The CAP theorem and the solution involving the use of consensus algorithms and decentralisation

The **CAP theorem** (**c**onsistency, **a**vailability and **p**artition[262]) describes an IT phenomenon involving distributed data storage systems (such as blockchains). According to this theorem, when using distributed data storage systems it is only possible to achieve two of the following three characteristics:

1. <u>Consistency</u>
   (every read operation contains the previous write operations/errors);
2. <u>Availability</u>
   (every request is answered); and
3. <u>Partition</u>
   (the network continues to function even when multiple data transfers are lost).

Partition is essential in distributed systems, as transmission errors and participant failures occur on a regular basis. So it is necessary to choose either consistency or availability. In the case of blockchain systems, **availability is usually chosen over consistency**. This may sound surprising, but it is a solution to a temporary lack of consistency. Through the use of **consensus algorithms**, a transaction is only viewed as confirmed after the mining of a block. Thus, it is irrelevant in the first few seconds

[262] Consistency, availability and partition.

whether all participants have the same information. It is rather unlikely that the block will be challenged after it has been confirmed by several other participants (**decentralisation**), creating consistency.[263]

This is achieved through an:

- immutable
- register (database)
- of all transactions
- that is created through consensus-building
- and can be viewed publicly.

This register is managed and stored by the entire system (all users) – thus, in a **decentralised** manner (the blockchain).[264] As a result, it is not necessary to trust a central entity, as everyone has all of the information about all of the transactions. In other words, the system is designed and can be checked by users themselves to **enable trust in the way the system works.**[265]

2.4 The opportunities for attacks on TT-systems (attack vectors)

Trustworthy-Technologies solve the problem that participants in public networks usually cannot be trusted (see the remarks above on the potential solutions). If the network participants were trustworthy and they did not attempt to alter the transmitted messages to their own benefit, trustworthy-technologies would be unnecessary. But if TT are used to solve these problems, then new problems arise as a result of new opportunities for attacks. The most important – the 51% attack – will now be presented in order to be able to answer the question of what makes a trustworthy technology in particular trustworthy. The race attack, which attacks the finality of blockchain transactions, will then be presented as a second example.

---

263 On the entire CAP theorem paragraph, see VAN HIJFTE, Blockchain Platforms, p. 27.

264 On decentralisation, see also *A.* FRICK, Zivilrechtliche Aspekte von Token im Zusammenhang mit dem liechtensteinischen Token- und VT-Dienstleister-Gesetz, p. 14.

265 See NÄGELE, Sekundärmarkt für Security Token (Secondary Market for Security Tokens), p. 8; and, in particular, HAWLITSCHEK/NOTHEISEN/TEUBNER, The limits of trust-free systems: A literature review on blockchain technology and trust in the sharing economy, Electronic Commerce Research and Applications 2018, p. 57; Völkel also views immutability of the transaction history as a key feature that contributes to trustworthiness; VÖLKEL, Vertrauen in die Blockchain und das Sachenrecht, ZFR 2020/218, p. 492 f.; on decentralisation, see also *A.* FRICK, Zivilrechtliche Aspekte von Token im Zusammenhang mit dem liechtensteinischen Token- und VT-Dienstleister-Gesetz, p. 14.

The 51% attack

The **51% attack** is surely the most well-known blockchain attack. The principle behind it is easy to explain: If someone controls 51% of the participants (nodes) on a blockchain network, then this person can use the consensus algorithm to achieve the desired result. This attack scenario is used to be able to "spend" tokens more than once (**double spending**) or, for example, to block the acceptance of new transactions. However, it is not possible to simply change the blockchain history.[266] Thus, with a 51% attack it is not possible to change, for example, transactions that occurred two years ago. Instead, this attack aims at transactions occurring in the present moment and that are about to take place.

The **costs of a 51% attack** on a blockchain network vary, in particular, based on the network's hash rate[267] and the algorithm used. In the case of Bitcoin, for example, on 7 February 2021 a 51% attack cost around USD 700,000 per hour, while the cost for Ethereum on that date was around USD 400,000 per hour.[268] It is important to understand that the network can only be influenced for as long as the attack lasts. Once the 51% majority is lost, the network can reject the manipulated transactions. It is easy to see that such attacks do not make financial sense on large blockchain networks (number of nodes or hash rate[269]) like Bitcoin and Ethereum.[270] There have in the past been several such attacks on small blockchains, but the damage was "only" in the millions. The much greater "damage" is the **loss of trust and reputation** on the part of the attacked blockchain.[271] The **Aeternity** blockchain, which was developed in Liechtenstein, was attacked using a 51% attack in December 2020 and January 2021. During these attacks, 29 million AE tokens (worth about USD 2.7 million as of

---

[266] VAN HIJFTE, Blockchain Platforms, p. 63 f.

[267] Hash rate refers to the computing power that network participants provide. It is indicated in hashes per time unit (seconds) that are possible as a result of the computing power that is provided.

[268] CRYPTO51, Cost of a 51% Attack for Different Cryptocurrencies, https://www.crypto51.app/ (accessed on 7 February 2021).

[269] Indicated in hashes per second.

[270] On the disproportionate nature of such attacks, see also *A.* FRICK, Zivilrechtliche Aspekte von Token im Zusammenhang mit dem liechtensteinischen Token- und VT-Dienstleister-Gesetz, p. 15.

[271] VAN HIJFTE, Blockchain Platforms, p. 64.

7 February 2021[272]) were "stolen". According to Aeternity, the tokens were subsequently blocked and "retrieved".

The "race" attack – why the number of confirmations (finality) is relevant

The victim of a race attack is someone who accepts payments in cryptocurrencies. The attacker first makes a payment to a merchant who accepts cryptocurrencies as a means of payment. Immediately afterwards, they make a second payment to another merchant or to themselves with the "same" cryptocurrency. If the merchant does not want to make the client wait for multiple confirmations of the transaction[273] (known as the **finality** of the transaction) and accepts the payment with zero confirmed blocks, the second transaction can be mined and accepted in the next block. The first transaction then remains unconfirmed. If the merchant has already delivered the service or the goods, they remain unpaid.[274] These attacks have occurred on Bitcoin ATM operators in Switzerland who did not want to make their clients wait "unnecessarily". Oftentimes, merchants who wish to accept larger sums in bitcoin face the dilemma of having to wait for the necessary confirmations. And their clients are often extremely impatient and demanding.

3 The publication of software source codes ("open source")

Now we turn to the criterion for publication of the software source code. The publication of the source code for the trustworthy-technologies makes it possible for everyone – at least anyone who can understand software code – to **see how the software works**. For example, it can be checked to see if there are any backdoors[275], or if it is possible to alter the results after the fact without being noticed. The publication of the source code (the rules) makes it possible to see this in advance.[276] The question of whether the source code for software is publicly available[277] depends on the developers.

---

[272] COINMARKETCAP, Aeternity price today, AE marketcap, chart, and info | CoinMarketCap, https://coinmarketcap.com/currencies/aeternity (accessed on 7 February 2021).

[273] In the case of Bitcoin, for example, a new block is added to the blockchain around every 10 minutes. Thus, it would be necessary to wait an hour to be sure that the transaction is almost immutable; see the remarks on "finality" in Part 2, Section 2, II, 1.2).

[274] VAN HIJFTE, Blockchain Platforms, p. 64.

[275] Although these are not always easy to find.

[276] See the criterion "rules defined in advance"; BuA No. 54/2019, p. 131.

[277] Source code is usually published on github.com; for example, "https://github.com/bitcoin", "https://github.com/ethereum/" or "https://github.com/aeternity".

If the source code is published on github.com, for example, all of the steps and changes can be followed. It can also be seen how the project develops further. For example, it is possible to see how many people actively work on the development of the software, how many changes are made to it, etc. If new tokens are published, for example, on the basis of Ethereum based on the ERC-20 standard token, it has become established practice to publish the **token smart-contract** in plain language[278]. Thus, the smart-contract for the Aeternity ERC-20 AE token can be found on etherscan.io[279]. The Aeternity ERC-20 token expires after about[280] two years and then can no longer be transferred. In the case of Aeternity, it was clearly specified that the ERC-20 token was only intended to be used to finance the development of the new Aeternity blockchain and that it would then be converted into project tokens on the basis of the migration smart-contract. The time limit was specified as two years, which naturally put some pressure on the project team. This example really shows how transparent the processes can be made.

If a "TT-system" is developed by a profit-oriented company, then it has an interest in keeping the source code secret. This is mainly for financial reasons, of course. For example, it is intended to safeguard the investments in development costs. With open source software, anyone can make a copy. Although the publication of the source code goes a long way towards being able to critically assess how TT-systems work, this is not a constituent feature of a "TT" pursuant to the TVTG. There are other ways[281] to see how the source code works and learn the defined rules in advance.

II The functional constituent features of the definitions of TT and TT-systems

In the previous sections, it was shown, using the examples of Bitcoin and Ethereum, what trustworthy-technologies meant to the Government when it created the TVTG. The functional definitions included in the TVTG will now be examined and classified on the basis of the foregoing:

---

278 The source code of the token smart contracts is not deployed automatically.

279 ETHERSCAN.IO, Aeternity (AE) contract address.

280 As Ethereum has no direct time system, the block height is used for this purpose, as it can be converted into an approximate time. The average time needed until the next block is mined is used.

281 For example, reviews by independent third parties.

Pursuant to Art. 2, para. 1(a) TVTG, **trustworthy-technologies (TT)** are[282]:

> *"Technologies through which the (1) integrity of Tokens, the (2) clear assignment of Tokens to TT-identifiers and the (3) disposal over Tokens is ensured."*

TT-systems are based on TT and, pursuant to Art. 2, para. 1(b) TVTG, are:

> *"(4) Transaction systems which allow for the secure transfer and storage of Tokens and the rendering of services based on this by means of trustworthy technology."*

1 (1) Integrity of tokens

The wording of Art. 2, 1(a) TVTG defines the criterion for "integrity". This integrity, which must be ensured by the technology, refers to the token. What the token is technically depends on the TT-system used. This also ensures how the integrity is safeguarded, regardless of the system. The legislative materials refer to "integrity" in terms of IT, where it is generally used to mean the accuracy and soundness of data.[283] For this reason, it essentially means the **soundness of the token**, i.e. the syntactic level (for data[284]).[285] This feature is less important for intrinsic tokens, as these tokens do not contain any further data. In the case of extrinsic tokens, in contrast, the tokens can contain information whose integrity must be protected. For example, tokens can contain a work pursuant to the Copyright Act, where every character counts. TT usually use hash functions to ensure integrity[286].

2 (2) The clear assignment of tokens to TT-identifiers

The assignment of TT-identifiers is reflected both in the definition of "TT" pursuant to Art. 2, para. 1(a) TVTG and in the legal definition of the token in Art. 2, para. 1(c) TVTG. The assignment of TT-identifiers is discussed in detail in Part 3, § 5, "(4) The Assignment to TT-identifiers". In the following, it is to be briefly outlined how the assignment is ensured. In the case of Bitcoin, for example, it is checked to see whether the unlocking script fulfils the locking script (validation of the transaction) before a new assignment can be made. The power of disposal is thus checked automatically

---

[282] The figures in parentheses were added here and in subsequent paragraphs to make it easier to refer to the text and are not found in the legislative text.

[283] BuA No. 54/2019. p. 130; see also VÖLKEL, Vertrauen in die Blockchain und das Sachenrecht, ZFR 2020/218, p. 493.

[284] See the remarks on information as data in Part 3, Section 2, A, II.

[285] On security against manipulation, see also *A.* FRICK, Zivilrechtliche Aspekte von Token im Zusammenhang mit dem liechtensteinischen Token- und VT-Dienstleister-Gesetz, p. 13.

[286] See the remarks on hash functions in Part 2, Section 2, I, 3.

by the systems. As the terms must be defined so they can be checked by an algorithm, no intermediary is required. The stored information about transactions must then also be protected against manipulation. It must be clear when someone wishes to alter an old transaction, for example, by changing the assignment so the tokens are assigned to another TT-identifier. With blockchain systems, the term "immutability" is used, which is ensured through the use of **hash functions** and through the interlocking of the blocks with one another[287].

3 (3) Disposal over tokens

In the case of the "disposal over tokens" there are, in my view, no other requirements for the technology that would not otherwise be necessary. Therefore, this is a somewhat restrictive criterion. If it is no longer possible – not just in the short term – to dispose of the tokens (for example, because they were destroyed[288]), then they are no longer tokens pursuant to the TVTG. However, the extreme ease at which transfers of data can take place presents the challenge that the law intended to address here. While tokens must be transferable, it must not be possible to copy them readily (restriction of the ability to copy[289]). Most technological implementations in this area are based on **decentralisation** and a **consensus algorithm**. The number of participants in the network (nodes) that store copies of the data is relevant for protection against failure as well as the integrity and immutability of the data. The more copies there are, the more likely it is that one will be able to prove a certain data status.[290]

4 (4) TT-systems

TT-systems are based on TT and are **transaction systems** which allow for the **secure transfer** and (secure) **storage of tokens** and the **rendering of services based on this** by means of trustworthy technology. The criteria for secure transfer and secure storage should be understood as general criteria. In particular, secure storage refers to the digital representation of rights and their integrity (meaning tokens), not the

[287] Also through the use of the hash function.

[288] See the remarks on the burn function in Part 3, Section 2, B, III, 2.4.

[289] On this point, see the remarks on double spending in Part 3, Section 3, A, II, 2.

[290] A centrally managed database with a nice graphical user interface (a traditional website) should not be classified as a TT system. The administrator of the website can see any changes to the data status.

storage of the TT-key.[291] See the remarks on the integrity of tokens, which also encompasses the secure storage of the tokens. As already noted, however, it is not the TT-key that is stored securely, but rather, figuratively speaking, the lock (in the case of Bitcoin, the locking script) that they key fits.

Secure transfer as a constituent feature is also not discussed in greater detail and is in turn dependent on integrity. It must be ensured that when the token is transferred to a TT-identifier, the holder of the TT-key can actually dispose of it. In the case of Bitcoin, for example, this is done through the locking and unlocking scripts (lock-key principle). Secure transfer is then reflected in the transfer provisions pursuant to Art. 6 TVTG, which, in turn, refers to the regulations of the TT-system. Here, the TT-system requires a "completed transaction", which, as already noted, presents a major challenge for most systems.[292] When a transaction is considered completed varies, depending on the TT-system. For this reason, the provisions of Art. 6 TVTG will be considered in more detail below in order to better understand why secure transfer was included as a constituent feature of TT-systems. In addition, an examination of the transfer of tokens is necessary in preparation for the chapter on the representation of rights.

III The transfer of tokens through the disposal over tokens pursuant to Art. 6 TVTG

1 Art. 6 and disposals over tokens by means of separate transfer regulations

With Art. 5 and 6, the TVTG introduces **separate assignment and transfer regulations**, which will be presented below. The civil law section[293] of the TVTG specifies that, as a general rule, the rights that are represented by tokens are transferred with the tokens.[294] In addition, the TVTG connects further legal consequences to the transfer of tokens, such as acquisition in good faith pursuant to Art. 9 TVTG. It is therefore all the more important to provide clarity on the circumstances under which

---

[291] In my view, Wild does not accurately portray the original references, as she writes that the storage refers to the digital representation of "information" and its integrity. In its report and application, the Government talked about the digital representation of rights, meaning tokens. WILD, Zivilrecht und Token-Ökonomie in Liechtenstein. Eine Analyse der zivilrechtlichen Bestimmungen des TVTG unter Berücksichtigung des Wertrechts (2020), p. 28; on the original, see BuA No. 54/2019, p. 139.

[292] On finality, see the remarks in Part 2, Section 2, II, 1.2.

[293] See II. Civil basis, Art. 3 to 10 TVTG.

[294] See Art. 7 TVTG and the further remarks on the representation of rights in Part 3, Section 4.

disposals over tokens are **legally valid** and thus the **represented right is transferred**.

Pursuant to Art. 6 TVTG, disposal over a token requires that:

1. the transfer of the token is **carried out in accordance with the rules of the TT-system**;[295]
2. the transferor and the transferee both declare[296] that they **want to transfer** the right of disposal over the token[297]; and
3. the transferor has the[298] **right of disposal** pursuant to the provisions of Art. 5 TVTG.[299]

If, in accordance with the law, the requirements for the disposal over a token are met, then this also results in the disposal over the right represented by the token. The broad applicability of this "**coordination requirement**"[300] was probably unique when the TVTG entered into force and will be examined in detail in the chapter on representation.[301] If the authorised transferor and the transferee agree on the transfer of the right of disposal over the token and the transfer of the represented right, the right represented by the token will – provided it is possible[302] in accordance with the law or suitable measures – be transferred.[303]

---

[295] Whereby a limited right in rem to a token can also be created without a transfer, provided that this right is apparent to third parties and the date the right in rem is created is clearly defined.

[296] Thus, there must be a compulsory underlying transaction.

[297] Or that they want to establish a limited right in rem.

[298] Acquisitions in good faith pursuant to Art. 9 TVTG remain reserved.

[299] See also NÄGELE, Sekundärmarkt für Security Token, p. 10 f.

[300] BuA No. 54/2019, p. 168; see also *A.* FRICK, Zivilrechtliche Aspekte von Token im Zusammenhang mit dem liechtensteinischen Token- und VT-Dienstleister-Gesetz, p. 38; WILD, Zivilrecht und Token-Ökonomie in Liechtenstein, p. 65 f.; LINS/PRAICHEUX, Digital and blockchain-based legal regimes: An EEA case study based on innovative legislations, SPWR 2020, p. 318; NÄGELE, Sekundärmarkt für Security Token, p. 11.

[301] See also OMLOR, Digitales Eigentum an Blockchain-Token – rechtsvergleichende Entwicklungslinien, ZVglRWiss 2020, p. 57.

[302] Art. 7, para. 1 TVTG must be read together with Art. 7, para. 2 TVTG. This paragraph discusses cases when "the legal effect under (1) does not come into force by law"; NÄGELE, Sekundärmarkt für Security Token, p. 11.

[303] NÄGELE, Sekundärmarkt für Security Token, p. 11.

Thus, the conditions pursuant to the TVTG for the transfer of the token and the conditions for the transfer of the represented right must be met. The coordination mandated by the coordination requirement in Art. 7 TVTG will be enforced. The first step, therefore, is to determine the conditions under which the token will be effectively transferred.

2 Transfer in accordance with the rules of the TT-system

Neither the legislative text of the TVTG nor the relevant legislative materials specify exactly what a transfer in accordance with the rules of the TT-system is. A distinction must be made between transactions that are on-chain, i.e. carried out directly on the TT-system, and so-called off-chain transactions, which are carried out without knowledge of the TT-system, usually through physical handover of the TT-key. Regardless of the type of transaction that is being considered, the **reference to the system rules** is grounded in the need for **technology neutrality**.[304] Consequently, it is necessary to review how tokens are transferred on each TT-system. This will be done subsequently.

2.1 On-chain transfers

In practice, on-chain transactions are usually simplified with the help of technical tools such as "wallet"software, which makes it possible to easily carry out transactions on multiple TT-systems. Thus, it is possible to transfer both bitcoins and ethers and all tokens based on Ethereum with a single application. However, the technical aspects of these token transfers are very different. The way on-chain transactions involving Bitcoin's and Ethereum's system tokens are carried out has already been discussed in Part 3 , § 2, B, II. See the remarks on tokens in the proper sense in Part 3, Section 2, B, III. However, as off-chain transactions have not yet been discussed, I will look at them below.

---

304 Falker, Teichmann also assign great significance to the TVTG in the future because of its technology neutrality; FALKER/TEICHMANN, InTeR 2020, p. 62.

2.2 Off-chain transfers

Transfer through the physical (off-chain) handover of TT-keys (e.g. through hardware wallets)

A popular method for fulfilling over-the-counter (OTC) transactions (purchase of cryptocurrencies) is the **physical handover** of hardware wallets and thus the TT-key for the token that is the subject of the contract.

Hardware wallets are physical devices that store the TT-key in the device itself. It is usually necessary to enter a PIN code or a password directly in the hardware wallet in order to access the TT-key. As these devices generally do not have a direct connection to the internet, they are considered relatively secure. In terms of the classification of data[305], hardware wallets are at the structural level. Physical handover of the device has no impact at the semantic level. Consequently, there are no transactions on the TT-system. The transaction therefore occurs outside the blockchain, which is where the term "**off-chain**"comes from. The hardware wallet, together with the TT-key stored in it, is handed over. But what does this mean for the transfer rules pursuant to Art. 6 TVTG? Once the parties have agreed that ownership of the hardware wallet is to be transferred as well, then the method must also be in accordance with the principles of property law.[306]

However, the transfer of the hardware wallet under property law does not mean that the right of disposal over the token has also been transferred, but only the power of disposal pursuant to Art. 5, para. 1 TVTG. The owner of the hardware wallet can now – provided they know the PIN code for the hardware wallet – dispose of the tokens. But they are not the person with the right of disposal pursuant to Art. 5 TVTG. If the parties have agreed on the transfer of the right of disposal and on handover of the hardware wallet as the mode of transfer, then this involves disposal over tokens pursuant to Art. 6, para. 1(a) TVTG. The law does not however specifically say whether an off-chain transaction is a "transfer of the token concluded in line with the regulations of the TT-System" pursuant to Art. 6, para. 2(a). As already noted, the transaction does not take place on the TT-system, and the TT-key and TT-identifier remain the same. The TT-system does not "notice" this transaction either. In my view, within

---

305 See the remarks on the different levels of data in Part 3, Section 2, A, II.

306 See also the report and application, which, to put it briefly, states that the specified off-chain transactions are fulfilled through the hand-to-hand transfer of the hardware wallet: BuA No. 54/2019, p. 193; see also *A.* FRICK, Zivilrechtliche Aspekte von Token im Zusammenhang mit dem liechtensteinischen Token- und VT-Dienstleister-Gesetz, p. 19.

the framework of the technological interpretation it must be assumed that a transfer of the TT-key must also be included under the specified provision. The TVTG had such transactions in mind and dealt with them in the legislative materials. Therefore, according to the rules of the TT-system, the conditions are always fulfilled when someone receives the power of disposal as a result of the handover of the TT-key, irrespective of whether the transaction is on-chain or off-chain.[307]

The presumed high level of legal security when physically transferring property that creates a power of disposal over tokens renders the producers of special hardware wallets, such as OpenDime, useful.[308] Such wallets in pen-drive-form work in a manner similar to bearer instruments. Anyone can read the TT-identifier by inserting the pen-drive into a computer or mobile phone. The TT-identifier can be used to check how many tokens have been assigned to this TT-identifier. The TT-key is stored in a separate storage device. Only after it has been manipulated mechanically (by piercing a conductor) does the protected area of the USB stick with the TT-key become accessible and it is possible to read the TT-key. As a result, the tokens can be transferred again. From this moment, however, the bitcoins can be used by anyone who has access to the USB stick. The holder of the TT-key has the power of disposal over the tokens. The question then is whether the power of disposal has been obtained because the person possesses the USB stick in accordance with the principles of property law or because they have manipulated it mechanically. The BuA requires "knowledge of the TT-key".[309] In my view, it must suffice if it is possible to easily gain knowledge, in contrast with hardware wallets protected by a PIN code. With such devices, possession of the physical wallet alone does not grant the power of disposal. Knowledge of the PIN code is also necessary.

[307] The Government wants Art. 6 TVTG to solely apply to on-chain transactions and refers to property law for off-chain transactions. In my view, this does not go far enough, as the other provisions of Art. 6 TVTG govern the conditions of effective disposal; a transaction on the TT system does not meet the definition in Art. 6, para. 1(a) TVTG, even where there is justification as a result of securities or usufruct rights pursuant to Art. 6, para. 1(b) and para. 2(a) TVTG, if they are apparent to third parties, which is ensured by the physical handover; see BuA No. 54/2019, p. 192 f.

[308] OPENDIME, World's First Bitcoin Credit Stick Wallet, https://opendime.com/ (Accessed 23 February 2021).

[309] BuA No. 54/2019, p. 63.

Payment of share capital using cryptocurrencies via the analogous practice of contributions in kind

The different types of transaction in practice can also be seen, for example, in payments by legal entities. The Office of Justice of the Principality of Liechtenstein (AJU) permits the payment of share capital using cryptocurrencies – currently in bitcoins and ethers[310] (see information sheet 02/2021).[311] Here, the AJU applies the principles of payments via contributions in kind.[312] The **cryptocurrency** being contributed must be **clearly identified** in a contribution in kind agreement and its value must be at least equal – both when the public deed is drawn up and when it is recorded – to the share capital pursuant to the company's articles of incorporation.[313] There is no need for an expert report, which is normally required for contributions in kind[314], as payment via cryptocurrencies involves elements of payment by means of cash contributions. This is justified with the fact that the reference prices of the key cryptocurrencies are published on the website[315] of the Tax Authority and, thus, bitcoin and ether have a market value. Among other things, the AJU requires the articles of incorporation to include the following information:

- *"Subject of the contribution in kind;*
- *Name of the contributor."*[316]

There may be an impression that the AJU implicitly requires the use of a physical carrier (an object) for the TT-key or an object that conveys the power of disposal over

310 The information sheet incorrectly refers to the TT-systems (i.e. blockchain) as Bitcoin and Ethereum and not the cryptocurrencies bitcoins and ethers. But the cryptocurrencies are what is meant, as can also be seen by the abbreviation BTC used for bitcoin.

311 Office of Justice of the Principality of Liechtenstein, Merkblatt zur Liberierung von Gesellschaftskapital mit einer Kryptowährung, https://www.llv.li/files/onlineschalter/Dokument-3306.pdf (accessed on 27 February 2021).

312 With reference to the provisions on contributions in kind in the Persons and Companies Act (PGR) and the Commercial Register Ordinance (HRV).

313 For this reason, the AJU recommends including a "safety margin" in the contribution in kind agreement.

314 For joint stock companies, see, for example, Art. 55a, para. 2a of the Ordinance of 11 February 2003 on the Commercial Register (Commercial Register Ordinance, or HRV), Liechtenstein Law Gazette (2003).

315 The major cryptocurrencies are maintained as foreign currencies and can be accessed online; Swiss Federal Tax Administration, ICTax - Income & Capital Taxes, https://www.ictax.admin.ch/extern/de.html#/ratelist/2021 (accessed on 27 February 2021).

316 Office of Justice of the Principality of Liechtenstein, Merkblatt zur Liberierung von Gesellschaftskapital mit einer Kryptowährung.

the cryptocurrency being contributed (off-chain) when payment is made by cryptocurrency. In my view, however, it must also be possible to provide proof of the power of disposal by means of confirmation from the TT service provider (TT-token custodian, TT-key custodian and TT-protector).

The off-chain transfer of book-entry securities in the form of tokens

Another question that arises with off-chain transfers relates to the transfer of book-entry securities. In the case of book-entry securities, the shareholder in the company is the person entered in the book-entry securities register. If the book-entry securities register is maintained on a TT-system and there is an off-chain transaction as described above, the transferor of the right of disposal remains the shareholder, as long as they are entered in the book-entry securities register. The book-entry securities register is not updated in the event of an off-chain transaction. In addition, no information is entered prior to the whitelisting of the new TT-identifier. In other words, the book-entry securities register does not know the identity of the new shareholder and the new shareholder is not entered in the register by name. As previously noted, the **book-entry securities register** has a **constitutive character**. Thus, if book-entry securities are transferred by means of physical handover (structural level) of the TT-key (semantic level), the person obliged pursuant to Art. 7, para. 2 TVTG must ensure, by means of suitable measures, that the represented right is transferred as well. The debtor could be informed of the change of person behind the TT-identifier. There is still a big question mark over whether this method is sufficient. The debtor might manually alter the whitelist and reassign the TT-identifier to the new shareholder. For this and other reasons, it is advisable to request the corresponding on-chain transaction. Using off-chain transactions makes it all the more difficult to ensure security. For example, if someone simply hands over a hardware wallet and PIN code to the purchaser, the latter can dispose of the TT-key and change the PIN code. But this does not ensure that the seller can no longer dispose of the TT-key. They could have simply made a copy of the key.[317] If the transaction takes place on-chain, it is a case involving the provisions of Art. 7, para. 1 TVTG, as the disposal over the token also results in the updating of the book-entry securities register and the by law disposal results in the transfer of the right represented in the token.

[317] Thus, OTC sales involving the handover of hardware wallets that have already been initialised result in damage, as the person handing over the wallet transferred the tokens with a copy of the TT key to another TT-identifier when the payment was received.

B Conclusion on the definitions of "TT" and "TT-system"

The meaning of trustworthy-technologies and TT-systems could not be more important. The subject, purpose and scope of the general, civil law and supervisory law provisions always refer to trustworthy-technologies. In Art. 7, para. 1 and para. 2 TVTG, in particular, the aim of the law is to tightly connect the represented right and the token in a way that ensures that the right cannot be asserted or transferred to others without the token. It is sufficient for the purpose of demonstrating ownership if the token holder demonstrates the right to dispose of the token (identification-function). A payment by the debtor to the person identified in such a way liberates the debt (liberation-function). If a service provider does not use TT or TT-systems, then the service provider is not a TT-service provider and may not refer to itself as such (designation protection). However, this also means that if no TT-system is used for the service provision, then the service provider cannot be registered as a TT-service provider.

These wide-ranging legal consequences create the legal certainty that legislators intended when they drafted the TVTG. But why weren't these legal consequences assigned to digital transactions with no intermediaries before the development of TT and TT-systems, and what distinguishes a TT-system from a "normal" database application? This takes us to the crux of the term "trustworthy-technologies". Obviously, there are technologies that make it possible to carry out transactions with little or no trust in the other actors and to connect this to wide-ranging legal consequences. We trust the technology, not the actors. The term "trustless" technologies is also used in IT. Trustless (or "trust-free") systems refers to systems that operate without the trust of users in order to provide certain functions. In the case of TT-systems, which by definition must be "trustless", it refers to systems that provide storage and transaction systems for which "trustworthy" intermediaries are usually used. As the terms TT and TT-systems are defined in a technology-neutral way and are designed to be as broad as possible, they must be interpreted by the legal practitioner. However, there is no fixed catalogue of criteria that can be used. Instead, a holistic view must be taken of whether the criteria meet the definitions: Trustworthy-Technologies (TT) are technologies through which the integrity of tokens, the clear assignment of tokens to TT-identifiers and the disposal over tokens is ensured. TT-systems are based on TT and are transaction systems which allow for the secure transfer and storage of tokens and the rendering of services based on this by means of trustworthy technology.

Legislators used Bitcoin and Ethereum as models of TT and TT-systems. Looking at the technological structure makes it clear as to what makes a technology a TT and what makes a system a TT-system. In doing so, the major attack scenarios need to be taken into account. The often-cited 51% attack only has an effect while it is under way. For this reason, however, it is not possible to simply change the blockchain history. Thus, with a 51% attack it is not possible to change, for example, transactions that occurred two years ago. The fact that a TT-system was the victim of a 51% attack does not automatically exclude if from being classified as a TT-system. But it does show how important the number of nodes or the hash rate of a network is for assessing how easily it can be manipulated and thus how trustworthy it is. To date, it has been assumed that Bitcoin and Ethereum are TT and TT-systems. But while a system may fulfil the other conditions for "TT" and "TT-systems", if it is relatively easy for unauthorised users to change them to their advantage, then they are not TT and thus TT-systems. However, most major blockchains and DLT systems can only be manipulated with great effort. In other words, if the system is immutable with a probability bordering on certainty, then it is a TT-system. However, if the system is structured in a way that makes it easy to change (e.g. a central simple database, such as is used on web servers), then neither the registration system nor the civil law provisions apply. To date, there have been few problems as regards inclusion, as, for the most part, established systems are used.

§ 4 (3) The representation of rights

A General information about the representation of rights

As previously explained, the TVTG created a new legal object, the token.[318] This token can be described as a "**container**" that <u>can</u> **represent rights**. Just like a security, when it serves as a representation, the token combines something of value (rights in rem, claims and rights of membership, etc.) with something with almost no value (the token).[319] The civil law section of the TVTG is largely based on the traditional notions of securities.[320] In the case of cryptocurrencies with no other functions, like Bitcoin, the token does not represent any rights or claims against an issuer.[321] In this case, depending on the value attributed to the token by users, the token itself is the

---

[318] BuA No. 54/2019, p. 59.

[319] Similar to securities, see MEIER-HAYOZ/CRONE, Wertpapierrecht[3] (2018), p. 1.

[320] BuA No. 54/2019, p. 165.

[321] Instead, the token is created by the network itself through mining.

"thing of value". In the legislative materials on the TVTG, the Government also refers to an "**empty container**". In the law, empty tokens are implicitly included in the "can" in "can represent rights" as specified in the legal definition of tokens. *Möllenkamp/Shmatenko* distinguish between **intrinsic** and **extrinsic** tokens. Pursuant to the TVTG, intrinsic tokens are empty tokens that do not represent any rights. Extrinsic tokens are tokens that represent rights and thus derive their value from an external asset.[322] Thus tokens do not have to represent rights (intrinsic tokens), but they can (extrinsic tokens).

I The Token-Container-Model {"TCM"}

The term "**Token-Container-Model**" was coined by NÄGELE[323] to provide legal practitioners with an easy way of understanding how the TVTG enables "tokenisation".[324] No new rights are created as a result of **tokenisation**, the **representation of rights**.[325] Consequently, tokenisation does not alter the legal nature of the original rights ("substance over form"). What changes is instead the transfer of the token in accordance with Art. 6 TVTG, and, depending on the right which is represented by the token, the transfer of the represented right ex lege through disposal over the token (Art. 7 para. 1 TVTG) or the transfer through suitable measures (Art. 7 para. 2 TVTG).[326]

The provisions, particularly those regarding the representation of rights, require interpretation. The teleological interpretation of the legislation must keep in mind the reasons for the introduction of the TVTG. The TVTG, *"with the 'token', has introduced a new legal object in order to enable the representation of 'real' value on TT-systems in a legally secure manner and thus to tap the full application potential of the token economy."*[327] This potential of the token economy requires the **justifiable trust of users**

[322] MÖLLENKAMP/SHMATENKO, Blockchain und Kryptowährungen, in *Hoeren/Sieber/Holznagel* (ed.), Handbuch Multimedia-Recht (1999), margin no. 30.

[323] Nägele first spoke publicly of the Token-Container-Model as a speaker at the seminar "Blockchain meets Liechtenstein" on 6 September 2019: UNIVERSITY OF LIECHTENSTEIN, Blockchain meets Liechtenstein.

[324] See, for example, the remarks on the Token-Container-Model in NÄGELE/XANDER in *Piska/Völkel*, p. 394 ff.

[325] On the representation of rights, see also WILD, Zivilrecht und Token-Ökonomie in Liechtenstein, p. 29 f.

[326] BuA No. 54/2019, p. 58 ff.

[327] BuA No. 54/2019, p. 6.

in the transactions (transfer protection). The person acquiring the right represented by a token must always be able to trust that they will receive the represented right when the token is transferred (trust in the legal transaction).[328] It is with this purpose and the explanatory basis of the civil law section of the TVTG in mind that the provisions related to the representation of rights will be interpreted below.

1 Intrinsic tokens – empty containers pursuant to the Token-Container-Model

Intrinsic tokens (empty tokens) do not derive their value or their benefits from external rights. For example, **Bitcoin** does not represent **a claim against an issuer** or anyone else – there is no issuer[329]. A person with the power of disposal over a TT-identifier to which a bitcoin is assigned cannot really do a lot with it. They mainly have the ability to transfer the bitcoin to someone else. In most cases, to put it simply, the bitcoin is "assigned" to a new TT-identifier. Because of Bitcoin's transaction model, it is entirely irrelevant which of the 21 million[330] bitcoins someone has the power of disposal over. The value of a bitcoin is largely based on its scarcity (21 million) and its acceptance by the users to whom a bitcoin has been assigned. Bitcoin was also developed as a means of payment – "a peer-to-peer electronic cash system"[331] – and is intended to fulfil the functions of money. Therefore, a bitcoin is an example of an intrinsic, empty token according to the TVTG.[332]

Ether can be presented as a second example of an intrinsic token. Ether also do not derive their value or benefits from external rights. In contrast to bitcoin, however, ether do not have a fixed limit. On 12 February 2021, there were about 114 million

[328] Wild views the connection between tokens and right as somewhat tenuous and would prefer to apply the identification and discharge function pursuant to Art. 8 TVTG only to book-entry securities; it will be shown below why this proposed restriction to book-entry securities should not be implemented and there is generally a strong connection between tokens and represented rights in practice; WILD, Zivilrecht und Token-Ökonomie in Liechtenstein, p. 79; see the following remarks on the functions of tokens when representing rights.

[329] The maximum specified number of bitcoins is 21 million. New bitcoins are mined by network participants (miners).

[330] The smallest unit is the satoshi. Properly speaking, reference would therefore have to be made as to the number of satoshis someone has or receives.

[331] Title of the Bitcoin white paper; NAKAMOTO, (PSEUDONYM), Bitcoin: A Peer-to-Peer Electronic Cash System.

[332] Based on the assignment of tokens using a TT-identifier, Omlor says that tokens that do not represent any rights should not be included under the term "token". He doubts that rights can be derived from "ownership" of bitcoins. This argument is not persuasive, as it does not take account of the fact that tokens can have an intrinsic value and are therefore included in the term "token" pursuant to the TVTG; OMLOR, , ZVglRWiss 2020, p. 43 f.

ethers.[333] Ethers should not be confused with other tokens based on Ethereum that might derive their value from external assets.

2 Are intrinsic tokens a generic or a specific obligation?

Looking at the technical structure of tokens, they can be divided into **fungible** and **non-fungible tokens (NFT)**. In general, "fungibility" refers to the characteristics of goods, currencies and securities as well as tokens, such as dimensions, number, weight – or in the case of tokens, the smart-contract that is used – that makes them definable and easily exchangeable or interchangeable.[334] In legal terms, therefore, they are a **generic obligation** and in the case of bitcoin, it does not matter which bitcoins or satoshis the creditor receives.[335]

In contrast, non-fungible tokens ("NFT") are **specific obligations** – they involve specific tokens[336]. The ERC-721 standard for non-fungible tokens ("NFT") was published on github.com in September 2017.[337] The main difference with the ERC-20 standard is that, within the framework of the ERC-721 standard, each token can be identified on the basis of the same smart-contract using a unique "tokenID". For this reason, tokens have, for example, different ages, are uncommon to different degrees or have a different output, for example, an image, when used in decentralised applications (dApps). Because of their individual description, **ERC-721-compatible tokens are a specific obligation.**[338]

It may at first glance appear that there is no case where an intrinsic token that represents a specific obligation is non-fungible (NFT). Therefore, it is not suitable to use these tokens as a means of payment, as they cannot be divided and cannot be exchanged. The first "broad" application for non-fungible, intrinsic tokens was the game

[333] ETHERSCAN.IO, Ether Total Supply and Market Capitalization Chart, https://etherscan.io/stat/supply (accessed on 12 February 2021).

[334] Without addressing tokens, see BREUER, Definition: Fungibilität, Springer Fachmedien Wiesbaden GmbH.

[335] From the perspective of the duties of care, however, tokens can no longer be easily exchanged because of their use in the past for criminal purposes. For example, various service providers review the "origin" of cryptocurrencies using so-called "chain analysis tools". If the tokens are associated with criminal activities, then they are no longer accepted. It can be said that the tokens are contaminated and users prefer to receive "clean" bitcoins. Consequently, contaminated bitcoins would no longer be accepted for an obligation and the debtor would sometimes fall into default.

[336] For example, through the use of a unique identifier (UID).

[337] See also the remarks on ERC-721 in Part 3, Section 2, B, III, 2.3.

[338] ETHEREUM, ERC-721 Non-Fungible Token Standard.

"**CryptoKitties**"[339]. In this game, users can buy, sell, raise and collect virtual cats. On 12 May 2018, a CryptoKitty was auctioned for USD 140,000.[340]

3 Extrinsic tokens – containers "filled" with rights

Depending on the type of right represented, the technical structure of the container (smart-contract) is more relevant for **extrinsic tokens** than it is for intrinsic tokens. A distinction between fungible and non-fungible tokens must also be made for extrinsic tokens. Fungible extrinsic tokens represent generic obligations, i.e. fractions or ratios of rights (e.g. co-ownership rights). When using, for example, stablecoins as a means of payment or generally to represent generic obligations (co-ownership shares), fungible tokens need to be used. With this token it does not matter which fraction or ratio someone receives, as they are all exchangeable.

If the represented obligation is a **specific obligation** – it is for the specific payment or this particular token – non-fungible tokens must be used to represent it. These clear tokens are suitable for representing, for example, ownership rights to property, proof of identity, confirmation of academic grades[341], votes cast during elections, licensing applications and much more.[342]

II The functions of tokens when representing rights

1 Art. 8 TVTG – the identification and liberation-function when representing rights

When rights are represented, the question is whether the **identification and liberation-function** pursuant to Art. 8 TVTG should apply to all tokens or, as WILD suggests[343], only to book-entry securities. While Art. 8 TVTG is difficult to overestimate, it specifies that:

---

339 DAPPER LABS INC., CryptoKitties, https://www.cryptokitties.co/catalogue/latest-cattributes (accessed on 12 February 2021).

340 MALA, Who Spends $140,000 on a CryptoKitty? The New York Times,.

341 The University of Basel has been creating certificates on the basis of Ethereum since 2018; see UNIVERSITY OF BASEL, Zertifikate basierend auf Blockchain-Technologie, https://cif.unibas.ch/de/blog/details/news/zertifikate-basierend-auf-blockchain-technologie (accessed on 21 January 2021).

342 VAN HIJFTE, Blockchain Platforms, p. 29.

343 According to Wild, Art. 8 TVTG should therefore only be applied to book-entry securities; the arguments against the restriction to book-entry securities will be presented below; WILD, Zivilrecht und Token-Ökonomie in Liechtenstein, p. 79 ff.

1. *"The person possessing the right of disposal reported by the TT-system is considered the lawful holder of the right represented in the Token in respect of the Obligor"* and
2. *"By payment, the Obligor is withdrawn from his obligation against the person who has the power of disposal as reported by the TT-system, unless he knew, or should have known with due care, that he is not the lawful owner of the right. "*[344]

However, there is no restriction to book-entry securities pursuant to Art. 8 TVTG. According to the wording of the law, Art. 8 TVTG thus grants all tokens that represent rights (extrinsic tokens) the identification and liberation-function.

"In other words, tokens are digital representations of analogue rights that cannot be transferred or asserted without the token (Art. 6 TVTG). The person with the right to dispose over the token is considered the lawful holder of the right (Art. 8, para. 1 TVTG), and the obligor is withdrawn as the holder of the right as a result of the payment to the person with the right of disposal (Art. 8, para. 2 TVTG)."[345]

The cited law, in turn, fits in with the overall system of the civil law provisions of the TVTG, which has as its objective the "token economy", which is not solely restricted to book-entry securities. In future, legal transactions will primarily take place digitally. Based on the provisions of Art. 6 and 7 TVTG, tokens fulfil the transport function similar to the transport function of securities. In the version of the TVTG during the consultation process, the identification-function in Art. 9[346] was limited to tokens that "embody" a claim or membership right[347].[348] This restriction of the identification-function was (rightfully) criticised during the consultation period and the Government expanded the identification-function to include all tokens by modifying the wording of the law in BuA No. 54/2019:

[344] See Art. 8, para. 1 and 2 TVTG.

[345] Because of an editorial error, the BuA refers to Art. 8, p. 2 instead of Art. 8, para. 2; BuA No. 54/2019, p. 166.

[346] Now Art. 8 TVTG.

[347] At the time, the Government used the word "embody" rather than "represent".

[348] Consultation report on the Blockchain Act, p. 143.

"The Government shares the concerns expressed in the statement and is expanding the identification and liberation-function to include all [extrinsic][349] tokens and not just those tokens that represent a claim or membership right."[350]

The expansion did not include all tokens, but rather all extrinsic tokens. This has resulted in the following situation:

1.1 The situation regarding intrinsic tokens

As the addition of brackets to the government quote from the report and application by the author shows, the expansion of Art. 8 TVTG should not include all tokens, but rather only all extrinsic tokens. Art. 8 TVTG should not apply to **intrinsic tokens**, i.e. tokens that do not represent rights. However, this is clear from the wording of Art. 8, para. 1 TVTG, which talks about the "represented right". Para. 2 of this law refers to para. 1, which is why the represented right is meant here, even if it only talks about the "right". Thus, this restriction to extrinsic tokens is appropriate. Let's take Bitcoin as an example. Here, there is no division between the fate of the token and the fate of the asset. There is no "right represented in the token". However, there are no obligors arising from the token to whom it is necessary to provide identification (identification-function). If there are no obligors, then there is also no one who has to make a payment, and as a result the liberation-function does not apply. Art. 8, para. 1 TVTG is thus not significant for intrinsic tokens and Art. 8 TVTG is thus not applicable to intrinsic tokens.

1.2 The situation regarding book-entry securities

In the case of **book-entry securities** that are maintained on TT-systems (book-entry security tokens), the holder of the right is the holder of the right of disposal[351] and the token serves as identification to assert the rights against legal entities (the shareholder is the person who is listed in the book-entry securities register). The **entry** in the book-entry securities register has a **constitutive effect** pursuant to Section 81a, para. 3 SchlT PGR. The book-entry securities register is public on TT-systems and creates the necessary publicity. In the case of securities, the identification-function ensures the marketability of securities and secures legal transactions. Art. 8, para. 2 TVTG provides book-entry security tokens with the identification and liberation-

[349] The Government refers here to all tokens, but based on the clear wording in Art. 8 TVTG, it clearly means all extrinsic tokens. See the remarks below.

[350] Emphasis added by the author. BuA No. 54/2019, p. 208.

[351] See the coordination requirement pursuant to Art. 7 TVTG.

function also.[352] Once the obligor makes payment to the person with the right of disposal as reported on the TT-system, they are released from their payment obligation (liberation-function). The applicability of Art. 8 TVTG to book-entry security tokens appears to be disputed.

1.3 The situation regarding extrinsic tokens

In contrast, the applicability of Art. 8 TVTG to extrinsic tokens is disputed. The expansion of the legal text to include all extrinsic tokens following the consultation was, in my view, correct and necessary. Only in this way are all[353] extrinsic tokens – and not only "book-entry security tokens"[354] – **functionally equivalent to securities**.

The Government justified the expansion on the basis of the **high level of reliability**. It based this reliability on the **legal responsibility** assigned by the TT-system.[355] The representation of rights in tokens only makes sense and demonstrates the advantages of tokens (reliability) within the framework of the token economy as a result of the identification and liberation-function of extrinsic tokens.[356] The token and the TT-system serve – together with the other corresponding measures[357] – as a **means of**

---

[352] Section 81a, para. 6 SchlT PGR provides for the identification and discharge function. In my view, Art. 8 TVTG, as a special law, takes precedence over this provision when maintaining the book-entry securities register using TT. Para. 6 of this law thus refers to a situation when a book-entry securities register is maintained with TT.

[353] It is not clear, based on the legal clarification and the legislative materials why Wild, who wants to apply Art. 8 TVTG solely to tokens that represent book-entry securities (in fact, only the claims and rights of membership are represented and not the book-entry securities; instead, here the tokens are the book-entry securities); see WILD, Zivilrecht und Token-Ökonomie in Liechtenstein, p. 79 ff.

[354] In the case of book-entry securities, the token is the book-entry security, i.e. there is no representation in the proper sense. The token derives its value from an external asset, but it is classified as an extrinsic token, which is why Art. 8 TVTG applies.

[355] BuA No. 54/2019, p. 207.

[356] A separate question that needs to be considered is which suitable measures pursuant to Art. 7, para. 2 TVTG can be taken if the effects of the disposal over the token do no come into effect by law. If such measures are not possible or are economically untenable, then tokenisation cannot be carried out. See, in particular, the remarks on (3b) rights to property.

[357] See the tokenisation clause below.

publicity[358] and the high level of reliability of the publicity justifies the identification and liberation-function.[359]

III The tokenisation-clause for extrinsic tokens

With respect to the representation of rights in tokens, there are – depending on the right represented – different requirements for successful tokenisation. On the one hand, when representing absolute rights, as is the case, in particular, with the rights to property, then the **publicity requirements**, for example, need to be observed. Thus, a physical object must normally be handed over in order for ownership to be transferred. This makes it clear to everyone to whom the property must now be reassigned. On the other hand, in the case of all extrinsic tokens, the parties must agree that – depending on the right – exercising the right is associated with the right of disposal over the token (identification-function) and, conversely, that a debtor can only make payment to the person with the right of disposal over the token in a manner that liberates the debt (liberation-function). The goal is always for tokens and the represented right to share the same fate. If the claims represented by the token by law cannot be transferred, then Art. 7, para. 2 TVTG once again takes effect. Suitable measures for claims pursuant to Art. 7, para. 2 TVTG include: in particular, purely contractual arrangements, corresponding contractual clauses or bond or issue conditions for a financing instrument. Claims are transferred solely in accordance with the provisions of the TVTG and there is no assignment under the provisions of civil or corporate law. If there is a third-party effect[360] on the prohibition against assignment – as is the case in Liechtenstein – then the effective exclusion of a parallel disposal over the represented claim is ensured.[361]

---

[358] In particular, see also the situation in Switzerland involving book-entry securities that are maintained by a central securities depository in a public register; MEIER-HAYOZ/CRONE, Wertpapierrecht[3], p. 327 f.

[359] See also the note as an alternative method for book-entry claims; THÖNI in *Fenyves/Kerschner/Vonkilch*, ABGB, Sections 1375 to 1410[3] (2011), Section 1392, margin no. 75.

[360] Liechtenstein did not adopt Section 1396a of the Austrian Civil Code, and as a result prohibitions against assignment are fully effective and the debtor may also invoke third parties; THÖNI in *Fenyves/Kerschner/Vonkilch*, ABGB, Sections 1375 to 1410[3] (2011), Section 1393, margin nos. 79 and 84.

[361] BuA No. 54/2019, p. 171 ff.

One may find a solution to this challenge in traditional securities. The paper, i.e. the security, is property pursuant to property law and it is thus possible to use it to transfer, for example, shareholder rights (bearer share). The **certificate clause** (securities clause) in securities law plays a major role in establishing the connection between the right and the certificate.[362] Within the framework of freedom of contract, the person with the right and the obligor assign specific functions in connection with the assertion of the right.[363] Book-entry securities are register rights. Thus, if shareholder rights are represented by the token, the certificate clause is no longer necessary. The register rights are entirely digital. This is a sensible development and whenever relative rights are represented by tokens, registers maintained by the debtor using TT-systems are an effective means for identifying the creditor and discharging the debtor pursuant to Art. 8 TVTG. As already noted, this should apply for more than just book-entry securities. New approaches are needed in order to also enable the applicability of Art. 8 TVTG to extrinsic tokens that are not maintained in a register by the debtor. Now, let's return to securities. One approach would be for the parties to agree on a clause similar to a "securities clause" within the framework of freedom of contract. Here, the token assumes the functions of the certificate. As an example, this could be called, let's say, the "**tokenisation-clause**":

"**Transfer of rights will only take place via a token,**
payment only to the person with the right of disposal over the token".

Such a clause could, if, for example, in the case of property it were only applied to the property itself, also **create the publicity** that is required. This would make it clear to everyone that a transfer is only possible via tokens and that performance only releases the individual from debt who is authorized to dispose of the token. This might involve the application of a **clear identifying feature** to the property. The feature would then be referenced in the token, e.g. the tokenID. This would create the connection between the token and the property or the right to the property and meet the publicity requirements.

The creation of a unique token identification number (UTIN) is also conceivable. It would then be easy to find the token via a simple internet search or by scanning a QR code on the object whose rights have been tokenised. The advantage of this solution is that publicity is maintained and anyone can immediately see that the property does

[362] See the presentation clause and identification clause as well as the different forms of securities, MEIER-HAYOZ/CRONE, Wertpapierrecht[3], p. 1 ff.

[363] MEIER-HAYOZ/CRONE, Wertpapierrecht[3], p. 4 f.

not have to be in the possession of the owner. The debtor would only make payment to the person with the right of disposal as agreed.

Another solution to the publicity requirement would be the introduction of a central register with all of the rights represented in tokens. However, this would be a purely domestic solution and, in my view, would present as many hurdles as it would solve problems. Even if an obligation to inspect the national register were introduced for the transfer of rights to property, there would be little advantage in terms of publicity. Quite the contrary. A third level would be added to the two current levels, which are already difficult to coordinate: a central register documenting the tokenisation.

Implementation via a "tokenisation-clause" would not require any modification of the law and could be carried out within the framework of the development of the law. This concept will be examined below in relation to the representation of rights in tokens. However, the tokenisation-clause could be protected by existing law, such as in correspondence with the provisions of Section 272 of the Criminal Code (StGB) on breaking an official seal. It would therefore be worth considering the introduction of a penalty in relation to the removal of the tokenisation-clause from an object.

IV Interim conclusion on the representation of rights

Tokens can be described as "containers" that can represent rights. This model is also called the Token-Container-Model (TCM). Similar to a security, when it represents something the token combines a thing of value (claims or rights of membership, rights to property or other absolute or relative rights) with something that has almost no value (the token). If the token does not represent anything of value – in other words, if it is an empty container – then the token itself is the "thing of value". Thus, tokens do not have to represent rights (intrinsic tokens), but they can (extrinsic tokens).

When rights are represented, the identification and liberation-function pursuant to Art. 8 TVTG must be applied to all extrinsic tokens and not just book-entry securities. Art. 8 TVTG does not apply to intrinsic tokens, i.e. tokens that do not represent rights. With respect to the representation of rights in extrinsic tokens, in contrast, there are – depending on the right represented – different requirements for successful tokenisation. When absolute rights are being represented, the publicity requirements, for example, must be observed. In the case of extrinsic tokens, the parties must agree that – depending on the right – exercising the right is associated with the right of disposal over the token (identification-function) and, conversely, that a debtor can only make payment to the person with the right of disposal over the token in a manner that liberates the debt (liberation-function). Tokens and the represented right should share the same fate. If the claims represented by the token cannot be transferred by law, then Art. 7, para. 2 TVTG once again takes effect, which requires suitable measures, depending on the requirements. One suitable measure would be a tokenisation-clause. Here, the token assumes the functions of the certificate in the case of the certificate clause. Such a clause could, if, in the case of property for example, it were only applied to the property itself, create the publicity that is required. This would make it clear to everyone that a transfer is only possible via tokens and that the payment only releases the individual with the right of disposal from debt.

B (3a) Claims or rights of membership against a person

I Representation of claims

Pursuant to Section 1392 of the Civil Code, the claims arising from an existing obligation can be transferred to a new creditor through a legal transaction known as **cession**. The cession comes about through a **form-free consensual contract** between the transferor (assignor) and the transferee (assignee). The consent of the debtor is not required and the cession can also be formed through an **implied contract**.[364] However, the cession of a **contractual claim** does **not make the assignee a contracting party**. It is not the assignor's entire prior legal status that is transferred. The assignee merely assumes the assignor's **position as creditor**. In the case of synallagmatic contracts, this results in a **division of the contractual relationship**, with the assignee receiving the right[365] against the debtor arising from the contract, but the related obligations[366] remaining with the assignor.[367]

The **cession,** in being a causal disposal transaction (Modus), presupposes the existence of and requires a valid obligation-creating transaction (Titel); these transactions

[364] THÖNI in *Fenyves/Kerschner/Vonkilch*³, Section 1392, margin nos. 2 and 4.

[365] The counterpart of cession is the assumption of an obligation governed by Sections 1405 f., which enables a change of debtors; THÖNI in *Fenyves/Kerschner/Vonkilch*³, Section 1392, p. 109.

[366] If the parties wish to transfer the entire contractual status to the transferee, they must conclude a transfer of contract.

[367] THÖNI in *Fenyves/Kerschner/Vonkilch*³, Section 1392, margin no. 9.

are usually inseparable in the case of a standard full cession.[368] Uncertificated[369] claims that are not represented in tokens are generally transferred on the basis of the mere agreement between the transferor and the transferee of the assignment (transfer contract). Thus, ownership of the assigned claim passes to the assignee when the assignment agreement is concluded. An act of transfer is not required, as this is given by the assignment agreement itself.[370]

The transfer of the claim **does not result in any changes to the claim** (see Section 1394 ABGB). The debtor is entitled to all of the same rights and objections against the assignee that they had against the assignor.

Thus, in Liechtenstein **claims** can be transferred **form-free through cession**, **including through an implied contract**, provided the underlying legal transaction has no formal requirements. The rights and objections remain in force, as a result of which the assignee must respond to objections. If there are no additional formal requirements, then disposal over the token results in the transfer by law (ex lege) of the claim to the new holder of the right of disposal over the token.[371] Occasionally, additional measures must be taken to ensure that the token has the identification and liberation-function. These measures will be discussed below.

1 The applicability of the identification and liberation-function

When representing **claims** in (extrinsic) tokens, the question is whether Art. 8 TVTG applies. Based on Art. 8, para. 1 TVTG, the debtor can be sure that the person identified by the TT-system as the person with the right of disposal is also the lawful holder of the right represented in the token (**identification-function**). No further clarifications are necessary. Art. 8, para. 2 TVTG releases the debtor from the payment obligation after they make payment to the person identified in this manner (**liberation-function**). However, pursuant to Section 1395 ABGB, if the debtor has no knowledge of the cession, they can still make payment to the assignor and liberation the debt. But the coordination requirement specified in Art. 7, para. 2 TVTG must be observed in this case. The person with disposal over the token (the creditor) must subsequently

368 THÖNI in *Fenyves/Kerschner/Vonkilch*³, Section 1392, margin no. 11f.

369 Bearer instruments can only be transferred in accordance with the principles of property law; in contrast, bearer shares can, according to the prevailing view, also be transferred via cession; THÖNI in *Fenyves/Kerschner/Vonkilch*³, Section 1392, margin no. 16.

370 THÖNI in *Fenyves/Kerschner/Vonkilch*³, Section 1392, margin no. 15.

371 NÄGELE, Sekundärmarkt für Security Token, p. 12; *A.* FRICK, Zivilrechtliche Aspekte von Token im Zusammenhang mit dem liechtensteinischen Token- und VT-Dienstleister-Gesetz, p. 41.

ensure through suitable measures that the transfer of the right is carried out and that there is no competing disposal over the claim.

One suitable measure here is a **tokenisation-clause**. Before a given creditor can cede and assign their claim, they can agree with a given debtor that the "transfer of rights will only take place via a token, payment only to the person with the right of disposal over the token". This ensures that the debtor can no longer make payment to the assignor, thus carrying out the coordination.

2 Tokenisation using the example of a purchase contract for a watch

The TVTG enables tokens to represent rights and assigns tokens an identification and liberation-function pursuant to Art. 8. It does not provide for the **representation of obligations** in tokens. There are more problems here than the question of general meaningfulness alone. For example, a **change of debtors** is not immediately possible, while a change of creditors is[372]. Both documentation and tokenisation aim to make rights easier to transfer and exchange, among other things. This is not the case for obligations, as it depends on who the debtor is.

The **purchase contract** is the textbook example of a synallagmatic (mutual) contract. The purchaser is obliged to pay the purchase price and the claim, for example, upon handover of the property. In return ("do ut des"[373] exchange), the seller is obliged to hand the object of the purchase over to the purchaser (to transfer ownership to them) and to relinquish the claim to the purchase price against the purchaser. Only the claims and rights arising from the contractual relationship can be represented in the token. A distinction regarding how these are transferred is made depending on the claim. The **purchase price claim** is transferred via **cession**. As discussed in the section on cession, the holder of the right of disposal over the token (token holder, assignee) is, however, not the contracting party (the seller's/assignor's entire prior legal status is not transferred). In other words, the token holder does not have to hand over the object of the purchase or meet any of the seller's other ancillary obligations. The token holder (assignee) merely assumes the assignor's **position as creditor**. In the case of synallagmatic contracts such as a contract to purchase an object, this results in a division of the contractual relationship, with the token holder receiving the right arising from the contract against the purchaser (debtor). However,

[372] See the remarks on cession in Part 3, Section 4, B, I.

[373] From Roman law, "do ut des" means "I give so that you might give".

the **obligations** associated with the contract remain with the seller (assignor), as noted above.

Conversely, the purchaser cannot tokenise the obligation to pay the purchase price, but rather the claim to the transfer of ownership of the object of the purchase. As discussed in the chapter on the representation of property[374], representation pursuant to Art. 7, para. 1 TVTG often fails and suitable measures need to be specified, such as a substitute for the transfer of ownership or custody by a third party.

Thus, "tokenisation" is only available for **claims arising from purchase contracts**. Depending on the type of obligation, the obligations can be carried out fully automatically through smart-contracts.

II The representation of rights of membership and book-entry securities

Legal entities[375] may grant their members **membership shares** (share rights), provided that there is no law or articles of incorporation to the contrary. The membership cannot be divided, sold or bequeathed, but there may be alternate provisions in the law or the articles of incorporation.[376] The membership is transferred and a limited right in rem is created by means of a written contract pursuant to Art. 149, para.

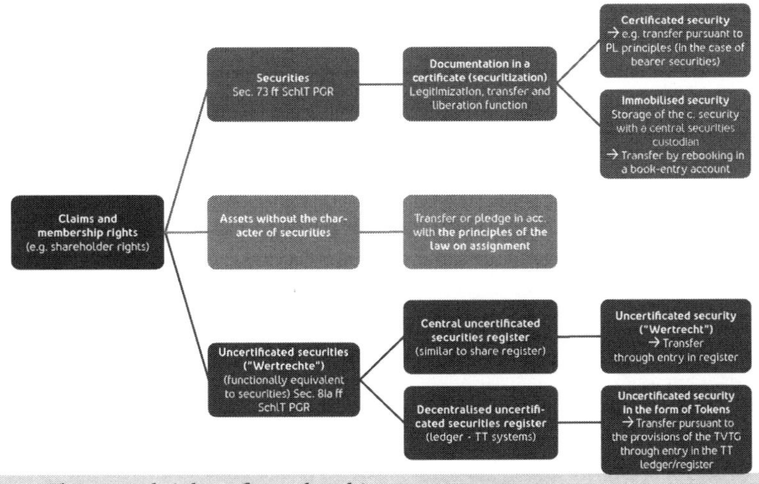

Figure 1 Claims and rights of membership

374 See the remarks in Part 3, Section 4, C.

375 The PGR calls legal entities "cell companies". See the heading of the second section before Art. 106 PGR.

376 See Art. 149, para. 1 and 2 PGR.

3 PGR. This does not include those cases in which there are securities or book-entry securities with the character of securities[377].[378] Thus, if rights of membership are not issued in the form of securities or as book-entry securities pursuant to Art. 81a, para. 1 SchlT PGR (certificated), then they are transferred by means of a contract (see Figure 1).[379]

1 From physical securities to claims and rights of membership to book-entry securities and an electronic register system using TT-systems

There are special transfer requirements for securities that following the principles of property law. The term and the form of securities is discussed in Sections 73 ff. SchlT PGR. **Securities are certificates** that manifest a right physically, preventing the right from being sold, claimed or otherwise transferred without the certificate.[380] They combine a right with a physical information carrier (property pursuant to property law), a certificate.[381] The debtor of a security is obliged to make payment when the security is presented and surrendered (the identification-function of the security). The transfer of the security as property or as a limited right in rem requires a written contract (title) and the surrender of the security (mode).[382]

Although it may now seem strange that the physical surrender of the certificate was the norm when transferring securities, this method already represents a major simplification for transferring rights of membership. Securitization in certificates was the first steps towards a more efficient capital market, in which the ease of transfers, in particular, plays an important role. In most cases, securities[383] serve as documentary

[377] Since the entry into force of the TVTG, any discussion of Liechtenstein law on securities is also understood to include book-entry securities; see BuA No. 54/2019, p. 111.

[378] However, the articles of incorporation can establish other provisions, such as the right of first refusal, the duty to obtain the consent of corporate bodies or members.

[379] Figure 1 from NÄGELE, Sekundärmarkt für Security Token, p. 13.

[380] Art. 73, para. 1 SchlT PGR; for a detailed view, see *A.* FRICK, Zivilrechtliche Aspekte von Token im Zusammenhang mit dem liechtensteinischen Token- und VT-Dienstleister-Gesetz, p. 23 f.; see also WILD, Zivilrecht und Token-Ökonomie in Liechtenstein, p. 85 f.

[381] BuA 54/2019, 108.

[382] Art. 75, para. 1 SchlT PGR.

[383] For example, savings books, bonds, debentures and convertible bonds.

evidence for claims to repayment and interest on the holder's capital against the issuer (debt security).[384]

If a token is intended to represent a claim that is securitized (in paper), the transfer of the token does not by law result in the transfer of the securitized right as well as by law the right represented by the token pursuant to Art. 7, para. 1 TVTG.[385] Instead, the transfer of the security requires the transfer of the certificate (paper) in compliance with the mode in accordance with the rules of property law. Pursuant to Art. 7, para. 2 TVTG, the obliged person must therefore ensure that the legal effect of the "transfer of the security" is carried out through suitable measures.[386] Thus, the "tokenisation" of claims already documented in securities makes little sense, as it results in little in terms of efficiency gains.[387]

However, the problem of physical surrender occurs with global securities trading as well. Securities have been immobilised due to the constantly growing transaction volumes – to further improve efficiency. As a result of this immobilisation, a multi-level custodial system was developed by custodians (central securities depository) in which certificates no longer needed to be surrendered, and instead the transfer was carried out de facto by means of electronic account transfer processes (securities transfer system).[388] As a further step towards improved efficiency, in some countries, such as Germany, Austria, Luxembourg and Switzerland, company shares were certificated in the form of collective certificates (global certificates).[389] The – continued – requirement that a certificate be issued when the shares were documented in the form of a securities certificate was called into question was another major stage in this development. This resulted in the so-called **dematerialisation of securities**, making it no longer necessary to document the security rights in the form of a certificate.[390]

---

384 *G.* Leser/*G.* Leser/Habsburg-Lothringen, Finanzinstrumente - Aktien, Anleihen, Rohstoffe, Fonds und Derivate im Überblick. Inkl. virtuelle Währungssysteme (Blockchain, ICO, Bitcoin, Ethereum und andere Kryptowährungen)^2 (2019), p. 14; on the entire paragraph, see Nägele, Sekundärmarkt für Security Token, p. 14.

385 BuA No. 54/2019, p. 169.

386 Another option for meeting these requirements, albeit one that is somewhat outdated, is the surrender of the physical securities. The surrender of physical certificates is almost inconceivable in modern global securities trading because of the transaction volume.

387 Book-entry securities save the parties involved from the laborious process of dealing with physical securities.

388 Schwarz, Globaler Effektenhandel, p. 29 ff.

389 Schwarz, Globaler Effektenhandel, p. 45 ff.

390 Schwarz, Globaler Effektenhandel, p. 44 f.

The next major step in the rationalisation of securities was the **complete disappearance of physical form**. This has been the case in Liechtenstein since 1 January 2020. In place of certificates there would be purely electronic entries in a register, so-called "book-entry securities".[391]

2 The term "book-entry securities" in accordance with Art. 81a SchlT PGR – "functionally equivalent securities in tokenised form"

So-called book-entry securities occupy a special place in the TVTG, although this term does not appear in the text of the law itself, as it was included by legislators in the final section of the PGR. Even before the TVTG, Liechtenstein law recognised immobilised and dematerialised securities, i.e. **book-entry securities** without the character of securities.[392] In its original version of 1926, the PGR specified in Art. 149, para. 3 that membership shares must be issued to legal entities as book-entry securities. However, these shares were transferred or pledged in accordance with the **principles of assignment law**, which would exclude acquisition in good faith. Within the framework of the TVTG, book-entry securities were codified in Art. 81a, para. 1 SchlT PGR:[393] Consequently, book-entry securities are *"rights with the same functions as securities"* and *"fungible securities"*[394]. As a result, documentation in the form of a certificate is no longer necessary, and claims can be issued in the form of tokens from the outset (book-entry securities). The basis for Art. 81a SchlT PGR was Art. 973c of the Swiss Code of Obligations, although Liechtenstein legislators went further than the authors of the original law. Art. 973c, para. 1 of the Swiss Code of Obligations has since been amended to take account of developments related to distributed electronic register technology, with the addition of new provisions in Art. 937d to 937i SCO.

---

[391] SCHWARZ, Globaler Effektenhandel, p. 51 f., p. 51 f.; NÄGELE, Sekundärmarkt für Security Token (Secondary Market for Security Tokens), p. 15 f.

[392] In Germany, book-entry securities are called "debt register claims"; SCHWARZ, Globaler Effektenhandel, p. 52; in 1975, the Constitutional Court noted in a comment on a case that it is possible for the foundation rights to an institution to be issued as "book-entry securities without the character of securities"; see BuA No. 54/2019, p. 108 f.; with reference to StGH 1975/002 ElG 1973, 381, 383; on the long path of securities law to dematerialisation, see WILD, Zivilrecht und Token-Ökonomie in Liechtenstein, p. 85 f.; see also *A.* FRICK, Zivilrechtliche Aspekte von Token im Zusammenhang mit dem liechtensteinischen Token- und VT-Dienstleister-Gesetz, p. 26.

[393] BuA No. 54/2019, p. 108 ff.

[394] BuA No. 54/2019, p. 110; see also WILD, Zivilrecht und Token-Ökonomie in Liechtenstein, p. 86.

In order for tokens to be **functionally equivalent to securities**, they must have the same functions as securities documented in the form of a certificate when they represent rights that can be represented by securities. These are:

1. The "**identification-function**"[395]: Right-owners identify themselves by verifying their possession of the power of disposal over the token;
2. The "**liberation-function**"[396]: Liberates the debtor upon payment of the holder of the power of disposal over the token;
3. The "**transport-function**"[397]: The token makes it possible to transfer rights;
4. The "**transaction-protection-function**"[398]: The protection of bona fide rights; and
5. A "**objection restriction**"[399]: A restriction on objections aimed at entries in the book-entry securities register.[400]

Book-entry securities pursuant to Art. 81a SchlT PGR therefore have all of the functions of a security when TT-systems are used => **functional equivalence**.[401]

Here, the tokens do not represent book-entry securities; they are fully digital book-entry securities. However, as they derive their value from an external asset, they are extrinsic tokens. Pursuant to Art. 81a SchlT PGR, the debtor (legal entity) can also maintain the **book-entry securities register** using trustworthy-technologies pursuant to the TVTG.[402] Pursuant to Art. 81a, para. 4 SchlT PGR, transfers of book-entry securities in the form of tokens are **solely based on the provisions of the TVTG**.[403]

---

395 Called "identification" in the heading of Art. 8 TVTG.

396 Called "discharge" in the heading of Art. 8 TVTG.

397 See Art. 6 and 7 TVTG.

398 Implemented in Art. 9 TVTG.

399 At any rate, the restriction on objections should apply for tokens that represent book-entry securities; see: BuA No. 54/2019, p. 110; whether a restriction on objections makes sense for other extrinsic tokens must be determined in each individual case.

400 For more on the specified functions, see BuA No. 54/2019, p. 110.

401 Nägele, Sekundärmarkt für Security Token, p. 20; BuA No. 54/2019, p. 111; Wild, Zivilrecht und Token-Ökonomie in Liechtenstein, p. 87.

402 Art. 81a, para. 2 SchlT PGR.

403 Nägele, Sekundärmarkt für Security Token, p. 16.

A major restriction in issuing book-entry securities is that **only those rights that can be certificated in the form of a security** can be issued **as book-entry securities.**[404] Consequently, since the entry into force of the TVTG, any discussion of Liechtenstein law on securities is understood to include book-entry securities also.[405] There are further restrictions based on the legal form of the entity.[406] In addition to **joint stock companies**[407], as the prime example[408], in Liechtenstein securities – and thus book-entry securities – can, for instance, be issued via membership in **(special) associations**[409], registered cooperatives[410], associations with limited liability (trade unions)[411], silent partnerships[412] and **institutions**[413]. Since the **GmbH** revision of 2016, it is no longer possible to document in the form of a certificate and thus tokenise limited liability companies (LLC/GmbH)[414]. When issuing book-entry securities[415] via legal positions under company law, the requirements related to company law must be observed in addition to the requirements related to securities law. The content of the book-entry securities is based mainly on the company's articles of incorporation and shareholder resolutions.[416]

---

404 BuA No. 54/2019, p. 116 ff.

405 Which is why legislators decided against amending all laws; see BuA No. 54/2019, p. 111.

406 Wild also relies on the respective company form, WILD, Zivilrecht und Token-Ökonomie in Liechtenstein, p. 88.

407 See Art. 267 ff. and Art. 323 ff. PGR.

408 In practice, almost all shares are issued as securities; see BuA No. 54/2019, p. 117.

409 Art. 259, para. 1 PGR

410 According to Art. 401, para. 3 PGR; this is in contrast to Swiss cooperatives, for which there is an express legal prohibition against certification in the form of a security; see MEIER-HAYOZ/CRONE, Wertpapierrecht[3], p. 4.

411 Art. 380, para. 3 PGR.

412 Art. 772, para. 4 PGR.

413 Art. 540, para. 5 PGR.

414 Art. 409 has been repealed and Art. 391, para. 5 PGR amended; based on the materials, the reasons for this are likely the lack of relevance and the better suitability of joint stock companies; in view of the developments related to the TVTG it would, in my view, be worth considering a reintroduction of an option to document securities as certificates in modified form; see GOVERNMENT OF THE PRINCIPALITY OF LIECHTENSTEIN, BuA No. 68/2016, p. 26.

415 And securities.

416 BuA No. 54/2019, p. 116; NÄGELE, Sekundärmarkt für Security Token, p. 16 f.; WILD, Zivilrecht und Token-Ökonomie in Liechtenstein, p. 86.

3 The transfer of book-entry securities using the example of bearer shares in a joint stock company in the form of tokens

The example of bearer shares in the form of book-entry rights in a joint stock company can be used to demonstrate the transfer of book-entry securities. Before they were immobilised[417] in accordance with the requirements of securities law described above, bearer shares were transferred in the form of a certificate in accordance with the principles of property law (title and mode). Bearer shares must now be held in safekeeping by a securities depository designated by the company.[418] Pursuant to Art. 326a, para. 2(1) PGR, the custodial regime does not apply to exchange-listed joint stock companies – on the basis of the applicable special provisions contained therein. Book-entry securities must be booked with the securities depository when they are issued rather than stored pursuant to Art. 326a, para. 1 PGR. All of the book-entry-securities holdings must be booked in a holding account with the depository; certificates no longer need to be stored, as they no longer exist.[419]

Firstly, we will take a brief look at how bearer shares documented in certificates (securities) are transferred using a depository in order to be able to compare to book-entry securities.[420]

Shareholders wishing to transfer bearer shares in accordance with Art. 326h PGR must notify the securities depository accordingly. The transfer becomes effective when the acquiring party is entered in the register (**constitutive effect**).[421] All of the requirements under securities law and company law must be met cumulatively. The certificate must be transferred in accordance with the principles of property law. This is achieved in the form of an instruction of ownership ("Besitzanweisung") pursuant to Art. 503 PL by the selling shareholder, as the indirect, dependent possessor, to the custodian, as the direct, independent possessor. Once the transfer of the certificate

---

417 And introduction of a sanction mechanism for the maintenance of the share register for registered shares by LLG 2013, No. 67.

418 BuA No. 54/2019, p. 117 ff.

419 BuA No. 54/2019, p. 117.

420 BuA No. 69/2012, p. 18; on the entire paragraph, NÄGELE, Sekundärmarkt für Security Token (Secondary Market for Security Tokens), p. 17 f.

421 BuA No. 54/2019, p. 118; on the constitutive effect of the entry in the book-entry securities register, see, in particular, WILD, Zivilrecht und Token-Ökonomie in Liechtenstein, p. 89 f.

is complete, the security is deemed transferred under civil law. However, the company – from the perspective of company law – only recognises the person entered in the depository register as the shareholder.[422]

Applying this dichotomy to compare it with the issue and transfer of book-entry securities in accordance with Art. 81a SchlT PGR, the transfer of bearer shares in the form of book-entry securities can be carried out, on the one hand, by:[423]

1. entering the acquiring party in the book-entry securities register of the legal entity pursuant to Art. 81a, para. 4 SchlT PGR; and, on the other hand, by
2. entering the acquiring party in the securities depository register pursuant to Art. 326h, para. 3 in conjunction with Art. 326c PGR.

These two registers must be coordinated[424], whereby a securities depository pursuant to Art. 326b PRG may also maintain the book-entry securities register.[425]

In other words, a simple transaction on a TT-system can be used to transfer a bearer share in the form of a book-entry security.

III Claims and rights of membership in the form of book-entry securities in (security) tokens and their classification under regulatory law

While regulatory law is not the subject of this book, a classification should be undertaken at this point in order to be able to delineate between the TVTG and regulatory law. In addition, the question of whether tokens that represent rights to financial instruments maintain their characteristic as securities must be answered.

The functional equivalence of book-entry securities makes it possible to treat book-entry securities equally without any restrictions under regulatory law. Of particular interest from the regulatory law perspective is the classification among financial instruments. Such tokens are also referred to as “**security tokens**”. An especially **dense and extensive set of rules** applies to security tokens, both when they are first offered publicly (primary market) and when they are subsequently traded (secondary

[422] BuA No. 54/2019, p. 118; on the entire paragraph, see NÄGELE, Sekundärmarkt für Security Token (Secondary Market for Security Tokens), p. 18.

[423] BuA No. 54/2019, p. 118.

[424] Or maintained as a joint register, which is made easier by the use of TT-systems.

[425] BuA No. 54/2019, p. 117 ff.; on the entire paragraph, see: NÄGELE, Sekundärmarkt für Security Token (Secondary Market for Security Tokens), p. 18 f.

market).[426] Financial market law provisions apply in addition to the **provisions of the TVTG**. A public offering of security tokens may therefore involve both obligations under prospectus law and registration and other obligations pursuant to the TVTG. The Liechtenstein Financial Market Authority, when assessing the applicability of the provisions of financial market law (see FMA Communication 2019/1[427] and FMA Communication 2019/2[428]) and thus its jurisdiction, applies the principle of "substance over form". This technology-neutral approach[429] is to be welcomed[430]. Security tokens should therefore be classified as such pursuant to financial market regulations.[431]

As the competent regulatory authority, the FMA approved its first **securities prospectus** for securities in the form of security tokens in summer 2018.[432] It is worth noting that this answered the question of whether securities issued in the form of tokens retained the **characteristic of securities** and thus approval of the prospectus by the FMA was possible. In October 2019, the FMA, in FMA Communication 2019/2[433], established additional requirements for securities prospectuses when issuing security tokens. According to this communication, the Securities Prospectus Act and EU Regulation 2017/1129[434], which is directly relevant, are also applicable **if the**

---

426 For example, companies that offer tokens for public sale have long attempted to avoid having them classified as financial instruments and e-money in order evade this heavily regulated environment.

427 FINANCIAL MARKET AUTHORITY (FMA), FMA Communication 2019/1, https://www.fma-li.li/files/list/fma-mitteilung-2019-01.pdf (accessed on 11 April 2020), p. 2.

428 FINANCIAL MARKET AUTHORITY (FMA), FMA Communication 2019/2, https://www.fma-li.li/files/list/fma-mittteilung-2019-2-emittenten-wp-st.pdf (accessed on 24/03/2020), p. 4.

429 FMA, FMA Communication 2019/2, p. 5.

430 The technology-neutral approach corresponds to the practice of the US regulatory authority, the US Securities and Exchange Commission (SEC); on this point, see: "A change in the structure of a securities offering does not change the fundamental point that when a security is being offered, our securities laws must be followed. Said another way, replacing a traditional corporate interest recorded in a central ledger with an enterprise interest recorded through a blockchain entry on a distributed ledger may change the form of the transaction, but it does not change the substance": CLAYTON, Statement on Cryptocurrencies and Initial Coin Offerings, https://www.sec.gov/news/public-statement/statement-clayton-2017-12-11 (accessed on 11 April 2020).

431 See also BuA 54/2019, 44.

432 FMA, FMA Communication 2019/2, p. 5.

433 FMA, FMA Communication 2019/2.

434 Regulation (EU) 2017/1129 of the European Parliament and of the Council of 14 June 2017 on the prospectus to be published when securities are offered to the public or admitted to trading on a regulated market, and repealing Directive 2003/71/EC (text with EEA relevance) (Prospectus Regulation), OJ EC 2017/168, p. 12.

token fulfils the characteristics of a security. By approving multiple prospectuses, the FMA affirmed this characteristic an equal number of times.[435] When assessing the fulfilment of the characteristic of a security, the FMA assesses three criteria:

1. Tradability,
2. Transferability, and
3. Standardisation.[436]

For the question of tradability it is relevant whether the security can be traded on the capital market, whereby the term "capital market" must be interpreted broadly.[437] As far as can be determined, the first "blockchain-based"[438] **multilateral trading facility (MTF)** [439]in the European Economic Area (EEA) was approved in Liechtenstein (subject to conditions).[440] Tradability was ensured by no later than this point.[441] The transferability criterion is usually ensured within the system by means of the token's transfer-function.[442] The conditions must still remain to ensure that the transfer is also successful pursuant to the TVTG (this is the case for book-entry securities by law). Finally, standardisation is also not problematic to implement from a technical

---

435 FMA, List of approved prospectuses to 20 July 2019.

436 NÄGELE, Sekundärmarkt für Security Token (Secondary Market for Security Tokens), p. 21 ff.; FMA, FMA Communication 2019/2, p. 5.

437 A virtual marketplace alone is sufficient for tradability on a capital market; see PAULMAYER, Initial Coin Offerings (ICOs) und Initial Token Offerings (ITOs) als prospektpflichtiges Angebot nach KMG? ZFR 2017/259, p. 533 with further references.

438 The operators appear to include the listing of blockchain-based financial instruments here.

439 Multilateral trading facility (MTF).

440 On this point, see also the article dated 29 April 2020 by three Austrian FMA staff members who were unable to locate any trading platform in the EEA that purposely and openly listed DLT-based transferable securities; PEKLER/RIRSCH/TOMANEK, Kapitalmarktrechtliche Hindernisse für den Handel von Security Token, ZFR 2020/73, p. 172; see the press release of the advising law firm Ashurst; as of the date this paper was submitted, the MTF was still not entered in the register maintained by the FMA. Last reviewed on 6 May 2021; see in Ashurst LLP, Ashurst press release (Ashurst advises Nomisma on Europe's first MiFID II license for a blockchain-based MTF) (26 April 2020, https://www.ashurst.com/en/news-and-insights/news-deals-and-awards/ashurst-advises-nomisma-on-europes-first-mifid-ii-license-for-a-blockchain-based-mtf).

441 NÄGELE, Sekundärmarkt für Security Token (Secondary Market for Security Tokens), p. 23 f.

442 Transfer restrictions such as whitelisting that are not in the standard should be planned for security tokens.

standpoint. A large number of tokens of the same type[443] are created[444] on a regular basis. It is not necessary for the security to be issued in paper form (certificate).[445] The FMA holds this view as well and assesses the characteristic of securities on the basis of the aforementioned three criteria. **Documentation** of the security in certificate form is therefore **not a mandatory condition**. Here, the FMA explicitly speaks of the principal of "substance over form".[446] Even when applying the principle of "substance over form", it can be concluded that, when financial instrument rights are represented by tokens, the regulatory provisions on financial instruments must be applied if the represented rights are subject to these provisions. By contrast, the form and designation (in tokenised form or as a certificate) play a subordinate role.[447] Conversely, this also means that tokens **that represent other rights** are **not to be classified as financial instruments**[448] and should not be subject to financial market regulations.[449] With respect to the issue and subsequent obligations[450], the FMA does not see "any significant differences between securities prospectuses for the issue of securities and securities prospectuses for the issue of security tokens".[451]

443 Tokens pursuant to the ERC-20 standard are generally fungible and easy to generate in large numbers.

444 In addition to the three criteria, the Austrian Financial Market Authority (öFMA) also reviews whether the right is "embodied". Here, the AFMA views the connection between the claim and holding the security as relevant. The overwhelming view is that the use of trustworthy technologies can affirm embodiment (representation), as tokens have an identification-function; SCHOPPER/RASCHNER, ÖBA 2019, p. 212 ff. with further references; the TVTG assumes that the rights will be represented and not embodied; see BuA No. 54/2019, p. 142.

445 With further references. PATZ, Handelsplattformen für Kryptowährungen und Kryptoassets, BKR 2019, p. 436.

446 FMA, FMA Communication 2019/2, p. 4.

447 FMA, FMA Communication 2019/2, p. 5.

448 In order to account for Bitcoin, in particular, Germany, in Art. 1, para. 11, clause 1, no. 10 of the German Banking Act (Kreditwesengesetz, or KWG), created a catch-all clause in order to take account of all of the various forms of "cryptoassets" that do not already fall under another category of financial instrument; see FEDERAL FINANCIAL SUPERVISORY AUTHORITY, information sheet: Guidance notice on the crypto custody business, https://www.bafin.de/DE/Aufsicht/BankenFinanzdienstleister/Zulassung/Kryptoverwahrgeschaeft/kryptoverwahrgeschaeft_node.html (accessed on 19 April 2020); German Act on Banking (Banking Act, or KWG), Federal Gazette. (1961), Art. 1, para. 11, clause 1, no. 10.

449 Of course, other reasons for the applicability of securities law remain reserved. See also BuA No. 54/2019, p. 44.

450 FMA, FMA Communication 2019/2, p. 6.

451 On the entire paragraph, see also NÄGELE, Sekundärmarkt für Security Token, p. 23 ff.

IV The creation of limited rights in rem of book-entry securities in accordance with Art. 81a, para. 4 SchlT PGR

Limited rights in rem to book-entry securities are created by entering the person with the right in the book-entry securities register. In practice, the creation of pledging and usufruct rights are especially relevant. If the book-entry securities register is maintained using trustworthy-technologies pursuant to the TVTG, the disposal over the book-entry securities is governed exclusively by the provisions of the TVTG.[452]

Entry in the book-entry securities register also has **constitutive effect** here and enables non-possessory liens. This is property law, as both the owner and the pledgee are listed in the register. Art. 365, para. 1 PL specifies that the law enables the assertion of exceptions to the principle on the pledging of chattels. Such an exception can be found in Art. 81a, para. 4 SchlT PGR.[453]

The creation of a right of lien to book-entry securities in the form of tokens requires – in addition to the other conditions – an entry in the book-entry securities register; possession of the pledged asset is not necessary.

V Conclusion on claims or rights of membership against a person

In Liechtenstein, claims can be transferred form-free and implicitly through cession, provided the underlying legal transaction has no formal requirements. The transfer of the claim does not result in any changes to the claim (see Section 1394 ABGB). The rights and objections remain in force, as a result of which the assignee must respond to objections. The debtor is entitled to all of the same rights and objections against the assignee that they had against the assignor. If there are no additional formal requirements, then disposal over the token results in the transfer by law of the claim to the new holder of the right of disposal over the token. Corresponding additional measures must be taken to ensure that the token has the identification and liberation-function and to guarantee successful transfer.

Legal entities may grant their members membership shares (share rights), provided that there is no law or articles of incorporation to the contrary. The membership cannot be divided, sold or bequeathed, but there may be alternate provisions in the law or the articles of incorporation. Book-entry securities occupy a special place in the

[452] See Art. 81a, para. 4 SchlT PGR and BuA No. 54/2019, p. 114.

[453] BuA No. 54/2019, p. 114.

TVTG, although this term does not appear in the text of the law itself, as it was included by legislators in the final section of the PGR. Even before the TVTG, Liechtenstein law recognised immobilised and dematerialised securities, i.e. book-entry securities without the character of securities. Within the framework of the TVTG, book-entry securities were codified in Art. 81a, para. 1 SchlT PGR: Consequently, book-entry securities are "rights with the same functions as securities" and "fungible securities". As a result, documentation in the form of a certificate is no longer necessary, and claims can be issued in the form of tokens from the beginning (book-entry securities). In order for tokens to be functionally equivalent to securities, they must have the same functions as securities documented in the form of a certificate when they represent rights that can be represented by securities. A major restriction in issuing book-entry securities is that only those rights that can be certificated in the form of a security can be issued as book-entry securities. The transfer is dichotomous in the case of book-entry securities. Thus, bearer shares in the form of book-entry securities are transferred, on the one hand, by entering the acquiring party in the book-entry securities register (constitutive effect) of the legal entity pursuant to Art. 81a, para. 4 SchlT PGR, and, on the other hand, by entering the acquiring party in the securities depository register pursuant to Art. 326h, para. 3 in conjunction with Art. 326c PGR. These two registers must be coordinated, whereby a securities depository pursuant to Art. 326b PRG may also maintain the book-entry securities register.

C (3b) Rights to property

In addition to book-entry securities, the representation of rights to property was of particular interest to the Government when it developed the TVTG. It aimed to find a system that made it possible to combine the advantages of TT-systems with the property law system in a way that ensured a compatible solution. In turn, this solution was supposed to lead – in most cases – to the synchronisation of the analogue world (property) and the digital world (token). These are referred to, somewhat unfortunately, as "digital twins".[454] This is unfortunate because twins are ultimately their own subjects and in most cases tokens are only intended to represent rights.

[454] UNIDROIT, Exploratory workshop on digital assets and private law, https://www.unidroit.org/89-news-and-events/2941-unidroit-exploratory-workshop-on-digital-assets-and-private-law (accessed on 15 February 2021).

To date, there have been few scholarly articles that have looked at the civil law provisions of the TVTG.[455] As expected, there is significant tension between the digital "token world" and the analogue world – especially when it comes to representing rights to physical property under property law. For example, on p. 165 of BuA 54/2019, the Government says: *"The represented right is generally transferred by means of the transfer of the token in accordance with the rules of the TT-system (see Art. 7)".*[456] The word "generally" in this sentence should be viewed as a programmatic interpretative aid. It is not intended to indicate any difference between digital and analogue assets. The TVTG uses the representation[457], assignment and transfer concepts found in securities law as a basis. However, it does so with the difference that rather than involving the surrender of a physical object (a certificate), it involves a token. Property law applies to the surrender of the certificate, while the TVTG applies to the surrender of the token.[458]

The question is whether the regulations on tokens take precedence over the regulations on the represented property. In a response to a question arising during the consultation, the Government states in BuA No. 54/2019:

> *"But disposal over a token (title and mode) does not replace the instruction of ownership or the hand-to-hand transfer of the property itself, provided that the token represents the property right."*[459]

Thus, the Government has **not given precedence** to the regulations on tokens over the regulations on property; instead it has classified them in a system. In its introductory remarks in Report and Application 54/2019 on the TVTG, the Government stated that, in order to **ensure legal certainty** in the "offline world" - depending on the category of represented right (property, claim) - it must be clarified that disposal by

---

[455] To date, the most detailed is WILD, Zivilrecht und Token-Ökonomie in Liechtenstein; see also RIETZLER/*M.* FRICK/CASELLINI in *Piska/Völkel*; NÄGELE, Sekundärmarkt für Security Token; SILBERNAGL, Zivilrechtliche Regelungen des liechtensteinischen Blockchaingesetzes (TVTG) - Möglichkeiten für Österreich? Zak 2020/7; *A.* FRICK, Zivilrechtliche Aspekte von Token im Zusammenhang mit dem liechtensteinischen Token- und VT-Dienstleister-Gesetz; LINS/PRAICHEUX, SPWR 2020; WURZER, SPWR 2019; DEUBER/KHORRAMI JAHROMI, Liechtensteiner Blockchain-Gesetzgebung: Vorbild für Deutschland? MMR 2020; VÖLKEL, Vertrauen in die Blockchain und das Sachenrecht, ZFR 2020/218; RASCHAUER/SILBERNAGL, Grundsatzfragen des liechtensteinischen „Blockchain-Gesetzes" – TVTG, ZFR 2020/3.

[456] BuA No. 54/2019, p. 165.

[457] The BuA uses the term "presentation" rather than "representation" here. This is clearly an editorial oversight; BuA No. 54/2019, p. 165.

[458] BuA No. 54/2019, p. 165.

[459] BuA No. 54/2019, p. 198.

means of tokens (over the represented property) is possible. Since it would per se be possible to undertake a clarification in the relevant laws, but would only affect assets that are subject to Liechtenstein law, this was not undertaken – with the exception of book-entry securities. In other words, property law has not been changed and it has not been said that the transfer of property rights represented in tokens – similar to securities – occurs through tokens (in the case of securities, through the surrender of the security). Instead, the Government chose a functional approach that enables a broader application. This approach does not require any changes to the individual laws. Here, too, there is said to be a coordination requirement as a result of the imposition of corresponding obligations on the person obliged as a result of their disposal over the token pursuant to Art. 7, para. 2 TVTG.[460]

For this reason, a detailed analysis will be presented below considering whether the system of the representation of rights in tokens and disposal over tokens in accordance with the provisions of the TVTG, as well as the TT-system used together with the instruments available to the obliged person as a result of the disposal under property law (in particular, the instruction of ownership, constructive possession and hand-to-hand transfer), enables them to meet their obligations.

I The coordination requirement pursuant to Art. 7, para. 2 TVTG in the case of the representation of rights to property

In Art. 7, para. 1 and para. 2 TVTG, the aim of the law is to **closely connect the represented right and the token** in a way that – similar to securities – ensures that the right **cannot be asserted or transferred to others** without the token.[461] This primarily involves **commercial security**, which in turn presupposes that the **legal subject** (user) can trust the legal appearance of the tokens. In other words, if the token represents the right to own a watch, then it must suffice for the purpose of demonstrating ownership for the token holder to demonstrate the right to dispose of the token (**identification-function** pursuant to Art. 8, para. 1 TVTG). A payment by

[460] BuA 54/2019 states that this obligation is supposed to apply to the token generator. However, Art. 7, para. 2 TVTG imposes this obligation on the obliged person as a result of their disposal over the token; BuA No. 54/2019, p. 64.

[461] On securities, see MEIER-HAYOZ/CRONE, Wertpapierrecht[3], p. 1; for a somewhat tenuous connection, see WILD, Zivilrecht und Token-Ökonomie in Liechtenstein, p. 78 f.

the debtor to the person identified in this manner liberates the debt (**liberation-function** pursuant to Art. 8, para. 2 TVTG).[462]

Therefore, the conditions for satisfying the coordination requirement in Art. 7, para. 2 TVTG will be analysed based on the represented right. At first glance, Art. 7 TVTG does not allow for any flexibility in situations where there is no synchronisation between the analogue and digital worlds. Either the synchronisation is brought about by law pursuant to Art. 7, para. 1 TVTG (e.g. in the case of book-entry securities based on the new provisions of Art. 81a SchlT PGR), or through **suitable measures** pursuant to Art. 7, para. 2 TVTG. The TVTG (correctly) does not stipulate precisely which measure must be taken here. This enables as broad an application as possible through adequate measures for the representation of rights to property. BuA 54/2019 specifies **organisational, structural and legal measures** that can be considered in order to achieve coordination. The examples that are listed include **storing the property with a depository** or transferring ownership to a nominee. "*This intermediary is then obliged by contract and/or law to recognise only that person as the owner or creditor who is the person entitled to dispose over the corresponding token in accordance with the rules of the TT-system.*"[463] This example shows that the Government also views Art. 8 TVTG as applicable for the representation of rights.

According to Art. 7, para. 2(b), the suitable measures must also ensure that "*competing disposal over the represented right is excluded*". "Disposal" here refers to disposal in the analogue world (disposal over the represented right). For example, if a token represents ownership of a watch, the wording of the contract must ensure that the intermediary conveys ownership to the person currently entitled to dispose of the token (tokenisation-clause). It is doubtful that legislators intended to go so far as to also exclude the intermediary from selling the watch to a third party. However, it is possible to see in this provision the government's intent to give disposal over the token (in the digital world) a certain precedence over a competing disposal in the analogue world.[464] This thesis is further supported by the fact that neither the TVTG nor the legislative materials include a scenario in which "*an asset in the analogue*

---

462 In this context, the TVTG can also be seen as the further development of securities law, which has always been shaped by the available technological opportunities. Securities law is now facing the next great revolution as a result of developments related to blockchain/DLT. The trend in securities law of replacing certificates (paper) through digitalisation or registration is nothing new; MEIER-HAYOZ/CRONE, Wertpapierrecht[3], p. 1.

463 BuA No. 54/2019, p. 171.

464 BuA No. 54/2019, p. 170 ff.

world is sold and surrendered"[465] without a corresponding transaction in the digital world. WILD proposes an analogous application of Art. 7, para. 2 TVTG here.[466] In this scenario, the seller of the asset in the analogue world is obliged to ensure a corresponding transfer of the right of disposal over the token. The TVTG does not provide for such a situation. Instead, **competing disposal** over the represented right must be excluded to ensure that the situation does not arise. The Government correctly concludes in BuA 54/2019 that if coordination cannot be ensured with a reasonable amount of effort, then "*the issue of a token that represents the corresponding analogue assets is economically untenable*".[467] The analogous application of Art. 7, para. 2 TVTG proposed by WILD is not necessary to achieve an adequate solution. This will be discussed in detail below.

Disposal over tokens has already been discussed at length elsewhere, so the focus will now be on disposal over the right represented in the token.

II The transfer of ownership through a substitute for the transfer of ownership

In the legislative materials, the Government explained how the full rights of ownership represented in the token should be transferred: The transfer requires:

- an obligatory transaction (title) related to the token and the right;
- disposal over the token (mode) in accordance with the rules of the TT-system;[468] and
- disposal over the rights represented in the token through an instruction of ownership or hand-to-hand surrender of the property.[469]

For this reason, when representing the rights to property, in addition to the requirements under the TVTG regarding the transfer of the token, the property must also be transferred in accordance with the principles of property law. The provisions of Art. 7, para. 2, which are vaguely formulated, make it possible – depending on the situa-

[465] WILD, Zivilrecht und Token-Ökonomie in Liechtenstein, p. 64 f.

[466] WILD, Zivilrecht und Token-Ökonomie in Liechtenstein, p. 65.

[467] BuA No. 54/2019, p. 172.

[468] Not explicitly required in the specified point in BuA 54/2019, but it does result directly from Art. 6, para. 2 TVTG.

[469] BuA No. 54/2019, p. 202.

tion – to find suitable solutions for ensuring adherence to the coordination requirement and the synchronisation of the digital and analogue world.[470] In the case of transfers of possession and ownership, aside from the[471] hand-to-hand[472] surrender of property, which is fairly uninteresting in practice, the forms of acquisition without possession (Art. 187 PL), e.g. through substitutes for the transfer of ownership, such as the instruction of ownership[473] in accordance with Art. 503 PL, play a central role.[474] It is important to note here that the **substitutes for the transfer of ownership** are **often formless.** [475]

1 The instruction of ownership pursuant to Art. 503 PL

The title "Without surrender" alone makes it clear that Art. 503 PL creates opportunities for transferring possession (as a precondition for the transfer of ownership) without surrendering the property. An instruction of ownership ("Besitzanweisung")is thus always carried out in conjunction with another legal transaction, e.g. the sale of an object.

The instruction of ownership requires:

- indirect possession by the seller,
- direct possession by a third party (intermediary) on the basis of a special legal relationship and
- a legal agreement between the seller and the purchaser that the third party will hold the property for the purchaser in future (possession contract).[476]

---

[470] BuA No. 54/2019, p. 169.

[471] See the detailed analysis of the watch example with the de facto surrender of the watch; WILD, Zivilrecht und Token-Ökonomie in Liechtenstein, p. 65 f.

[472] As in such cases, TT-systems would only have to serve documentation purposes.

[473] In response to the consultation: *"But disposal over a token (title and mode) do not replace the instruction of ownership or the hand-to-hand surrender of the property itself, provided the token represents the ownership of property."* BuA No. 54/2019, p. 198.

[474] OPILIO, Liechtensteinisches Sachenrecht, p. 437; BuA No. 54/2019, p. 198, 203; see also *A.* FRICK, Zivilrechtliche Aspekte von Token im Zusammenhang mit dem liechtensteinischen Token- und VT-Dienstleister-Gesetz, p. 41.

[475] On the formless instruction of ownership, see CRONE/KESSLER/ANGSTMANN, Token in der Blockchain – privatrechtliche Aspekte der Distributed Ledger Technologie, SJZ 2018/114, p. 345.

[476] *J.* SCHMID/HÜRLIMANN-KAUP, Sachenrecht[4] (2012), p. 37 f.

An instruction of ownership requires mediate possession ("gestufter Besitz"); the seller must surrender the property to the intermediary (third party) prior to instruction of ownership. Art. 503, para. 1 PL states that the intermediary must remain in possession of the property on the basis of "a special legal relationship" (**possession contract**). The following are examples of a special legal relationship on the basis of which the intermediary can be given actual control over the property: usufruct in rem or compulsory rights, such as leases, loans, work contracts, commissions or storage.[477] The dependent possessor maintains their position; the **seller's indirect possession** is transferred.[478]

The legal agreement between the seller and the purchaser represents a contract (**possession contract**)[479] for which no written form is specified and for which substitution is available. However, it does not involve a cession of the right to recover possession. The validity of the transfer of possession no longer depends on the validity of the transfer – at least **after** the dependent possessor has been notified. The transfer of possession **takes place immediately** after the **conclusion of the possession contract**. While Art. 503 PL specifies that the transfer of possession to the intermediary only becomes effective when the seller notifies[480] the intermediary (the direct possessor), the transfer of possession applies erga omnes before the notification of the bailee. Thus, notification of the independent possessor (intermediary) of the transfer of possession is not a prerequisite for the transfer of possession.[481] Even if the intermediary asserts their possession on the basis of a contract with the seller and the purchaser refuses to assume or continue this legal relationship, the transfer of possession takes place upon conclusion of the possession contract.[482]

This recognition of the instruction of ownership – **even without notification of the intermediary** – is based on the following considerations: In accordance with the rules of mediate possession, the purchaser becomes the owner as soon as the intermediary possesses the property on their behalf. Thus, if the intermediary agrees to maintain possession on behalf of the purchaser, the latter becomes the owner when

---

477 *J.* SCHMID/HÜRLIMANN-KAUP, Sachenrecht[4], p. 37.

478 STARK/LINDENMANN, Der Besitz, Art. 919-941 ZGB Schweizerisches Zivilgesetzbuch, in *Hausheer/Zobl/Leemann/Gmür/Becker/Meier-Hayoz* (ed.), Berner Kommentar[2] (1996), p. 139.

479 STARK/LINDENMANN in *Hausheer/Zobl/Leemann/Gmür/Becker/Meier-Hayoz*, p. 141.

480 Or communication.

481 STARK/LINDENMANN in *Hausheer/Zobl/Leemann/Gmür/Becker/Meier-Hayoz*, p. 141 ff.

482 STARK/LINDENMANN in *Hausheer/Zobl/Leemann/Gmür/Becker/Meier-Hayoz*, p. 143.

the notice is sent to the intermediary. However, even before the notice is sent to the intermediary and even if the intermediary refuses to take possession for the purchaser, the purchaser becomes the owner on the basis of the multi-level mediate possession ("dopppelt gestuften Besitzes"). The special rule regarding the instruction of ownership is not decisive for the acquisition of ownership. This is because with double-stepped possession, the seller remains the indirect owner. The intermediary (third party) has direct possession on behalf of the seller and conveys possession to the purchaser. This is intended to prevent problems from occurring with the ownership arrangement that has been agreed in the possession contract (of which the intermediary now holds in possession for the purchaser). This applies for as long as the intermediary maintains possession for the seller.[483]

The notice to the intermediary is a **formless declaration of intent** that requires acknowledgement of receipt from the seller, which is addressed to the intermediary (the direct possessor) of the property. The **purchaser** can serve as the **seller's representative**. They may be **authorised** to do so in the possession contract. The sale may be express or **implicit**.[484] In doing so, the seller exercises a right that is available to them on the basis of their legal relationship with the intermediary. The seller remains the owner until there is a change of intent on the part of the intermediary. The seller does not cease to be the interim owner directly as a result of the possession contract, but rather upon the seller's declaration of intent.

The notice requires acknowledgement of receipt because the **intermediary's legal situation has changed significantly**.[485] A sale by an unauthorised party to the intermediary via a instruction of ownership is, in itself, not legally relevant. If the intermediary trusts the unauthorised party and hands over the property to them, then they have been deceived. Based on the contractual relationship with the indirect owner, the intermediary becomes liable to the latter for damages if they can no longer hand over the property.[486]

Even before the notice, the **purchaser** receives the **legal status** on the basis of which they **have a right** according to the basic contract between them and the seller. If rights in rem are the subject of the basic contract, the purchaser has the right in

---

[483] STARK/LINDENMANN in *Hausheer/Zobl/Leemann/Gmür/Becker/Meier-Hayoz*, p. 145 f.

[484] STARK/LINDENMANN in *Hausheer/Zobl/Leemann/Gmür/Becker/Meier-Hayoz*, p. 146.

[485] STARK/LINDENMANN in *Hausheer/Zobl/Leemann/Gmür/Becker/Meier-Hayoz*, p. 145.

[486] STARK/LINDENMANN in *Hausheer/Zobl/Leemann/Gmür/Becker/Meier-Hayoz*, p. 146.

rem and may assert their right in the event of the insolvency of the seller or the intermediary. Even if the **basic contract proves to be invalid, but the possession contract is valid**, the purchaser nevertheless receives the legal status of owner.[487]

If, upon the instruction of ownership, **the intermediary sells and surrenders** the **property entrusted to them** to a third party, the latter **acquires**[488] the property in accordance with Art. 512 PL, provided that they act **in good faith**[489].[490]

The special case involving cash and bearer instruments in accordance with Art. 514 PL[491] is to be noted, by which the cash and bearer instruments cannot be reclaimed from a recipient acting in good faith even if the possessor was dispossessed of them against their will.

1.1 Instruction of ownership in the case of rights represented in tokens

The provisions related to the instruction of ownership ("Besitzanweisung")will now be applied to rights represented in tokens. In the **possession contract**, the direct possessor undertakes to surrender (tokenisation-clause) the property only to the person entitled to dispose over the token (identification-function).[492] The notification obligation is implicitly waived and replaced with the token's identification-function. The **legal responsibility** identified by the TT-system offers a **high degree of reliability** (commercial security).[493] The statutory regulation of the identification-function of (extrinsic) tokens and the high degree of reliability therefore justify the use, in the case of notification of possession, of the token's identification-function in the

487 STARK/LINDENMANN in *Hausheer/Zobl/Leemann/Gmür/Becker/Meier-Hayoz*, p. 145 f.

488 This is in contrasted to acquisition in good faith, as in this case the seller's "actual possession" is required pursuant to Art. 367 of the Austrian General Civil Code; this does not apply for the instruction of ownership, only for the physical surrender and the traditio brevi manu. If a third party holds the property that has been sold in custody, then ownership is acquired through the actual "delivery" of the property to the purchaser; LEUPOLD, Gutgläubiger Erwerb, in *Kerschner/Fenyves/Klang* (ed.), ABGB, Art. 353 to 379[3] (2011), 620, margin no. 51.

489 See Art. 933 of the Swiss Civil Code; Swiss Civil Code (SCC), Federal Gazette (1907).

490 With further references. STARK/LINDENMANN in *Hausheer/Zobl/Leemann/Gmür/Becker/Meier-Hayoz*, p. 150.

491 See Art. 935 SCC.

492 For more on the legal nature of the security, see ZOBL, Das Fahrnispfand, Art. 888-906 ZGB, mit kurzem Überblick über das Versatzpfand (Art. 907-915 ZGB), in *Hausheer/Zobl/Leemann/Gmür/Becker/Meier-Hayoz* (ed.), Berner Kommentar[2] (1996), p. 353.

493 BuA No. 54/2019, p. 207.

form a (tokenisation) clause in the possession contract – in place of the obligation to notify the third party in direct possession of the property.[494]

The Liechtenstein Supreme Court also allows the effective transfer of bearer shares through a instruction of ownership, whereby the possession contract can also be formed through **conclusive statements and actions** (implicit):

"The transfer of ownership, including ownership of bearer shares, can be carried out via a so-called instruction of ownership also. This represents a contract between the seller and the purchaser in which the so-called intermediary (securities depository) is not involved. The possession contract can also be formed through conclusive statements and actions. In practice, it often coincides with the legal declaration regarding the transfer of ownership to the property (bearer share)."[495]

Thus, a **possession contract in the case of the representation of rights to property** can be concluded simply by having the intermediary hand over the property with the notice: Surrender only to the holder of the power of disposal over the token with the tokenID "123Sample" (**tokenisation-clause**). The parties can also implicitly agree to waive notification (communication). The intermediary is also no worse off: The identification-function pursuant to Art. 8 TVTG can functionally replace the notification of the intermediary pursuant to Art. 503, para. 2 PL with the instruction of ownership. This is appropriate, as the intermediary can easily and with a high level of certainty check to whom the seller wishes to transfer the legal status as owner (and thus, for example, to whom ownership of the property has been transferred). For this reason, the intermediary does not run the risk of becoming liable for damages because they have fallen victim to deceit by an unauthorised party. They observe the possession contract and only surrender it to the token holder. The possession contract that has been concluded implicitly is construed to make clear that the intermediary always conveys direct possession to the person who has the power of disposal over the token (identification and liberation-function). The same result would be achieved with the instruction of ownership if such an agreement were not possible. This is because the seller – implicitly – authorises the purchaser to provide the statement to the intermediary. Because the declaration of intent requires acknowledgement of receipt, it is possible for this to be done via a corresponding function in an app or another automated notification – triggered by transactions on the TT-system.

494 See also the note as an alternative method for book-entry claims; THÖNI in *Fenyves/Kerschner/Vonkilch*³, Section 1392, p. 152 f.

495 See guiding principle 1e in OGH Decision 19. 7. 2005, 9 CG.2000.137.

The **assignment** on the TT-system **will only not match the assignment** in accordance with the principles of property law in the analogue world if the **intermediary** is **no longer willing to convey** possession and they sell and surrender the property to a person acting in good faith. However, this is also true with a traditional instruction of ownership and cannot be solved any better if there is no universal register of all rights and a clear assignment thereof.[496]

With respect to the representation of rights to property, in particular, it is worth checking the **publicity effect** of a **tokenisation-clause** applied to the property: "The transfer of rights will only take place via a token, payment only to the person with the right of disposal over the token".[497] In addition, it may be possible to include a QR code on the property that leads to a website or an app. This would make it possible to easily display data from the TT-system. In my view, a corresponding symbol would have to suffice to exclude good faith. In this case, the purchaser would no longer become the owner from an unauthorised person and this would better meet the coordination requirement. The inclusion of a symbol would exclude a good faith acquisition from a non-token holder. The third party can review whether tokenisation has occurred. Only the good faith acquisition of the token would still be protected pursuant to Art. 9 TVTG. Otherwise, the bona fide provisions of the TVTG as a lex specialis in addition to property law would often be ineffective.

2 Constructive possession pursuant to Art. 503 PL

In addition to the instruction of ownership, another option for transferring possession without surrendering the property is **constructive possession** (constitutum possessorium, possessory agreement). Here, possession is transferred through a mere agreement when the current, usually direct possessor transfers independent possession to a third party (the purchaser), while simultaneously retaining the property as the dependent possessor on the basis of a special legal relationship (e.g. custody, lease, loan, usufruct)[498]. A special legal relationship does not have to be expressly agreed. It can also result from the circumstances (however, fungibles must always be separated out).[499] If there is no special legal relationship, the purchaser does not acquire indirect possession and thus does not acquire ownership either.[500] The special

[496] As already noted, this would not represent an adequate solution at present.

[497] See the remarks on the tokenisation clause in Part 3, Section 4, A, III.

[498] STARK/LINDENMANN in *Hausheer/Zobl/Leemann/Gmür/Becker/Meier-Hayoz*, p. 153-156.

[499] STARK/LINDENMANN in *Hausheer/Zobl/Leemann/Gmür/Becker/Meier-Hayoz*, p. 156.

[500] STARK/LINDENMANN in *Hausheer/Zobl/Leemann/Gmür/Becker/Meier-Hayoz*, p. 155.

legal relationship may not be based on the settlement of the main transaction alone. However, it must not be legally independent of the main transaction. For example, the custody fee can generally be paid through the purchase price or for a certain amount of time, or custody can be made a condition of the purchase.[501]

Constructive possession makes it possible to forgo the otherwise necessary back and forth of movable property when certain legal transactions coincide. For example, if a sale transaction (purchase) coincides with another legal transaction between the parties (lease) concerning the same property, what would otherwise be a double transfer is replaced by an agreement under which the previous owner retains custody of the property as the representative of the new owner. Common cases involving constructive possession include the sale of property that the seller subsequently leases or a bank that sells its client securities and then maintains custody of them.[502]

The condition[503] is that possession can only be transferred by means of constructive possession if the transferor (seller) himself is the (direct, independent) possessor.[504] A co-possessor can transfer their co-possession and thus co-ownership, if applicable, by means of constructive possession.[505] However, transfers by means of security using constructive possession are not permitted, as this would breach Art. 187 PL (Art. 717 SCC) by circumventing the **principle on the pledging of chattels**.

Furthermore, in the case of constructive possession, possession is transferred to the purchaser when an agreement is reached on the possession contract. This question is relevant when acquiring property from an unauthorised party based on Art. 512 PL[506] in the event that the purchaser subsequently learns that the seller lacked authorisation. They acted in good faith when the possession contract was concluded and became the owner, and they are not harmed by the subsequent loss of good faith. This also applies if they act in bad faith before the special legal transaction (e.g. the rental contract) ends. Ownership is also transferred in this case.

---

[501] STARK/LINDENMANN in *Hausheer/Zobl/Leemann/Gmür/Becker/Meier-Hayoz*, p. 156.

[502] STARK/LINDENMANN in *Hausheer/Zobl/Leemann/Gmür/Becker/Meier-Hayoz*, p. 151.

[503] With the exception of an anticipatory agreement, in which the property is not acquired upon conclusion of the contracts or, in the case of a contract for work and services, has not yet been completed; see STARK/LINDENMANN in *Hausheer/Zobl/Leemann/Gmür/Becker/Meier-Hayoz*, p. 151; see margin no. 46.

[504] STARK/LINDENMANN in *Hausheer/Zobl/Leemann/Gmür/Becker/Meier-Hayoz*, p. 152.

[505] STARK/LINDENMANN in *Hausheer/Zobl/Leemann/Gmür/Becker/Meier-Hayoz*, p. 153.

[506] The basis for Art. 512 PL is Art. 933 SCC.

2.1 Constructive possession in the case of rights represented in tokens

Constructive possession can be used for a transfer without surrender in cases where the owner wishes to transfer ownership while simultaneously being able, for example, to lease the property from the new owner. If the purchaser wishes to transfer the property again, a notification of possession may be used. For this reason, constructive possession is not highly relevant in practice. The aim of representing rights in tokens is usually to make them easier to transfer and exchange, which is not the case here.

III The problem of competing disposals in the case of the representation of rights to property

It bears repeating[507] that the identification-function applies to all (extrinsic) tokens, not only those tokens that are book-entry securities pursuant to the PGR.[508] The liberation-function arising from Art. 8 TVTG must be applied to all extrinsic tokens – in particular, to tokens that represent rights to property, provided corresponding measures such as, in particular, the agreement over the tokenisation-clause, have been taken.[509] Therefore, it must be ensured through suitable measures that when a right is represented in a token the debtor can only make payment to the person with the right to dispose over the token, thus discharging the debt.[510]

In order to better understand the rules of possession, the purposes they serve will be explained below. In rem rights, such as ownership of property, apply to everyone (erga omnes), and therefore have an absolute character. As everyone must respect the rights, they must also be recognised by everyone. For this reason, a certain amount

---

[507] See Part 3, Section 4, A, III.

[508] During the consultation period, critics questioned why the identification and fulfilment function was only applicable to claims and rights of membership and not to ownership rights to property. According to the critics, transactions involving such ownership rights were just as deserving of protection. In BuA 54/2019, the Government stated that it shares "*the concerns expressed in the statement and is expanding the identification and discharge function to include all tokens and not just those tokens that represent a claim or right of membership.*" BuA No. 54/2019, p. 208.

[509] See also the general remarks on the representation of rights and, in particular, BuA No. 54/2019, p. 208.

[510] "*The obligor refers to any debtor who can make payment to the person authorised to dispose over the token in discharge of the debt (discharge function for the person obliged by the right represented in the token, not the obligor as a result of the disposal over the token*") BuA No. 54/2019, p. 208.

of publicity of the rights pertaining to the property is required – known as the **publicity principle**.

In the case of **movable property**, property law primarily specifies **possession** as the means of publicity, although there are also certain registers (retention of title register[511], the register of cattle pledges, the ship register[512] and the aircraft register[513]). The main means of publicity for immovable property is the land register.[514] In turn, the **identification-function** is tied to the **means of publicity**. The outer appearance, such as possession in the case of movable property, justifies the assumption that there is an underlying right. The identification-function is expressed in two ways here. Firstly, the person identified through the means of publicity can claim the refutable presumption of being the holder of the relevant in rem right (Art. 509 PL). Secondly, a **third party** who relied in **good faith** on the **legal appearance** created, for example, by possession and trusting the acquired in rem rights to the property is, in some cases, **protected in its acquisition** (Art. 512 to 514).[515] In the case of **entrusted property** that is sold without authorisation by the **intermediary** to a third party acting in good faith, the principle of "*nemo plus iuris transferre potest quam ipse habet*"[516] is breached. The third party becomes the owner even though the transferring party did not hold the right of ownership.[517]

When they drafted the TVTG, Liechtenstein legislators explicitly gave the token an **identification-function** in Art. 8, para. 1. "*The person possessing the right of disposal reported by the TT-System is considered the lawful holder of the right represented in the Token*". The TVTG provides for the protection of an acquisition in good faith in Art. 9: "*Those who receive Tokens in good faith, free of charge, for the purpose of acquiring the right of disposal, or a restricted in rem right are to be protected in their acquisition, even if the transferring party was not entitled to the disposal over the Token, unless the recipient party had been aware of the lack of right of disposal, or should have been aware of such upon the exercise of due diligence.*" As a result, here, too, the

---

511 In Liechtenstein, the retention of title register was abolished as it had become obsolete, especially as the corresponding retentions can be agreed without a register; GOVERNMENT OF THE PRINCIPALITY OF LIECHTENSTEIN, BuA No. 141/2007, p. 41 f.

512 Does not exist in Liechtenstein.

513 In Liechtenstein, the Swiss Federal Act on the Aircraft Register applies.

514 *J.* SCHMID/HÜRLIMANN-KAUP, Sachenrecht[4], p. 15 f.

515 *J.* SCHMID/HÜRLIMANN-KAUP, Sachenrecht[4], p. 16.

516 Latin for "Nobody can transfer rights they do not have".

517 See *J.* SCHMID/HÜRLIMANN-KAUP, Sachenrecht[4], p. 16.

principle of "nemo transferre potest quam ipse habet" on the basis of the legal appearance attributed to the right to dispose over the token has been breached.

A **liberation-function** is thus assigned to the token by Art. 8, para. 2 TVTG, as "the Obligor, *by payment, is withdrawn from his obligation against the person who has the power of disposal as reported by the TT-system, unless he knew, or should have known with due care, that he is not the lawful owner of the right.*"

It should be noted here that the Government, based on the statements in Report and Application 54/2019 during the consultation period, reformulated Art. 7, para. 2 TVTG and clarified that, in the case of the representation of ownership to property, the person with the power of disposal over the token is allowed to demand the surrender of the property. *"As a lex specialis, the transfer provision pursuant to the TVTG takes precedence over the provisions of property law and applies as functionally equivalent to property law."*[518]

So what does this mean in the case of competing identification claims, as occurs, for example, in the following case: The person with the right of disposal over the token can prove their right of disposal, and at the same time a possessor may in good faith purchase and receive the property, ownership of which is represented in the token, from the intermediary to whom the property has been entrusted as the custodian: In this case, the token and possession are set against one another.

If sufficient measures had been taken (suitable measures pursuant to the coordination requirement), a note would have been affixed to the property (tokenisation-clause), which, in my view, would have prevented the good faith acquisition of the property. In this case, the person with the right of disposal over the token would have prevailed, as provided for in the law. But if there was no corresponding note, the third party would have acquired ownership in good faith. In this case, the possessor is protected and not the person with the right of disposal over the token. Pursuant to Art. 7, para. 2 TVTG, the latter may appeal to and indemnify the person obliged as a result of the disposal over the token. This is the case because the latter has not taken any suitable measures, contrary to the law.[519]

---

[518] BuA No. 54/2019, p. 202.

[519] See also RASCHAUER/SILBERNAGL, Grundsatzfragen des liechtensteinischen „Blockchain-Gesetzes" – TVTG, ZFR 2020/3, p. 13.

IV The special case of the physical validator

As has been shown, the synchronisation of the analogue and the digital world with respect to the representation of property rights through the coordination requirement in Art. 7, para. 2 TVTG represents a solution that is as flexible as possible. If the "person obliged as a result of the disposal over the token" does not meet their obligations to ensure synchronisation, they will – only – become liable for damages. No penalties are provided for in Art. 47 TVTG. As has also been shown, this can lead to cases where rights to property are represented in tokens and the tokens represent a legal appearance such as the possession of the property itself. For example, ownership of a watch is represented in a token, the token is transferred, while the watch is sold and surrendered to a third party acting in good faith without knowledge of the tokenisation. In this case, the third party is protected in their ownership, while the token holder has claims against the person obliged by the token. The obligor is the person who was obliged by the disposal over the token, which in most cases is not the token generator[520] or the token issuer[521], but rather the person who disposes over the token. This provision seems adequate, as only the person who is obliged as a result of their disposal over the token, as the person with the right of disposal over both the token and the right represented by it, may dispose of it or check their legal status in advance.[522] This may appear to represent an adequate solution for many cases involving negligible potential for damage (low value of the property represented).

In contrast, a separate role has been created for larger values to safeguard client protection. If, as part of a public offering of tokens that represent rights to property, basic information is to be published (Art. 33, para. 1(f) TVTG), it must include the following information:

- proof of a registered physical validator of the ownership of the property; and
- confirmation from the registered physical validator that the rights to property represented in the token are enforceable on the basis of the basic information.

In the case of a public offering of tokens by persons resident in Liechtenstein worth more than CHF 5 million (Art. 30 in conjunction with Art. 31, para. 1(c) TVTG) and provided no exceptions must be applied pursuant to Art. 31 TVTG, the basic information must be compiled and, in the case of the representation of rights to property,

---

520 Token generator pursuant to Art. 2, para. 1(l) TVTG.

521 Token issuer pursuant to Art. 2, para. 1(k) TVTG; except in the case of a token issuer's own issue, in which case the token issuer is also the obliged person.

522 BuA No. 54/2019, p. 202.

a registered physical validator designated. In Art. 2, para. 1(p), the TVTG defines the physical validator as a person who ensures the enforcement of rights in accordance with the agreement, in terms of property law, represented in tokens on TT-systems.[523] The physical validator establishes a connection between the physical property and the token by assuming **custody** of the property or **otherwise ensuring that the rights can be enforced in accordance with the agreement** in the event of any other **liability on the part of the physical validator**. The liability provision is included in the special internal control mechanisms in Art. 17, para. 1(e). Thus, the physical validator, with all of their assets, is liable along with the person obliged by the token. To ensure sufficient liability reserves, Art. 16, para. 1(e), cl. 1 and 2 TVTG provide for minimum capital of CHF 125,000 if the value of the property is less than CHF 10 million, and CHF 250,000 for represented property with a value of more than CHF 10 million.

In the case of a person with the right of disposal over a token that represents ownership of property held in custody by the physical validator, the latter would be well advised to withdraw the token from circulation after the surrender of the property (for example, by using a burn-function).

V The creation of a right of lien to movable property pursuant to Art. 365 PL, taking account of the principle on the pledging of chattels

The **pledge of chattels** pursuant to Art. 365 PL is the pledging of movable property that is acquired through the surrender of a pledged asset to secure a claim. An **instruction of ownership** ("Besitzanweisung") pursuant to Art. 503 PL is possible in place of the surrender of the property to the creditor. The property may no longer be given to or used by the debtor.[524] In line with the **publicity-principle**, possession of the property must be made apparent through physical surrender.[525] If physical surrender is not possible, then surrender may also be indicated by means of a symbol, provided this enables third parties to become aware of the pledge. Symbols that make it clear that the property may no longer be fully disposed over by the pledgor may be used (tokenisation-clause). Thus, it must be possible to deduce the pledge easily and

---

[523] If the rights to property worth CHF 5 million are represented in tokens which are not, however, offered for public sale, then a physical validator is not compulsory.

[524] Margin no. 7 Opilio, Liechtensteinisches Sachenrecht, p. 932.

[525] On the publicity principle, see also Raschauer/Silbernagl, Grundsatzfragen des liechtensteinischen „Blockchain-Gesetzes" – TVTG, ZFR 2020/3, p. 13.

with certainty. Depending on the pledged property, an indelible pledge slip, notification of the third-party debtor, book entries, blocking with a password or the designation of a custodian may be used.[526]

However, publicity is not an end in and of itself, but rather the result of a weighing of interests and thus the principle of the pledging of chattels serves a protective purpose. Third-party creditors who, on the basis of the possession infer not only the possessor's ownership, but also their creditworthiness, are protected. The possession generally conveys unencumbered ownership and should not convey a false impression regarding the possessor's financial situation to third-party creditors. In addition, the principle of the pledging of assets also aims to makes it possible for a third party to receive the property from the pledgor as a pledge or property without revealing an existing lien. This increases the suitability of the pledging of chattels as a means for securing credit and thus the "reliability in legal transactions".[527]

---

[526] Margin no. 8 and footnote 7 OPILIO, Liechtensteinisches Sachenrecht, p. 934.

[527] Margin no. 8 f. BAUER in *Honsell/Vogt/Geiser*, Basler Kommentar[5] (2015), Art. 884, p. 2127 f.

1 An illustration of the representation of rights to property using examples

1.1 Example 1 – Representation of ownership of a watch

The representation of rights to property will now be illustrated using two examples:

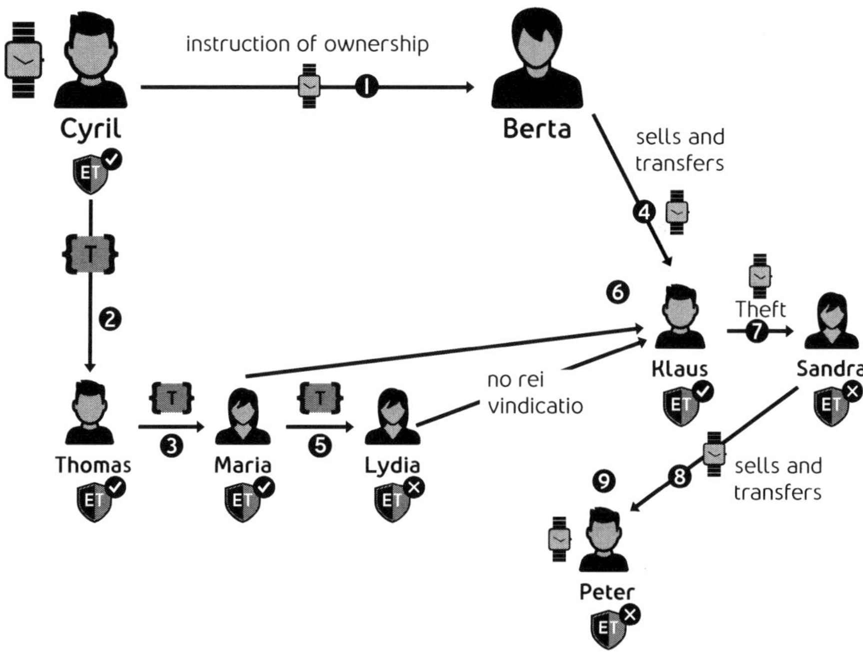

Figure 2 Representation of ownership of a watch

The transfer of a token that represents ownership of property (for example, a watch) requires a title over the two respective modes. This can be demonstrated using the example of a watch. The numbers in parentheses refer to the numbers in Figure 2:

Cyrill is the owner of a watch. The maker[528] of the watch has issued a blockchain-based certificate for the watch and transmitted a token for it to his TT-identifier. The

[528] According to Breitling, they are the first major luxury goods producer to offer a blockchain-based, digital identity for their products; the solution also serves as digital proof of ownership and is intended to make forgeries easier to identify. The watchmaker believes one of the major

watchmaker's blockchain-based certificate contains the watch's (unique) serial number, the watch model's GTIN[529] (Global Trade Item Number, also previously known as the EAN[530]), information about the materials used (e.g. 18 carat gold), the non-binding sales price, a description of the watch and other information (such as the purchase date).[531] The blockchain is also used to record, in particular, any maintenance and repairs that are carried out.[532] This certificate is publicly accessible via an unambiguous website that includes the certificate identifier in the URL. During the creation (minting) of the NFT, the variable string_uri[533] is filled in with the URL of the certificate website. In this way, the individual watch is clearly connected to a non-fungible extrinsic token[534] in accordance with the ERC-721 standard (tokenised), which is, in turn, assigned to a TT-identifier and can easily be transferred. Alternative: The tokenisation-clause is visibly engraved on the watch.

(1) Cyrill goes to Berta and gives her the watch, telling her that ownership of the watch is represented in the token with the tokenID "123example" (hereafter also called the "watch token") and installs the watchmaker's app on Berta's mobile phone, adding the token with the aforementioned tokenID. Cyrill explains to her that she can hand-over the watch to anyone with authorisation as demonstrated by the token (tokenisation-clause). Berta agrees and accepts the watch.

advantages for the owners of these products is that the watch owner can be identified more reliably and easily; BREITLING, Breitling press release, https://www.breitling.com/de-de/press-lounge/press-release/33479 (accessed on 16 February 2021).

529 WIKIPEDIA, Global Trade Item Number (GTIN), https://de.wikipedia.org/w/index.php?title=Global_Trade_Item_Number&oldid=208838895 (accessed on 18 February 2021).

530 WIKIPEDIA, European Article Number, https://de.wikipedia.org/w/index.php?title=European_Article_Number&oldid=208255311 (accessed 18 February 2021).

531 The certificate may contain a number of other elements; see ARIANEE PROJECT, Arianee Certificate Schema, https://docs.arianee.org/docs/ArianeeProductCertificate-i18n (accessed on 16 February 2021).

532 ARIANEE PROJECT, Arianee Event Schema, https://docs.arianee.org/docs/ArianeeEvent-i18n (accessed on 20 February 2021).

533 POA SOKOL EXPLORER, ArianeeSmartAsset (0x512C1FCF401133680f373a386F3f752b98070BC5), https://blockscout.com/poa/sokol/address/0x512C1FCF401133680f373a386F3f752b98070BC5/contracts (accessed on 20 February 2021).

534 For example, Breitling uses the Arianee protocol and so-called ArianeeSmartAssets; in addition to the tokenID needed to make the watch uniquely identifiable, the token smart contract also establishes the connection to the manufacturer's blockchain certificate, which, in turn, references the serial number. See the ArianeeSmartAsset smart contract: POA SOKOL EXPLORER, ArianeeSmartAsset (0x512C1FCF401133680f373a386F3f752b98070BC5).

(2) Cyrill lives in Vaduz and needs money. He would like to sell the watch to his friend Thomas, who lives in Uruguay, for 2.5 ethers. Thomas has already installed the watchmaker's app and provides Cyrill with his TT-identifier. In the background, the TT-system uses a smart-contract to review whether Thomas has sufficient ethers, blocks them and transfers the watch token to Thomas. At the same time, the 2.5 ethers are assigned to Cyrill's TT-identifier. The smart-contract also sends a message to Berta telling her that she can only make payment with liberation effect (liberation-function) to Thomas and convey possession to Thomas. Berta has configured the app to automatically confirm the receipt of such notices. There is almost no counterparty risk as a result of the use of a TT-system.

(3) Thomas saw that the watch is a special edition that is traded at a significantly higher value. Maria would like to acquire ownership of the watch for 5 ethers and comes to an agreement with Thomas. In turn, Thomas transfers the watch token to the TT-identifier as described in step 2, and Maria becomes the owner of the watch as the indirect possessor. Berta is the intermediary and the app, in turn, confirms receipt of the notice.

(4) Berta, too, has learned how valuable the watch that she directly possesses is. She is experiencing significant financial problems and sells and surrenders the watch to Klaus, who is not told by Berta that he has no authorisation to acquire ownership of the watch. Because the watch was entrusted to Berta, Klaus acquires ownership of the watch in good faith pursuant to Art. 512 PL. Alternative: As Klaus sees the tokenisation-clause, he is no longer acting in good faith and does not acquire ownership of the watch.

(5) Maria still does not know that Berta has sold the watch to Klaus and surrendered it to him. She sells the watch token to Lydia. However, as Berta no longer conveys possession for Maria, Maria loses her ownership and has a claim for damages against Berta arising from the possession contract.

(6) Lydia has no claim against Berta arising from the possession contract, as a corresponding contract has not been concluded. Lydia – and Maria – cannot proceed against Klaus using rei vindicatio and demand the surrender of the watch, as he acquired ownership in good faith. The rei vindicatio against Klaus would have been possible in the alternative. Pursuant to Art. 9 TVTG, Lydia acquires the right of disposal over the token, but not ownership of the represented right to the watch. However, because Maria sold the watch in title, she is liable to Lydia as a result of the

contract. Berta's criminal intent has resulted in the legal fate of the token and the property diverging.

(7) Sandra also has criminal intent and steals the watch from Klaus. Pursuant to Art. 513 PL, ownership of stolen property (res furtivae) cannot be acquired – within five years in the case of movable property.

(8) Sandra sells the stolen watch after one week and surrenders it to Peter, who is acting in good faith. He, too, does not become the owner pursuant to Art. 513 PL.

(9) As neither Sandra nor Peter are the owner of the watch, the question is who has the "better" right to the property: Klaus, Maria or Lydia? Klaus acted in good faith and acquired the property from Berta, who was not authorised to dispose over it, but who lost possession of it. Maria was the owner, but she lost indirect possession because Berta surrendered possession. Lydia was authorised to dispose over the watch token, but she was never the owner of the watch.

In accordance with the principles of property law, Klaus would be able to demand the surrender of the watch rei vindicatio from Peter within five years.

Certificates of authenticity are usually issued and the original invoice requested in the case of the sale of luxury watches. If Klaus had inquired about the watch's certificate of authenticity, he would have seen that the right to own it was represented in a token. He would have been able to view the TT-system himself to learn the TT-identifier to which the watch's serial number (via the watch token) had been assigned. In this case, he would not acquire ownership, as he would see that Berta is not entitled to dispose over the token. Based on the identification-function of the watch token, Lydia can demand the watch from Peter.[535] The same also applies in the case of the alternative.

[535] This is in contrast to the situation involving securities pursuant to Art. 504, para. 2 PL, according to which the recipient of the item acting in good faith takes precedence over the recipient of the security acting in good faith. In this case, possession of the item must be protected against the security, as the third party cannot simply check to see if a security exists.

1.2 Example 2 – Representation of ownership and usufruct rights in tokens to operate a snowboard rental business

Another example is the rental of snowboards at a ski resort (see Figure 3).

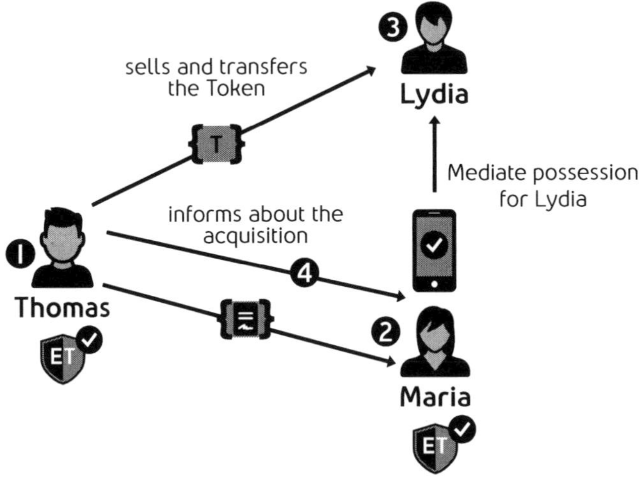

Figure 3 Representation of rights for snowboard rentals

(1) Thomas, the owner, tokenises the ownership of 10 snowboards and is the direct possessor in the beginning.

(2) He adds a tokenisation-clause to the snowboards: *"Transfer of rights will only take place via a token, payment only to the person with the right of disposal over the token"*. Under this is a QR code that downloads the necessary app when scanned in order to use the snowboard token. If this QR code is scanned with the corresponding app, it leads to a selection of the available tokens for the respective snowboard. The QR code therefore contains a link to the app as well as a unique tokenID for the respective NFT. In this way, Thomas labels a rack for the 10 snowboards next to the car park and adds a sign that reads "rent a snowboard easily with your mobile phone".

(3) Maria is interested, scans the QR code, downloads the app and accepts the terms of use.

(4) She finds her favourite snowboard, scans the QR code on the snowboard using the app and clicks on "Start rental".[536] The token to use the snowboard is automatically transferred to Maria's TT-identifier. Maria takes possession of the snowboard and becomes the direct possessor of it and conveys possession to Thomas on the basis of the agreements and, in particular, the rental contract.

(5) Thomas has had enough of the snowboard rental business and wishes to sell his 10 snowboards. Lydia finds Thomas's offering, downloads the app and sees the information and the picture of the snowboard that was just rented by Maria. Lydia clicks on "Purchase snowboard" and the token is transferred to her TT-identifier. A notice[537] appears on Maria's app informing her that Lydia is now the owner of the snowboard and that from now on she is renting the snowboard from Lydia, to which Maria agrees.

This example shows that the coordination could also function in the case of rentals as well as the potential here as a result of the representation of ownership and usufruct rights in tokens.

VI The special case of the representation of rights to real estate

If there are special formal requirements, such as entry in the land registry, representation in a token is still conceivable, but in most cases only serves documentation purposes and makes the process more difficult rather than making it easier. In Report and Application 54/2019, the Government clarified that the TVTG is <u>not</u> a lex specialis that applies in addition to the formal requirements pursuant to real estate law.[538] FRICK also views it as entirely conceivable for the ownership of real estate to be represented in a token.[539]

VII Conclusion on the representation of rights to property

Disposals over tokens do not per se take precedence over the disposal over the represented property itself. However, in Art. 7, para. 1 and para. 2 TVTG (coordination requirement), the aim of the law is to closely connect the represented right and the

[536] Maria also had the option of purchasing the snowboard.

[537] It is possible to configure the app settings so that such inquiries are always answered automatically.

[538] BuA No. 54/2019, p. 205.

[539] *A.* FRICK, Zivilrechtliche Aspekte von Token im Zusammenhang mit dem liechtensteinischen Token- und VT-Dienstleister-Gesetz, p. 42.

token in a way that – similar to securities – ensures the right cannot be asserted or transferred to others without the token. The synchronisation is either carried out by law (e.g. in the case of book-entry securities) or through suitable measures. The suitable measures must also ensure that "competing disposal over the represented right is excluded". "Disposal" here refers to disposal in the analogue world (disposal over the represented right).

For this reason, when representing the rights to property, in addition to the requirements under the TVTG regarding the transfer of the token, the property must also be transferred in accordance with the principles of property law. In the case of transfers of possession and ownership, aside from the hand-to-handsurrender of property, which is fairly uninteresting in practice, the forms of acquisition without possession, e.g. through formless substitutes for the transfer of ownership, such as the instruction of ownership or constructive possession, play a central role.

In the possession contract, the direct possessor undertakes to surrender the property only to the person entitled to dispose over the token (identification-function) (for example, by adding a tokenisation-clause). The notification obligation is implicitly waived and replaced with the token's identification-function. The legal responsibility identified by the TT-system offers a high degree of reliability (commercial security). The statutory regulation of the identification-function of (extrinsic) tokens and the high degree of reliability therefore justify the use, in the case of notification of possession, of the token's identification-function in the form a (tokenisation) clause in the possession contract – in place of the obligation to notify the third party in direct possession of the property.

D (3c) Other absolute or relative rights

I Intellectual property and protective rights

In addition to the aforementioned rights, tokens should also "*represent other rights, such as intellectual property rights*"[540]. Detailed statements on the representation of intellectual property rights can be found in the TVTG and the legislative materials for the TVTG. Intellectual property means intellectual creations in the broadest sense, which merit special protection by the law because of their economic significance. The creation of rights to intellectual property ("intellectual property rights") results in a separate legal entity. The person entitled to such rights assumes a position that is

[540] BuA No. 54/2019, p. 61.

similar to ownership. That is why the term "intellectual property rights" is used.[541] Both Switzerland and Liechtenstein apply **numerus clausus** for protected intellectual property rights:

- Copyrights and related protective rights (see the URG);
- Rights to topographies of semiconductor products (see the ToG[542]);
- Trademark rights and rights to geographic indications of origin (see MSchG[543]);
- Design rights (see the DesG[544] and the DesV[545]);
- Patent rights (see the Swiss Patents Act[546]).

In contrast to Switzerland, Liechtenstein does not have a Plant Variety Protection Act and, consequently, there are no protective rights for plant breeds. The protective rights for **trademarks** and **designs** solely arise **from their entry in a register** (constitutive effect of the register entry)[547]. The representation of the corresponding rights is not particularly useful if there is no corresponding amendment of the law. However, such purely register rights analogous to book-entry securities (see Art. 81a, para. 2 SchlT PGR) would be – de lege ferenda – best suited for maintaining the register using TT-systems. The main difference with book-entry securities is that the latter are entered in a book-entry securities register maintained by the debtor, while the design[548] and trademark[549] register is maintained by the Office of Economic Affairs. Of special interest for "tokenisation" are the copyrights that arise when the work is created.

---

541 KAISER/RÜETSCHI, Immaterialgüterrecht[3] (2017), p. 1.

542 Act of 19 May 1999 on the Protection of Topographies of Semiconductor Products (Topographies Act) (ToG), Liechtenstein Law Gazette (1999).

543 Act of 12 December 1996 on the Protection of Trademarks and Indications of Origin (Trademark Protection Act) (MSchG), Liechtenstein Law Gazette (1997).

544 Act of 11 September 2002 on the Protection of Design (Design Act) (DesG)), Liechtenstein Law Gazette (2002).

545 Ordinance of 29 October 2002 on the Protection of Design (Design Ordinance) (DesV), Liechtenstein Law Gazette (2002).

546 The Swiss Patents Act applies in Liechtenstein on the basis of Art. 5, para. 1(a) of the Treaty between the Swiss Confederation and the Principality of Liechtenstein on Patent Protection (Patent Treaty); Federal Act on Patents (Patents Act) (PatA), Federal Gazette (1954).

547 On trademarks, see Art. 5 MSchG and on design rights Art. 7 DesG.

548 Pursuant to Art. 54, para. 2 DesG in conjunction with Art. 1 DesV, the Office of Economic Affairs is the depository for designs.

549 Pursuant to Art. 29, para. 2 MSchG, trademarks must be deposited with the Office of Economic Affairs.

1 The representation of copyrights in tokens

Copyright pursuant to the URG protects the authors of works of literature and art as well as performers, directors of productions of sound and video recordings, broadcasters and the producers of databases[550]. The author is the natural person who created the work (**creation principle**).[551] The rights are acquired ipso jure by the person who created the work.[552] For this reason, only natural persons can be considered as creators.[553] Art. 7 URG governs co-copyright in cases where multiple people are the author and helped to create a work. In such cases, the participants have a collective copyright. They may only – provided that there is no agreement to the contrary – use the work with the consent of all participants.

Art. 8, para. 1 URG presumes – although this can be rebutted – that the person who is listed by name, pseudonym or symbol on the copies of the work or upon publication of the work is the author. The works do not have to be entered in a register or meet any other formal requirements. In some cases, this leads to disputes regarding evidence of authorship.[554] Art. 8, para. 2 URG allows publishers to exercise the rights to a work, provided the author remains unnamed or unknown in the event of a pseudonym or symbol. This presumption can also be rebutted. Where and in which form the author is designated is irrelevant. However, it must be done in a manner that makes its character as the author designation clear. In practice, the symbol © followed by the year and name has become common.[555]

Art. 18 URG uses the same wording as Art. 16 of the Swiss URG[556] and governs the ability to transfer and inherit the copyrights. Thus, with the exception of moral rights, which cannot be assigned, all of the author's rights of use (property rights) can be transferred to a third party. In particular, this includes all of the rights of use specified in Art. 10 URG, which can therefore be transferred individually or globally to a third party.[557] The transfer of copyrights has an in rem effect and applies erga omnes (to

[550] On databases, see, in particular, Part 3, Section 2, A, II, 3.

[551] Art. 6, para. 1 URG.

[552] See margin no. 1 Hug, Art. 6, in *Müller/Oertli* (ed.), Urheberrechtsgesetz (URG)[2] (2012), p. 58.

[553] See margin no. 3 Hug, Art. 6, in *Müller/Oertli*, p. 59.

[554] See margin no. 1 Hug, Art. 8, in *Müller/Oertli* (ed.), Urheberrechtsgesetz (URG)[2] (2012), p. 75.

[555] See margin no. 2-4 Hug, Art. 8, in *Müller/Oertli*, p. 75.

[556] Swiss Federal Act on Copyright and Related Rights (Copyright Act) (URG), Federal Gazette (1992).

[557] See margin no. 6 De Werra, Art. 16, in *Müller/Oertli* (ed.), Urheberrechtsgesetz (URG)[2] (2012), p. 135.

everyone, especially the author of the work). This is contrary to a licence, which is only contractually effective, i.e. inter partes (among the parties). The holder of a copyright which has been transferred can freely transfer this onwards. This is in contrast to a licensee, who generally cannot transfer or sub-license their contractual claim to a third party without the consent of the licensor.[558] The transfer of copyrights is causal, i.e. it requires an obligatory transaction and a disposal transaction.[559] It is form-free and may also be implicit.[560]

2 The representation of usage rights (property rights) to protected works in tokens

Property rights and rights of use can therefore be represented in tokens and these transferred form-free and even implicitly. Works in digital form can also be connected to a token by using the **hash function** and transferring the hash in the tokenID field of an ERC-721 token. The timestamp provided by trustworthy-technologies allows the holder of the right to prove that they created their work when the transaction occurred or the token was created. Thus, the token serves as **evidence of the creation of the work** and therefore the initial assignment to the person by whom the work was created (creator theory). In addition, the rights of use can be represented in the token, with which they can then be transferred and exercised.

If licences are to be represented in tokens, then the consent of the licensor is required for the transfer. This can be done automatically. Pursuant to Art. 7, para. 2 TVTG, the person obliged as a result of the disposal over the token must ensure, through suitable measures, that the licence is transferred with the token to the new person entitled to dispose over the token. This can also be done through the prior consent to free transferability on the part of the licensor.[561]

II Conclusion on other absolute or relative rights

Tokens can also represent other rights, such as intellectual property rights. The protective rights for trademarks and designs solely arise from their entry in a register

---

[558] See margin no. 7 De Werra in *Müller/Oertli*, p. 135.

[559] See margin no. 8 De Werra in *Müller/Oertli*, p. 136.

[560] See margin no. 33 De Werra in *Müller/Oertli*, p. 145.

[561] The granting of rights of use, especially of licences, is closely connected to the creation of the blockchain protocol in accordance with Bitcoin. Many protocols have financed their development through the sale of rights of use (utility tokens) within the framework of initial coin offerings (ICO).

(constitutive effect of the register entry), which makes representation in a token impractical. Property rights and rights of use can be represented in tokens and these transferred form-free and even implicitly. The timestamp provided by trustworthy-technologies allows the holder of the right to prove that they created their work when the transaction occurred or the token was created. Thus, the token serves as evidence of the creation of the work and therefore the initial assignment to the person by whom the work was created (creator theory). In addition, the rights of use can be represented in the token, with which they can then be transferred and exercised. If licences are to be represented in tokens, then the consent of the licensor is required for the transfer. This can be done automatically. A suitable measure pursuant to Art. 7, para. 2 to ensure that the licence is transferred with the token to the new person entitled to dispose over the token is the prior consent to free transfer on the part of the licensor.

§ 5 (4) The assignment to TT-identifiers

I Implementation in the TVTG

1 Introduction of a separate term for "public key" or "address"

According to the definition in Art. 2, para. 1(d) of the TVTG, the **TT-identifier** allows for the clear assignment of tokens. In the government's consultation report on the creation of the TVTG, there was a definition of the "public key" in Art. 5, para. 1, cl. 2. One criterion for the definition at the time – in addition to the assignment – was a "character string" used to create the key.[562] Due to criticism during the consultation period, the Government modified the definition and created the more functionally and technologically agnostic term "TT-identifier", with less of a technical implementation basis.[563] The character string criterion was also omitted. Applying this definition to the current technical implementation, it is clear that there are many forms of TT-identifiers for Bitcoin alone that are not "public keys". In practice, at least in the case of Ethereum and Bitcoin, the term "**address**" has become established in the sense of a paying agent. Sometimes, however, the "address" is equated – not entirely correctly – with the public key. Bitcoin addresses are character strings comprised of numbers and letters that serve as paying agents and can generally be disclosed. Put simply, bitcoins can be sent to the address. At the beginning of Bitcoin, it was possible

[562] Consultation report on the Blockchain Act, p. 139.

[563] Consultation report on the Blockchain Act, p. 145.

to "pay" to the IP address directly.[564] Logically speaking, this is not a public key. The characteristics of TT-identifiers and their legal delineation will be discussed below using the examples of Bitcoin and Ethereum.

II Assignment from a technical perspective and the technology-neutral approach

The Government therefore correctly refrained from using the term public key. In most cases, the public key is now no longer used for transactions. To ensure an approach that was as functionally and technologically neutral as possible, the term "**TT-identifier**" was introduced together with the "**TT-key**". The TVTG uses the TT-identifier to create the connection/assignment between tokens and legal subjects (persons).[565] The token is assigned to the TT-identifier, which is, in turn, controlled via a TT-key (power of disposal). The TT-key can be used by people to, for example, sign transactions. Even if multiple TT-keys are needed (multi-signature) or other conditions have been defined, the corresponding hashes for a locking script, for example, can also serve as the TT-identifier. The term "relationship model" between tokens and persons entitled to dispose over the token has become established.

1 Technical implementation with Bitcoin

1.1 General information about TT-identifiers with Bitcoin

In technical terms, the "addresses" with Bitcoin come in different variants. Based on the transaction model described above, bitcoins are not – as is the case with Ethereum – transferred from address to address, but rather from transaction to transaction.[566] In the case of a Bitcoin transaction, the input must meet the condition defined in the output in the locking script. Consequently, the locking script defines the token's **connecting point**, which allows for a **clear assignment** pursuant to the TVTG, i.e. the TT-identifier. The assignment is carried out by specifying the condition in the locking script. If someone can fulfil the condition, they are given the **power of disposal** over the token. In other words, they have the (TT) key that can be used to fulfil the condition specified in the locking script. Both the condition specified in the locking script (TT-identifier) and the key used to meet this condition (TT-key) come in various forms. There are locking scripts that request the signature of multiple TT-keys (multi-signature). There are also cases in which no conditions need to be fulfilled or for

---

[564] Footnote 39 VAN HIJFTE, Blockchain Platforms, p. 37.

[565] See Art. 2, para. 1(d) TVTG.

[566] On this point, see the remarks in Part 3, Section 2, B, II, 1.1.

which the conditions cannot be fulfilled. In the former case, anyone can transfer the bitcoins, while in the second, no one can transfer them. For example, the requirement can be set that 10 private keys must be used, or a password instead of a private key in order to transfer the bitcoins, or even no authorisation or similar.[567]

Whether all of the variants can be included in the definitions of the TVTG must now be looked at more closely:

1.2 Pay-to-public key hash (P2PKH) "addresses"

In the case of Bitcoin, the main distinction is drawn between addresses that begin with the number "1" and those that begin with the number "3". Bitcoin addresses derived from the public key (**pay-to-public key hash**, **"P2PKH"**[568]) begin with the number "1".[569] This form is based on a key pair comprised of a **public key** – hence the name "pay-to-public key hash" – and the **private key** that is necessary to unlock the public key. This technology, which is a core technology for blockchains, is called **asymmetric encryption** and was already explained in the introduction. The "addresses" (TT-identifiers) are derived from the respective public key through **hashing** and the subsequent **coding** (Base58Check). The coding enables the shortening of the character string[570], making it easier for people to read and contains an error control ("check" refers to the use of a "checksum"). Pursuant to the TVTG, in the case of these P2PKH addresses, the person who can use the private key – together with the hash from the public key – to create a signature from the private key is the person with the power of disposal.[571] Here, the signature is created with the private key (TT-key) from which the public key was derived. Of course, the private key cannot be found in the unlocking script or the locking script, as otherwise it would not be secure after each transaction. Thus, the signature only "proves" that a person knows the private key to the public key over which they have the power of disposal.

As is otherwise common practice, in the case of Bitcoin transactions there is no need for transaction rights, such as "collective signing rights". For this reason, Bitcoin has

---

567 BITCOIN WIKI, Transaction.

568 ANTONOPOULOS, Mastering Bitcoin, p. 81.

569 ANTONOPOULOS, Mastering Bitcoin, p. 64.

570 The Bitcoin Base58 alphabet is comprised of 58 characters and contains, for example, no characters that can be easily confused, such as the letter O and the number 0: "123456789ABCDEFGHJKLMNPQRSTUVWXYZabcdefghijkmnopqrstuvwxyz".

571 ANTONOPOULOS, Mastering Bitcoin, p. 82.

so-called "multi-signature" solutions. This simply means that more than one signature is required. Any number of signatures can be defined as necessary to carry out a transaction. This includes, for example, "two out of three" or even "three out of three". In the former case, three public keys are defined and at least two valid signatures are required. This helps to increase security (see collective signing right) and protects against the loss of a private key (for example, by storing a private key with a TT-key-custodian).[572]

At the beginning of Bitcoin, these multi-signaturerequirements were implemented directly in the locking script, which resulted in relatively large transactions[573] because of the long public key. In addition, the number of required signatures is limited. An example of a "two out of three" locking script would be:

"2 <Public Key A> <Public Key B> <Public Key C> 3 OP_CHECKMULTISIG"[574]

This locking script can be opened with the following unlocking script upon the signature of two private keys for the two public keys, B and C in this example:

" OP_0 <Signature B> <Signature C>"[575]

With P2PKH, the TT-identifier refers to the character string derived from the public key using hashing and coding (PubKHash). The private key in the key pair is included under the term "TT-key". With multi-signature locking scripts, several TT-identifiers are defined in the conditions and thus several TT-keys are necessary to be able to dispose over the bitcoin. Therefore, joint power of disposal has been defined – depending on the condition. This must be distinguished from the natural person or legal entity to whom the token has been economically assigned and who is therefore the person entitled to dispose over it pursuant to the TVTG.

1.3 Pay-to-script hash (P2SH) "addresses"

With Bitcoin, it is also possible to transfer bitcoins using a script, which is called "**pay-to-script hash**" ("**P2SH**"). These "addresses" always begin with the number "3"[576], but they are not derived from a public address (public key). However, they should

---

[572] ANTONOPOULOS, Mastering Bitcoin, p. 149 f.

[573] The transactions are large in terms of the amount of data.

[574] ANTONOPOULOS, Mastering Bitcoin, p. 150.

[575] ANTONOPOULOS, Mastering Bitcoin, p. 150.

[576] ANTONOPOULOS, Mastering Bitcoin, p. 65.

not – as is often the case in practice – be equated with multi-signature addresses.[577] This is because the addresses are often used to implement multi-signature requirements through a script. In the beginning, these multi-signature requirements were implemented directly in the locking script; see the remarks on P2PKH above. [578]

Pay-to-script hash (P2SH) was introduced in 2012.[579] In the case of P2SH, the locking script is comprised only of the hash for the "redeem script", which, in turn, contains a separate locking script. Instead of just a locking script and an unlocking script, a "redeem script" is also needed for a P2SH transaction. These P2SH addresses begin – as already noted – with the number "3" and can simply be used as a "recipient address" with any wallet software. The sender does not know the locking script or the requirements contained therein.[580] The result is a rather complex locking script with five long public keys (PubKey) and the simple unlocking script:

Locking script:

"2 PubKey1 PubKey2 PubKey3 PubKey4 PubKey5 5 OP_CHECKMULTISIG"

Unlocking script:

"Sig1 Sig2"

A redeem script with a relatively simple locking script and a more complex unlocking script:

Redeem script[581]:

"2 PubKey1 PubKey2 PubKey3 PubKey4 PubKey5 5 OP_CHECKMULTISIG"

Locking script:

"OP_HASH160 <20-byte hash of redeem script> OP_EQUAL"

Unlocking script:

"Sig1 Sig2 redeem script".[582]

[577] ANTONOPOULOS, Mastering Bitcoin, p. 81.

[578] ANTONOPOULOS, Mastering Bitcoin, p. 149 ff.

[579] ANTONOPOULOS, Mastering Bitcoin, p. 151.

[580] ANTONOPOULOS, Mastering Bitcoin, p. 151 f.

[581] The redeem script corresponds to the locking script in the above example.

[582] ANTONOPOULOS, Mastering Bitcoin, p. 152.

With P2SH, the conditions are no longer defined in the locking script and are also not included in the transaction output. Only a hash of the redeem script is defined in the locking script. However, without knowing the redeem script, it is also not possible to know the conditions that must be fulfilled in order to generate a suitable input. As a result, the complexity (the conditions in the redeem script) is transferred from the transferor to the recipient. The recipient not only needs the signatures defined in the redeem script (2 out of 5 in our case), but also the redeem script itself in order to be able to generate a new output. To put P2SH simply: Pay to a script, which results in this hash; the script is first needed when this output is transferred again.[583]

In order to make an address out of a script hash, the latter is recoded (Base85Check), which is why the P2SH address (e.g. "54c557e07dde5bb6cb791c7a540e0a4796f5e97e"), which begins with the number "5" is used to create a character string that begins with the number "3". In our example: "39RF6JqABiHdYHkfChV6USGMe6Nsr66Gzw".[584] This address can now be used immediately as a target address by wallets; it is shorter and for the specified reasons is no longer easily confused with characters and numbers.

In the case of P2SH, the bitcoin are assigned to P2SH addresses by the output. The P2SH addresses are therefore TT-identifiers pursuant to the TVTG. The person who knows the redeem script and can meet the conditions for it is the person with the power of disposal over P2SH addresses. In practice, the private keys are usually required in order to create the signatures for the public keys defined in the redeem script and be identified as the person entitled to dispose over the token. If several signatures are required, this is referred to as joint power of disposal. The right of disposal pursuant to the TVTG must be considered separately. In this example, it is therefore not the public keys that make it possible to allocate tokens clearly, but rather the redeem script or a coded hash of it, with the redeem script, in turn, containing public keys.

2 Technical implementation with Ethereum

As already described above, Ethereum refers not only to the decentralised storage of data in a database (blockchain), but also a global computer called the "Ethereum Virtual Machine" ("EVM"), which carries out the transactions and smart-contracts, which are paid for in ethers. There are two account types with Ethereum, **smart-**

583 ANTONOPOULOS, Mastering Bitcoin, p. 152.

584 ANTONOPOULOS, Mastering Bitcoin, p. 154.

contract accounts ("contract accounts") and accounts owned by external people with the right of disposal ("**externally owned accounts**", "**EOA**").[585] The "standard accounts" are the EOA, which are assigned to people or TT-identifiers (addresses) and enable transactions via private keys (TT-keys). Smart-contract accounts are only activated ("**triggered**") when they receive a transaction, and can only carry out other smart-contracts when they are triggered.[586] A transaction to a smart-contract address on Ethereum is carried out by the corresponding software code.[587] Thus, with Ethereum the conditions for token transfer can be structured much more flexibly than with the Bitcoin script function (locking script).

2.1 The Ethereum addresses that enable allocation to people (externally owned accounts, EOA)

With Ethereum, asymmetric encryption with a key pair comprised of a private and a public key also plays a central role (**asymmetric encryption**). The public key is thus derived from the private key. The addresses that create the connection to people via the private keys are the **EOA** in the form of character strings, which, in turn, are derived from the respective public key through hashing. The transactions are then enabled by means of the private key (TT-key). It can best be compared to Bitcoin's P2PKH addresses. The addresses used by Ethereum also involve hashes of public keys. In the case of Ethereum, "Keccak-256" is used as the hashing algorithm. However, the resulting hash is then shortened to 20 bytes and usually appears as "0x"[588].[589] This will be illustrated here using an example of a private key, a public key and an Ethereum EOA address:

Private key (**TT-key**):

"f8f8a2f43c8376ccb0871305060d7b27b0554d2cc72bccf41b2705608452f315"

from which the public key is derived:

"6e145ccef1033dea239875dd00dfb4fee6e3348b84985c92f103444683bae07b83b5c3..."

and the generated address (**TT-identifier**):

[585] ANTONOPOULOS/WOOD, Mastering Ethereum, p. 26 f.

[586] ANTONOPOULOS/WOOD, Mastering Ethereum, p. 27, see also p. 604.

[587] VAN HIJFTE, Blockchain Platforms, p. 157.

[588] This makes it clear that the address is in hex format.

[589] ANTONOPOULOS/WOOD, Mastering Ethereum, p. 73 f.

"0x001d3f1ef827552ae1114027bd3ecf1f086ba0f9".[590]

The address derived from the hash of the public key is the account at Ethereum and thus the TT-identifier. The private key is the TT-key.

In the case of Ethereum, there are not only addresses, but also a naming system (**Ethereum Name Service** – ENS), which can be considered similar to a domain name system ("DNS") for internet domain names. Instead of entering the web server's IP address in the browser – for example, 81.161.57.23 – the domain name "liechtenstein.li" can be entered. Thus, with Ethereum it is not necessary to note a complicated TT-identifier such as 0xF3561FaD89e1695f76abFB80477b3513DC6B8338, or even enter it in a wallet. Instead, the ENS name "naegele.eth" can simply be used in compatible wallets.[591] In my view, both the EOA address and the ENS name should be classified as TT-identifiers.

Pursuant to the TVTG, only EOA and ENS names can be included under "TT-identifiers". They clearly assign the tokens by ensuring that the person who is able to dispose over the token is the person who has the TT-key.

2.2 Smart-contract accounts – addresses that identify smart-contracts

In contrast, the smart-contract accounts represent a significant development of the Bitcoin scripting possibilities for which the conditions can be defined. Every smart-contract has a **smart-contract address**, the "**contract account**". The smart-contracts are only activated ("triggered") when they receive a transaction. [592] The transaction on a contract account on Ethereum results in the execution of the contract (software code) assigned to the account.[593] Thus, with Ethereum the conditions for token transfer can be structured much more flexibly than with the Bitcoin script function. However, a smart-contract has no private key that can be used to "check" it. Instead, who can carry out which functions is defined in the smart-contract. In general, for example, the person (owner identified using their EOA address) who deploys a smart-contract on the Ethereum blockchain is the one capable of generating (minting) new tokens. In order to carry out the minting function, the person who disposes

[590] ANTONOPOULOS/WOOD, Mastering Ethereum, p. 74.

[591] ANTONOPOULOS/WOOD, Mastering Ethereum, p. 281 ff.

[592] ANTONOPOULOS/WOOD, Mastering Ethereum, p. 604.

[593] VAN HIJFTE, Blockchain Platforms, p. 157.

over the private key for the public key and whose address is defined as the owner in the smart-contract must sign a transaction.

Tokens can also be sent to the address "oxo" on Ethereum and removed from a person's control, as no one can dispose over them anymore. If tokens are sent to smart-contract addresses, these are then processed by the smart-contract code and, where necessary, sent to an EOA address. However, it is also possible for the smart-contract to be accessed, for example, via a transaction in order to destroy the token (see **burn**-function). The tokens are not reassigned. Instead, they are made unusable or destroyed. Therefore, smart-contract addresses are not generally "TT-identifiers" pursuant to the TVTG.

III Conclusion on the assignment to TT-identifiers

According to the definition in Art. 2, para. 1 lit. d of the TVTG, the TT-identifier allows for the clear assignment of tokens. The use of the term public key has correctly been avoided. In most cases, the public key is now no longer used for transactions. To ensure an approach that was as functionally and technologically neutral as possible, the term "TT-identifier" was introduced together with the "TT-key". The TVTG uses the TT-identifier to create the connection/assignment between tokens and legal subjects (persons). The token is assigned to the TT-identifier, which is, in turn, controlled via a TT-key (power of disposal). The TT-key can be used by people to, for example, sign transactions. There are two account types with Ethereum, smart-contract accounts and externally owned accounts ("EOA"). The "standard accounts" are the EOA, which are assigned to people or TT-identifiers (addresses) and enable transactions via private keys (TT-keys). Smart-contract accounts are only activated when they receive a transaction and can only carry out other smart-contracts when they are triggered. A transaction to a smart-contract address on Ethereum is carried out by the corresponding software code. Thus, with Ethereum the conditions for token transfer can be structured much more flexibly than with the Bitcoin script function (locking script). Smart-contract accounts are not TT-identifiers pursuant to the TVTG.

PART 4 CONCLUSION

For Liechtenstein legislators, the drafting of the TVTG was important, on the one hand, to create legal certainty for companies and clients, and, on the other hand – nothing less than – to form a suitable basis for the token economy. There were many new paths that resulted in a coherent overall picture. As Prime Minister Adrian said in 2018, "blockchain" refers to more than just cryptocurrencies. However, in order for other assets, such as cars, music titles or securities to be traded using blockchain technology, it is necessary to have civil law regulations in addition to supervisory rules. The analysis was carried out on the basis of the individual constituent features of the legal definition of a token pursuant to the TVTG.

Firstly, the question of whether the term "information" used by the TVTG is the same as "data", and how to legally classify data and information. A minority view allows for the subjection of digital data to the concept in Liechtenstein. The prevailing opinion that it is not being subject to property law seems more convincing. This take into account the nature of digital data, which differs from the forces of nature, for example. In addition, a distinction must be made between the data carrier and the data stored on it. The data carrier is a movable good pursuant to property law, while the ideas stored on it are subject to and protected by intellectual property law. Digital data in the form of computer programs are not works pursuant to the Copyright Act, but they are treated as such and subject to special protection.

When the TVTG speaks of "information", it means "interpreted data" stored on TT-systems. The distinction between data and information is important here. What data and information (interpreted data) have in common is that they are not property pursuant to property law. The key delineating feature here is the lack of physicality of both data and information. Tokens and the information that makes up a token are different from the data that stores and processes this information. For this reason, the TVTG uses the term "information", which requires further explanation, rather than data as a constituent feature in its definition of the term "token". The interpreted data that makes up the information in a token varies depending on the token. The information that makes up a bitcoin is somewhat elusive and starts with the question of how many bitcoin have been allocated to a person with the right of disposal. The information about who "has" how many bitcoins cannot be seen directly in the database stored in a decentralised manner in the form of a blockchain, but is instead calculated by each full node and stored temporarily in a local database. The information that makes up a bitcoin is thus not a simple character string (syntactic level), but rather the result of a calculation (transaction model). In contrast to Bitcoin, Ethereum uses a model with account balances. As expected, the accounts have an account balance and – if someone wishes to carry out a transaction – the sender's account is checked to make sure there is a sufficient balance. If this is the case, the amount is credited to the recipient account and deducted from the sender account, which is called the account model. Thus, the information that makes up the ether is the result of an inquiry to determine how many ethers are allocated to which TT-identifier. However, in order to understand the term fully, it is important to look not only at how system tokens are created through mining and allocated and transferred as part of transactions, but also how tokens in the proper sense are technically structured through the programming of smart-contracts.

This is because, in addition to system tokens (coins), it has also become possible to create new tokens on the basis of existing TT. These tokens are technologically structured by smart-contracts. New tokens can be created relatively easily based on, for example, Ethereum or Aeternity in a modular system. These tokens are thus created not through mining, but rather through programming and deployment on an existing system. The information that makes up a token created in this way is therefore different than the information that makes up a system token. The token smart-contract defines the information that is available. Token standards describe a combination of functions that must be included in a smart-contract in order for them to be able to interact with other smart-contracts or software, such as crypto-exchanges or wallets. In other words, they therefore describe a certain minimum content. These smart-contracts are highly relevant to the legal classification. The respective token smart-contract must define whether a token is classified as a specific or generic obligation, whether there is an unchangeable, fixed number or a variable number of total tokens and whether there are restrictions on transfers. The major difference between the (fungible) ERC-20 standard token and the non-fungible token according to ERC-721 ("NFT"), for example, is the ability to clearly distinguish or identify them. In addition, there are many other standards, including several for security tokens (e.g. ERC-1400). In summary, it can be said that the constituent feature of information is that it includes the flexibility needed to encompass a wide variety of tokens, both system tokens and tokens based on other TT-systems.

Trustworthy-technologies (TT) and TT-systems were the next constituent features to be analysed. The meaning of TT and TT-systems are of utmost importance. The subject, purpose and scope of the general, civil law and supervisory law provisions always refer to trustworthy-technologies. If a service provider does not use TT or TT-systems, then the service provider is not a TT-service provider and may not refer to itself as such (designation protection). However, this also means that if no TT-system is used for the service provision, then the service provider cannot be registered as a TT-service provider. These wide-ranging legal consequences create the legal certainty that legislators intended when they drafted the TVTG. But why weren't these legal consequences assigned to digital transactions with no intermediaries before the development of TT and TT-systems, and what distinguishes a TT-system from a "normal" database application? This takes us to the crux of the term "trustworthy-technologies". Obviously, there are technologies that make it possible to carry out transactions with little or no trust in the other actors and to connect this to wide-ranging legal consequences. We trust the technology, not the actors. The term "trustless" technologies is also used in IT. As the terms TT and TT-systems are defined in a technology-neutral way and are designed to be as broad as possible, they must be interpreted by the legal practitioner. However, there is no fixed catalogue of criteria that can be used. Instead, a holistic view must be taken of whether the criteria meet the definitions: Trustworthy-Technologies (TT) are technologies through which the integrity of tokens, the clear assignment of tokens to TT-identifiers and the disposal over tokens is ensured. TT-systems are based on TT and are transaction systems which allow for the secure transfer and storage of tokens and the rendering of services based on this by means of trustworthy technology. Legislators thereby used Bitcoin and Ethereum as models of TT and TT-systems. Looking at the technological structure makes it clear as to what makes a technology a TT and what makes a system a TT-system. But while a system may fulfil the other conditions for "TT" and "TT-systems", if it is relatively easy for unauthorised users to change them to their advantage, then they are not TT and thus TT-systems. However, most major blockchains and DLT systems can only be manipulated with great effort. In other words, if the system is immutable with a probability bordering on certainty, then it is a TT-system. However, if the system is structured in a way that makes it easy to change (e.g. a central simple database, such as is used on web servers), then neither the registration system nor the civil law provisions apply. To date, there have been few problems as regards inclusion, as, for the most part, established systems are used.

The representation of rights was then discussed in more detail. For this purpose, tokens can be described as "containers" that can represent rights. This model is also called the Token-Container-Model (TCM). Similar to a security, when it represents something the token combines a thing of value (claims or rights of membership, rights to property or other absolute or relative rights) with something that has almost no value (the token). If the token does not represent anything of value – in other words, if it is an empty container – then the token itself is the "thing of value". Thus, tokens do not have to represent rights (intrinsic tokens), but they can (extrinsic tokens).

In Liechtenstein, claims can be transferred form-free and implicitly through cession, provided the underlying legal transaction has no formal requirements. The transfer of the claim does not result in any changes to the claim (see Section 1394 ABGB). The debtor is entitled to all of the same rights and objections against the assignee that they had against the assignor. The rights and objections remain in force, as a result of which the assignee must respond to objections. If there are no additional formal requirements, then disposal over the token results in the transfer by law of the claim to the new holder of the right of disposal over the token. Corresponding additional measures must be taken to ensure that the token has the identification and liberation-function and to guarantee successful transfer.

When rights are represented, the identification and liberation-function pursuant to Art. 8 TVTG must be applied to all extrinsic tokens and not just book-entry securities. Art. 8 TVTG does not apply to intrinsic tokens, i.e. tokens that do not represent rights. With respect to the representation of rights in extrinsic tokens, in contrast, there are – depending on the right represented – different requirements for successful tokenisation. When absolute rights are being represented, the publicity requirements, for example, must be observed. In the case of extrinsic tokens, the parties must agree that – depending on the right – exercising the right is associated with the right of disposal over the token (identification-function) and, conversely, that a debtor can only make payment to the person with the right of disposal over the token in a manner that liberates the debt (liberation-function).

Legal entities may then grant their members membership shares (share rights), provided that there is no law or regulation to the contrary. The membership cannot be divided, sold or bequeathed, but there may be alternate provisions in the law or the articles of incorporation. Book-entry securities occupy a special place in the TVTG, although this term does not appear in the text of the law itself, as it was included by legislators in the final section of the PGR. Even before the TVTG, Liechtenstein law recognised immobilised and dematerialised securities, i.e. book-entry securities without the character of securities. Within the framework of the TVTG, book-entry securities were codified in Art. 81a, para. 1 SchlT PGR: Consequently, book-entry securities are "rights with the same functions as securities" and "fungible securities". As a result, documentation in the form of a certificate is no longer necessary, and claims can be issued in the form of tokens from the outset (book-entry securities). In order for tokens to be functionally equivalent to securities, they must have the same functions as securities documented in the form of a certificate when they represent rights that can be represented by securities. A major restriction in issuing book-entry securities is that only those rights that can be certificated in the form of a security can be issued as book-entry securities. The transfer is dichotomous in the case of book-entry securities. Thus, bearer shares in the form of book-entry securities are transferred, on the one hand, by entering the acquiring party in the book-entry securities register (constitutive effect) of the legal entity pursuant to Art. 81a, para. 4 SchlT PGR, and, on the other hand, by entering the acquiring party in the securities depository register pursuant to Art. 326h, para. 3 in conjunction with Art. 326c PGR. These two registers must be coordinated, whereby a securities depository pursuant to Art. 326b PRG may also maintain the book-entry securities register.

In the case of property, the transfer cannot be carried out by law, as is the case with book-entry securities. However, tokens and the represented right should have the same fate. In turn, Art. 7, para. 2 TVTG takes effect, which requires suitable measures, depending on the requirements. One suitable measure would be a tokenisation-clause. Here, the token assumes the functions of the certificate in the case of the certificate clause. Such a clause could, if, in the case of property for example, it were only applied to the property itself, create the publicity that is required. This makes it clear to everyone that a transfer is only possible via tokens and that the payment only liberates the debt for the person with the right of disposal. In particular, the rights to property must be considered separately here. Disposals over tokens involving the representation of property do not per se take precedence over the disposal over the represented property itself. For this reason, when representing the rights to property, in addition to the requirements under the TVTG regarding the transfer of the token, the property must also be transferred in accordance with the principles of property law. In the case of transfers of possession and ownership, aside from the hand-to-hand-surrender of property, which is fairly uninteresting in practice, the forms of acquisition without possession, e.g. through formless substitutes for the transfer of ownership, such as the instruction of ownership or constructive possession, play a central role. In the possession contract, the direct possessor undertakes to surrender the property only to the person entitled to dispose over the token (identification-function) (for example, by adding a tokenisation-clause). The notification obligation is implicitly waived and replaced with the token's identification-function. The legal responsibility identified by the TT-system offers a high degree of reliability (commercial security). The statutory regulation of the identification-function of (extrinsic) tokens and the high degree of reliability therefore justify the use, in the case of notification of possession, of the token's identification-function in the form a (tokenisation) clause in the possession contract – in place of the obligation to notify the third party in direct possession of the property.

However, tokens can also represent other rights, such as intellectual property rights. The protective rights for trademarks and designs solely arise from their entry in a register (constitutive effect of the register entry), which makes representation in a token impractical. Property rights and rights of use can be represented in tokens and these transferred form-free and even implicitly. The timestamp provided by trustworthy-technologies allows the holder of the right to prove that they created their work when the transaction occurred or the token was created. Thus, the token serves as evidence of the creation of the work and therefore the initial assignment to the person by whom the work was created (creator theory). In addition, the rights of use can be represented in the token, with which they can then be transferred and exercised. If licences are to be represented in tokens, then the consent of the licensor is required for the transfer. This can be done automatically. A suitable measure pursuant to Art. 7, para. 2 TVTG to ensure that the licence is transferred with the token to the new person entitled to dispose over the token is the prior consent to free transfer on the part of the licensor.

Last but not least, the assignment to a TT-identifier had to be presented more precisely. According to the definition in Art. 2, para. 1 lit. d of the TVTG, the TT-identifier allows for the clear assignment of tokens. The use of the term "public key" or "address" has correctly been avoided. In most cases, the public key is now no longer used for transactions. To ensure an approach that was as functionally and technologically neutral as possible, the term "TT-identifier" was introduced together with the "TT-key". The TVTG uses the TT-identifier to create the connection/assignment between tokens and legal subjects (persons). The token is assigned to the TT-identifier, which is, in turn, controlled via a TT-key (power of disposal). The TT-key can be used by people to, for example, sign transactions.

On the whole, the Liechtenstein legislator were successful in introducing a suitable legal object into Liechtenstein law with the legal definition of the TVTG. Only after a close analysis of the features in context as a container for the transfer of rights in the token economy is it clear why the individual constituent features were specified the way they were. It also shows why the token was not only defined as a new legal object, but also separate transfer regulations were required. The legal definition is the focus of the TVTG, and the Token-Container-Model is already serving as the basis for foreign legislators, emphasising the level of innovation. By providing the legal definition, Liechtenstein created the basis for the tokenisation of rights. It will be exciting to see how the approach works in practice and how the technologies behind it develop further.

Glossary

Bitcoin

Bitcoin stands for the peer-to-peer network, for the open source software, for the decentralised ledger (blockchain), for the software development platform and for the transaction platform.[594]

bitcoins, BTC, XBT

The lower-case version refers to the unit of the cryptocurrency, which is abbreviated "BTC" or "XBT". According to the standard for currency abbreviations, currencies that are not issued by a state should start with an "X", followed by two letters that indicate the name of the currency.[595]

bitcoins are divided into:[596]

1 bitcoin	=	1 BTC
0.1 BTC	=	1 dBTC (1 Decibitcoin)
0.01 BTC	=	1 cBTC (1 Centbitcoin or bitcent)
0.001 BTC	=	1 mBTC (1 Millibitcoin or mbit)
0.000001 BTC	=	1 µBTC (1 Microbitcoin or µbit)
0.00000001 BTC	=	1 Satoshi (smallest divisible amount[597])

Coins and tokens

There is no uniform definition for the term "coin". Users of trustworthy-technologies pursuant to Art. 2, para. 1(a) TVTG (abbreviated as "TT") usually distinguish between tokens and coins[598], but sometimes these terms are used synonymously. The term "**coin**" is usually used to refer to system units – cryptocurrencies like bitcoin (BTC) or ether (ETH) – for the respective protocol (here, corresponding to Bitcoin or

[594] SIXT, Bitcoins und andere dezentrale Transaktionssysteme. Blockchains als Basis einer Kryptoökonomie (2017), p. 1.

[595] KERSCHER, Bitcoin. Funktionsweise, Risiken und Chancen der digitalen Währung[2] (2014), p. 10.

[596] KERSCHER, Bitcoin[2], p. 11.

[597] Named after the pseudonym "Satoshi Nakamoto".

[598] The best known examples are bitcoin and ether.

Ethereum).[599] In comparison, tokens are based on a blockchain such as Ethereum, which users pay to use in ether, the Ethereum coin. Tokens can have a wide variety of functions. Bitcoin was invented as a form of payment that requires no intermediary and is used to transfer assets. Access tokens grant access to a network or access to a service and during the period of initial coin offerings (ICOs) were often issued in order to finance the development of new blockchain protocols.[600] In this book, the definition in Art. 2, para. 1(c) TVTG is used for all manifestations of the term "token".[601]

Fiatmoney (money with no intrinsic value)

In the discussion on cryptocurrencies, the term "fiat"has become a synonym for government currencies, such as the Swiss franc or the euro. Fiat is Latin and comes from the verb "fieri", which can be translated as "let it be done" or "may it happen". A well-known example of the use of the verb "fieri" is the biblical quotation for the formation of the universe, "fiat lux" (let there be light). This involved a "creatio ex nihilio", the creation of something from nothing. Fiat money is a medium of exchange with no intrinsic value that is created as a means of payment (from nothing) through a legislative act. Its creation by the state is what distinguishes a CHF 100 banknote from a CHF 100 note printed by a game maker as play money. The banknote can be used to pay in a restaurant, the play money cannot. One of the key criteria to delineate banknotes from other forms is acceptance as a means of payment. Legal means of payment must be accepted by creditors in the respective jurisdiction; otherwise, they will be deemed to be in default of acceptance.[602] Acceptance is not, unless required by law, automatic or given for all time. For example, residents of Moscow preferred cigarettes as a means of payment over roubles in the 1980s.[603]

Miner

"Miners" are nodes that carry out the mining function. In the case of Bitcoin, for example, they do so for the purpose of adding a new block to the blockchain approx.

---

599 See also NÄGELE/BERGT, Kryptowährungen und Blockchain-Technologie im liechtensteinischen Aufsichtsrecht, LJZ 2018, p. 64 f.

600 LANGER/NÄGELE, Blockchain- und tokenbasierte Unternehmen in Liechtenstein, IWB 2018, p. 3 f.

601 With further references. NÄGELE, Sekundärmarkt für Security Token (2020), p. 9 f.

602 GOVERNMENT OF THE PRINCIPALITY OF LIECHTENSTEIN, BuA No. 54/2019, p. 12.

603 On fiat money and its creation by states, see MANKIW, Principles of Economics[2] (2001), p. 611; on "fiat" and the origin of the term, see Wikipedia's article on fiat money (accessed 23 January 2021, https://de.wikipedia.org/w/index.php?title=Fiatgeld&oldid=206054572).

every 10 minutes. In most cases, the miners do not save the entire blockchain (function: "full blockchain"). Instead, they only "know" the last block.

Node

"Nodes" are the participants in a network. For example, the participants in the Bitcoin blockchain network are referred to as "nodes". There are different types of nodes, each of which has a different function. While all of the nodes have equal rights, they do not necessarily have to carry out the same functions.

(Full) node

A "full node" carries out all four major functions that are necessary for the Bitcoin blockchain to function. These are:

- "(Network) routing node",
- "Full blockchain",
- "Mining" and
- "Wallet".

Each node must function as a "routing node". The other three functions are used in different combinations. The "full blockchain" function saves a copy of the entire blockchain database. Most "wallets" do not save a copy of the entire database. Instead, they (only) carry out the wallet function (see the term "wallet" below"). Miners also generally do not save a copy of the entire database (see the definition of mining).[604]

Smart-contract

Based on the various TT, in particular, Ethereum[605] and Aeternity[606], it is possible to create tokens with individual functions. The software programmer defines the scope of the functions for the respective token in the respective programming language[607]. To ensure that tokens remain as compatible with one another as possible, standards,

---

604 ANTONOPOULOS, Mastering Bitcoin. Programming the Open Blockchain (June 2017), p. 188 ff.

605 ETHEREUM, Ethereum is a global, open-source platform for decentralized applications, https://ethereum.org/ (accessed on 14 April 2020).

606 AETERNITY, a blockchain for scalable, secure and decentralized æpps, https://aeternity.com/ (accessed on 16 April 2020).

607 The programming language used for smart contracts on the Ethereum blockchain is called Solidity; ETHEREUM, Solidity, https://github.com/ethereum/solidity (accessed 12 February 2021); in the case of Aeternity, the language is called Sophia and is structured in a manner that is very similar to Solidity; AETERNITY, The Sophia Language, https://aeternity.com/documentation-hub/protocol/contracts/sophia (accessed on 12 February 2021).

like the ERC-20 standard[608], have been developed. However, tokens are generally only compatible with other tokens based on the same technology. A number of token issues, known as initial coin offerings ("ICOs"), contained tokens that were developed on the basis of the ERC-20 standard. Standardisation makes smart-contracts relatively easy to integrate with other tokens. This is particularly important when smart-contracts are intended to automatically initiate subsequent events with other smart-contracts. The best example of this is the initiation of a payment in a cryptocurrency.

Stablecoin

This is a token issued by an issuer whose value is based on various legal currencies, commodities, cryptocurrencies or a combination of these. In its draft "Markets in Crypto-assets" regulation, the European Commission uses the term "**asset-referenced token**" for stablecoins.[609]

Token economy

"**Token economy**" refers to the digitalisation of the economy through the "tokenisation" of assets.[610] To date, the term has not been scientifically defined and encompasses all applications of tokens in every sector of the economy, in particular, the financial market.[611] The tokenisation of assets creates greater legal certainty in digital transactions and increases the efficiency of and trust in the digital economy.[612] The token economy should therefore be viewed as part of the digitalisation of the economy and fits in with developments in recent decades.[613] **Tokens that represent rights** make the **assets** in smart-contracts **digitally accessible**. In other words, they

---

608 BUTERIN/VOGELSTELLER, ethereum/EIPs 20, https://github.com/ethereum/EIPs/blob/master/EIPS/eip-20.md (accessed on 2 February 2021).

609 EUROPEAN COMMISSION, Proposal for a Regulation on Markets in Crypto-assets (MiCA), https://eur-lex.europa.eu/legal-content/EN/TXT/?uri=CELEX:52020PC0593 (accessed 21 January 2021); see the overview of the different token classes in the MiCA, NÄGELE, MiCA – Markets in Crypto-assets Regulation and the DLT Pilot Regime – What impact might these proposed EU regulations have on Liechtenstein and the TVTG (aka Blockchain Act)? https://thomas-naegele.medium.com/mica-markets-in-crypto-assets-mica-and-dlt-pilot-regime-what-impacts-do-these-proposed-eu-fc3b85609dca.

610 HASLER, Rechtssicherheit für die Token-Ökonomie, NZZ Neue Zürcher Zeitung AG.

611 On the question of how tokenisation may change the financial market, see SUNYAEV/KANNENGIEẞER/BECK/TREIBLMAIER/LACITY/KRANZ/FRIDGEN/SPANKOWSKI/LUCKOW, Token Economy 2021, p. 16 f.

612 DÜNSER, Legalize Blockchain. How States Should Deal with Today's Most Promising Technology to Foster Prosperity (2020), p. 38 ff.

613 DÜNSER, Legalize Blockchain, p. 38 f.

can be disposed of through digital commands. This forms the basis of the token economy: A fully digital economy in which tokens can digitally represent rights.

Tokenisation

"Tokenisation" describes the process that is necessary for tokens to be able to represent rights. On the one hand, this includes the technical structure of the token in accordance with the requirements of the representation of the rights. It also includes the legal connection between the token and the right that is represented. The TVTG and the legislative materials call the token a type of "container to represent rights", and the phrase "Token-Container-Model" has now become established.[614] The "tokenisation" process is similar to securitisation under securities law.

Token holder = Person with the right of disposal over the token

The term "token holder" is usually used imprecisely in practice to mean the "owner" or "possessor" of the token. The term token holder is based on the notion of someone who "holds" the "token". But the TVTG does not refer to possession or ownership. In the TVTG system, the token holder is the person who has the **right of disposal** over a token (owner). This is different from the person who has the **power of disposal** over the token. This is comparable to an owner of a thing. While he can dispose of it, he may not be allowed to.

Wallet

The term wallet means several things. It primarily means the software application used as the user interface. The software makes it possible to dispose of the token, manages the TT-key and the TT-identifiers, shows the holdings and prepares and signs transactions.[615] This software application is also called "SPV wallet". "SPV" stands for "simplified payment verification". This is a node, i.e. a participant in a blockchain network, who carries out the wallet function. In contrast to a full node, a wallet node does not save a copy of the entire blockchain.

Timestamp

In TT-systems in the form of a blockchain, the blocks usually have a **timestamp**. Thus, blockchains are especially suited to documenting a certain (data) status at a

614 See also, for example, the remarks on the Token-Container-Model in NÄGELE/XANDER, ICOs und STOs im liechtensteinischen Recht, in *Piska/Völkel* (ed.), Blockchain Rules (2019), p. 394 ff.

615 ANTONOPOULOS, Mastering Bitcoin, p. 93.

certain time relatively easily and immutably. The "hash" of the data status is recorded in a transaction, which is then stamped with a timestamp when it is added to a block. This makes it possible for anyone to easily and publicly check when (precisely, to a few minutes exactly) the hash was "documented" by the blockchain by accessing a website. One potential application is the implementation of the digital signature using TT-systems.[616]

Central, decentralisedand distributed

In a centralised network, there is usually only one central server with control. However, this means that attacks only need to target the central server. The server thus

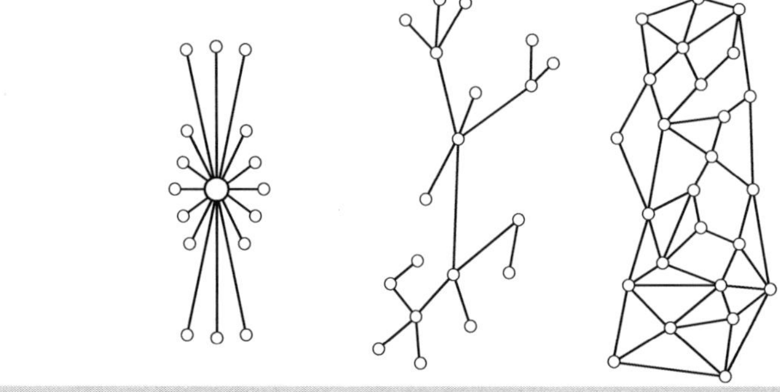

Figure 4 Central, Decentralised and Distributed

represents a potential single point of failure that could result in the failure of the entire network. This is because if the server fails, clients will no longer be able to exchange data. As a consequence, clients store their data in the server's central database so that everyone can access it. In contrast, decentralisation involves several servers that are connected to one another. The servers divide the tasks between themselves. This distribution and division of tasks between many decentralised servers makes the likelihood of a failure much lower than is the case with central systems (see figure: If one node that connects the branches to the network fails, however, these branches will lose their connection to the network). Decentralised networks are therefore a sub-form of distributed networks. The main differences between distributed and decentralised networks involve where and how decisions are taken and how

616 BlockAxs uses the Stellar blockchain to sign contracts digitally. As part of this process, a hash of the document is recorded in transactions on the Stellar blockchain: BLOCKAXS, Innovatives Vertragsmanagement der Zukunft, https://blockaxs.com/ (accessed on 25 February 2021).

information is distributed within the network.[617] In a distributed network, there are no central servers, meaning the failure of one participant will not have a negative impact (no single point of failure)[618]. See Figure 1[619]; each node ("participant") has multiple connections to the network and the failure of one node will not affect the overall system.

[617] See also EAGAR, What Is the Difference between Decentralized and Distributed Systems? EcoNova.

[618] Provided that there is no simultaneous failure of multiple participants, which in turn leads to a loss of data and system failures.

[619] Based on Fig. 1: Centralized, Decentralized and Distributed Networks; BARAN, On Distributed Communications. Introduction to Distributed Communications Networks (1964), p. 2.

List of sources and materials

1 Literature

ANTONOPOULOS, Mastering Bitcoin. Programming the Open Blockchain (June 2017).

ANTONOPOULOS/WOOD, Mastering Ethereum. Building Smart Contracts and DApps (2018).

BARAN, On Distributed Communications. Introduction to Distributed Communications Networks (1964).

BASHIR, Mastering Blockchain. Distributed Ledgers, Decentralization and Smart Contracts Explained (2017).

BLOCHER, Gewerblicher Rechtschutz und Urheberrecht (Commercial Legal Protection and Copyright Law), in *Jahnel* (ed.), IT-Recht[3] (IT Law) (2012).

BUCHLEITNER/RABL, Blockchain und Smart Contracts (Vom Ende der Institutionen) (Blockchain and Smart Contracts (the End of Institutions), (in ecolex 2017).

DÜNSER, Legalize Blockchain. How States Should Deal with Today's Most Promising Technology to Foster Prosperity (2020).

FRANK/BERNANKE, Principles of economics (2001).

A. FRICK, Zivilrechtliche Aspekte von Token im Zusammenhang mit dem liechtensteinischen Token- und VT-Dienstleister-Gesetz. Diplomarbeit Fakultät für Rechtswissenschaften der Universität Innsbruck (Civil Law Aspects of Tokens in Conjunction with the Liechtenstein Token and TT Service Provider Act. Dissertation for the Faculty of Law at the University of Innsbruck), Schaan, Innsbruck (2020).

HOEREN/SIEBER/HOLZNAGEL (ed.), Handbuch Multimedia-Recht (Rechtsfragen des elektronischen Geschäftsverkehrs) (Multimedia Law Manual (Legal Questions in Electronic Business Transactions)) (1999).

HONSELL/VOGT/GEISER, Basler Kommentar[5] (Basel Commentary) (2015).

JAHNEL (ed.), IT-Recht[3] (IT Law) (2012).

KAISER/RÜETSCHI, Immaterialgüterrecht[3] (Intellectual Property Rights) (2017).

KERSCHER, Bitcoin. Funktionsweise, Risiken und Chancen der digitalen Währung[2] (Bitcoin. Mechanics, Risks and Opportunities of the Digital Currency) (2014).

KERSKEN, IT-Handbuch für Fachinformatiker[6] (IT Manual for IT Specialists) (2013).

KOLLER/SEIDEL, Geld war gestern. [wie Bitcoin, Regionalgeld, Zeitbanken und Sharing Economy unser Leben verändern werden][1] (Money is History. How Bitcoin, Regional Money, Time Banks and the Sharing Economy will change Our Lives) (2014).

G. LESER/*G.* LESER/HABSBURG-LOTHRINGEN, Finanzinstrumente - Aktien, Anleihen, Rohstoffe, Fonds und Derivate im Überblick. Inkl. virtuelle Währungssysteme (Blockchain, ICO, Bitcoin, Ethereum und andere Kryptowährungen)[2] (Financial Instruments - Stocks, Bonds, Commodities, Funds and Derivatives at a glance. Incl. Virtual Currency Systems (Blockchain, ICOs, Bitcoin, Ethereum and Other Cryptocurrencies) (2019).

MANKIW, Principles of economics[2] (2001).

MEIER-HAYOZ/CRONE, Wertpapierrecht[3] (Securities Law) (2018).

MÜLLER/OERTLI (ed.), Urheberrechtsgesetz (URG) (Bundesgesetz über das Urheberrecht und verwandte Schutzrechte; mit Ausblick auf EU-Recht, deutsches Recht, Staatsverträge und die internationale Rechtsentwicklung)[2] (The Copyright Act (URG) (Federal Act on Copyright and Related Rights; with a Look at EU Law, German Law, Treaties and International Legal Developments) (2012).

NÄGELE/XANDER, ICOs und STOs im liechtensteinischen Recht (ICOs and STOs in Liechtenstein Law), in *Piska/Völkel* (ed.), Blockchain rules (2019).

NÄGELE/FELDKIRCHER/BERGT/ESNEAULT, National legal & regulatory frameworks in select European countries (VIII. LIECHTENSTEIN), in thinkBLOCKtank (ed.), Token Regulation Paper v1.0.

NÄGELE, Sekundärmarkt für Security Token (Secondary Market for Security Tokens) (2020).

PISKA/VÖLKEL (ed.), Blockchain rules (2019).

RIETZLER/*M.* FRICK/CASELLINI, Liechtensteinisches Blockchain Gesetz (Liechtenstein Blockchain Act), in *Piska/Völkel* (ed.), Blockchain rules (2019).

SALEH, Blockchain Without Waste: Proof-of-Stake (2018).

J. SCHMID/HÜRLIMANN-KAUP, Sachenrecht[4] (Property Law) (2012).

SCHUSTER/GRÜTZMACHER (ed.), IT-Recht (Kommentar)[1] (IT Law (Commentary)) (2018).

SCHWARZ, Globaler Effektenhandel. Eine rechtstatsächliche und rechtsvergleichende Studie zu Risiken, Dogmatik und Einzelfragen des Trading, Clearing und Settlement bei nationalen und internationalen Wertpapiertransaktionen (Global Securities Trading. A Practical and Comparative Study of Risks, Dogma and Individual Questions Related to the Trading, Clearing and Settlement of National and International Securities Transactions) (2016).

SIXT, Bitcoins und andere dezentrale Transaktionssysteme. Blockchains als Basis einer Kryptoökonomie (Sixt, Bitcoins and other Decentralised Transactions Systems. Blockchain as the Basis of a Crypto-Economy) (2017).

SONNTAG, Informationstechnologie: Grundlage (Information Technology: Principles), in *Jahnel* (ed.), IT-Recht[3] (IT Law) (2012).

SUNYAEV, Internet Computing. Principles of Distributed Systems and Emerging Internet-Based Technologies[1] (2020).

VAN HIJFTE, Blockchain Platforms. A Look at the Underbelly of Distributed Platforms (2020).

VOSHMGIR, Token economy. How blockchains and smart-contracts revolutionize the economy[1] (2019).

WIEGAND in *Honsell/Vogt/Geiser*, Basler Kommentar[5] (Basel Commentary) (2015), introductory remarks on Art. 641 ff.

WILD, Zivilrecht und Token-Ökonomie in Liechtenstein. Eine Analyse der zivilrechtlichen Bestimmungen des TVTG unter Berücksichtigung des Wertrechts (Civil Law and the Token Economy in Liechtenstein. An Analysis of the Civil Law Provisions of the TVTG, Taking Account of Book-entry Securities) (2020).

ZECH, introductory remarks on Art. 87a ff., in *Schuster/Grützmacher* (ed.), IT-Recht. Kommentar[1] (Commentary) (2018).

2 Journal articles

BÜCH, Die Blockchain und das Recht (Blockchain and the Law), p. 55, (in LJZ 2018).

DEUBER/KHORRAMI JAHROMI, Liechtensteiner Blockchain-Gesetzgebung: Vorbild für Deutschland? (Lösungsansatz für eine zivilrechtliche Behandlung von Token) (Liechtenstein Blockchain Law: A Model for Germany? (An Approach to the Civil Law Treatment of Tokens)), p. 576, (in MMR 2020).

ECKERT, Digitale Daten als Wirtschaftsgut: digitale Daten als Sache (Digital Data as an Economic Good: Digital Data as Property), p. 245, (in SJZ 2016).

EIGELSHOVEN/ULLRICH/GRONAU, Konsens-Algorithmen von Blockchain (Blockchain Consensus Algorithms), p. 29, (in I40M 2020).

FALKER/TEICHMANN, Liechtenstein – Das TVTG und Risiken der Blockchain-Technologie (The TVTG and Risks of Blockchain Technology), p. 62, (in InTeR 2020).

HANDLE, Der urheberrechtliche Schutz der Idee (Copyright Protection of Ideas), p. 233, (in SMI 2013).

HAWLITSCHEK/NOTHEISEN/TEUBNER, The limits of trust-free systems: A literature review on blockchain technology and trust in the sharing economy, p. 50, (in Electronic Commerce Research and Applications 2018).

LAMPORT/SHOSTAK/PEASE, The Byzantine generals problem, p. 382, (in ACM transactions on programming languages and systems 1982).

LANGER/NÄGELE, Blockchain- und tokenbasierte Unternehmen in Liechtenstein (Steuerliche und rechtliche Fragen und Antworten) (Blockchain- and Token-based Business in Liechtenstein (Tax and Legal Questions and Answers)), p. 1, (in IWB 2018).

LAYR/MARXER, Rechtsnatur und Übertragung von «Token» aus liechtensteinischer Perspektive (Legal Nature and The Transfer of "Tokens" from the Liechtenstein Perspective), p. 11, (in LJZ 2019).

LINS/PRAICHEUX, Digital and blockchain-based legal regimes: An EEA case study based on innovative legislations (Comparison of French and Liechtenstein domestic regulations), p. 311, (in SPWR 2020).

NÄGELE/BERGT, Kryptowährungen und Blockchain-Technologie im liechtensteinischen Aufsichtsrecht, p. 63, (in LJZ 2018).

NÄGELE/BONT, Tokenized structures and assets in Liechtenstein law, p. 633, (in Trusts Trustees 2019).

OMLOR, Digitales Eigentum an Blockchain-Token – rechtsvergleichende Entwicklungslinien (Digital Ownership of Blockchain Tokens – Comparative Law Lines of Development, p. 41, (in ZVglRWiss 2020).

PATZ, Handelsplattformen für Kryptowährungen und Kryptoassets (Trading Platforms for Cryptocurrencies and Cryptoassets), p. 435, (in BKR 2019).

PAULMAYER, Initial Coin Offerings (ICOs) und Initial Token Offerings (ITOs) als prospektpflichtiges Angebot nach KMG? (Do Initial Coin Offerings (ICOs) and Initial Token Offerings (ITOs) Require a Prospectus under the KMG?) p. 530 (in ZFR 2017/259).

PEKLER/RIRSCH/TOMANEK, Kapitalmarktrechtliche Hindernisse für den Handel von Security Token (Capital Market Law Obstacles to Trading Security Tokens), p. 172, (in ZFR 2020/73).

RASCHAUER/SILBERNAGL, Grundsatzfragen des liechtensteinischen „Blockchain-Gesetzes" – TVTG (Basic Questions about the Liechtenstein "Blockchain Act" – TVTG), p. 11 (in ZFR 2020/3).

A.SCHMID/SCHMIDT/ZECH, Rechte an Daten – zum Stand der Diskussion (sic!) (Rights to Data – The Status of the Discussion), p. 627 (in sic! 2018).

SCHOPPER/RASCHNER, Die aufsichtsrechtliche Einordnung von Krypto-Börsen in Österreich (The Classification of Crypto Exchanges in Austria under Regulatory Law, p. 249, (in ÖBA 2019).

SILBERNAGL, Zivilrechtliche Regelungen des liechtensteinischen Blockchaingesetzes (TVTG) - Möglichkeiten für Österreich? (Civil Law Provisions of the Liechtenstein Blockchain Act (TVTG) - Possibilities for Austria?) p. 9 (in Zak 2020/7).

SUNYAEV/KANNENGIEẞER/BECK/TREIBLMAIER/LACITY/KRANZ/FRIDGEN/SPANKOWSKI/LUCKOW, Token Economy, 2021).

THOUVENIN/FRÜH/LOMBARD, Eigentum an Sachdaten: Eine Standortbestimmung (Ownership of Technical Data: An Assessment), p. 25 (in SZW 2017).

VÖLKEL, Vertrauen in die Blockchain und das Sachrecht (Trusting in the Blockchain and Property Law), p. 492, (in ZFR 2020/218).

VON DER CRONE/KESSLER/ANGSTMANN, Token in der Blockchain – privatrechtliche Aspekte der Distributed Ledger Technologie (Tokens in the Blockchain – Private Law Aspects of Distributed Ledger Technology), p. 337, (in SJZ 2018/114).

WURZER, Practical Applications According to the Law on Tokens and TT Service Providers (Token- and TT Service Provider Act; TVTG), p. 221, (in SPWR 2019).

ZOGG, Bitcoin als Rechtsobjekt – eine zivilrechtliche Einordnung (Bitcoin as a Legal Object – A Civil Law Classification), p. 95 (in recht 2019).

3 Legal commentary

BAUER in *Honsell/Vogt/Geiser*, Basler Kommentar5 (Basel Commentary) (2015), Art. 884.

DE WERRA, Art. 16, in *Müller/Oertli* (ed.), Urheberrechtsgesetz (URG). Bundesgesetz über das Urheberrecht und verwandte Schutzrechte; mit Ausblick auf EU-Recht, deutsches Recht, Staatsverträge und die internationale Rechtsentwicklung)2 (The Copyright Act (URG). Federal Act on Copyright and Related Rights; with a Look at EU Law, German Law, Treaties and International Legal Developments) (2012).

FENYVES/KERSCHNER/VONKILCH, ABGB, Art. 1375 to 14103 / orig. by Heinrich Klang (2011).

HAUSHEER/ZOBL/LEEMANN/GMÜR/BECKER/MEIER-HAYOZ (ed.), Berner Kommentar (Kommentar zum schweizerischen Privatrecht)2 (Bern Commentary on Swiss Private Law) (1996).

HUG, Art. 6, in *Müller/Oertli* (ed.), Urheberrechtsgesetz (URG) (Copyright Act (URG)). Bundesgesetz über das Urheberrecht und verwandte Schutzrechte; mit Ausblick auf EU-Recht, deutsches Recht, Staatsverträge und die internationale Rechtsentwicklung)2 (The Copyright Act (URG). Federal Act on Copyright and Related Rights; with a Look at EU Law, German Law, Treaties and International Legal Developments) (2012).

HUG, Art. 8, in *Müller/Oertli* (ed.), Urheberrechtsgesetz (URG) (Copyright Act (URG)). Bundesgesetz über das Urheberrecht und verwandte Schutzrechte; mit Ausblick auf EU-Recht, deutsches Recht, Staatsverträge und die internationale Rechtsentwicklung)2 (The Copyright Act (URG). Federal Act on Copyright and Related Rights; with a Look at EU Law, German Law, Treaties and International Legal Developments) (2012).

KERSCHNER/FENYVES/KLANG (ed.), ABGB, Art. 353 to 379 / orig. by Heinrich Klang[3] (2011).

LEUPOLD, Gutgläubiger Erwerb (Good Faith Acquisition), in *Kerschner/Fenyves/Klang* (ed.), ABGB, Art. 353 to 379[3] (2011).

MÖLLENKAMP/SHMATENKO, Blockchain und Kryptowährungen (Blockchain and cryptocurrencies), in *Hoeren/Sieber/Holznagel* (ed.), Handbuch Multimedia-Recht. Rechtsfragen des elektronischen Geschäftsverkehrs (Multimedia Law Manual (Legal Questions in Electronic Business Transactions)) (1999).

OPILIO, Liechtensteinisches Sachenrecht. SR; Arbeitskommentar (Liechtenstein Property Law. PL; Commentary) (2010).

STARK/LINDENMANN, Der Besitz (Possession), Art. 919-941 ZGB Schweizerisches Zivilgesetzbuch (ZGB 924), in *Hausheer/Zobl/Leemann/Gmür/Becker/Meier-Hayoz* (ed.), Berner Kommentar. Kommentar zum schweizerischen Privatrecht[2] (Bern Commentary. Commentary on Swiss Private Law) (1996) p. 135–165.

THÖNI in *Fenyves/Kerschner/Vonkilch*, ABGB, Art. 1375 to 1410[3] (2011), Art. 1392.

THÖNI in *Fenyves/Kerschner/Vonkilch*, ABGB, Art. 1375 to 1410[3] (2011), Art. 1393.

ZOBL, Das Fahrnispfand, Art. 888-906 ZGB, mit kurzem Überblick über das Versatzpfand (Art. 907-915 ZGB) (Charges on Chattel, Art. 888-906 SCC, with a Brief Overview of Pawnbroking (Art. 907-915 SCC), in *Hausheer/Zobl/Leemann/Gmür/Becker/Meier-Hayoz* (ed.), Berner Kommentar. Kommentar zum schweizerischen Privatrecht[2] (Bern Commentary. Commentary on Swiss Private Law) (1996) p. 347–365.

4 Newspaper articles

ALBRICH, Unklare Rechtslage noch ein Hindernis für Bitcoin-Automaten (Unclear Legal Situation Still a Hindrance for Bitcoin ATMs), (in Liechtensteiner Volksblatt, 14 January 2019).

BREUER, Definition: Fungibilität, (in Springer Fachmedien Wiesbaden GmbH, 16 February 2018).

DEUTSCHE PRESSE AGENTUR, Bitcoin-Börse Mt.Gox insolvent (Bitcoin Exchange Mt. Gox Insolvent), (in FAZ, 28 February 2014).

EAGAR, What is the Difference between Decentralized and Distributed Systems? (in EcoNova, 4 November 2017).

HASLER, Rechtssicherheit für die Token-Ökonomie (Liechtenstein als Vorreiter) (Legal Certainty for the Token Economy (Liechtenstein as a Trendsetter)), (in NZZ Neue Zürcher Zeitung AG, 9 January 2019).

MALA, Who Spends $140,000 on a CryptoKitty? (in The New York Times, 18 May 2018).

SIEGEL, The DAO Attack: Understanding What Happened, (in CoinDesk, 25 June 2016).

5 Internet sources

AETERNITY, a blockchain for scalable, secure and decentralized æpps, https://aeternity.com/ (accessed on 16 April 2020), (in AETERNITY, A blockchain for scalable, secure and decentralized æpps).

AETERNITY, aepp-sophia-examples, https://github.com/aeternity/aepp-sophia-examples (accessed on 22 February 2021), (in AETERNITY, aepp-sophia-examples).

AETERNITY, æternity - a blockchain for scalable, secure and decentralized æpps, https://aeternity.com/#sophia (accessed on 22 February 2021), (in AETERNITY, Aeternity - a blockchain for scalable, secure and decentralized æpps).

AETERNITY, aeternity campaign - Twitter search / Twitter, https://twitter.com/search?q=aeternity%20campaign&src=typed_query&pf=on (accessed on 28 February 2021), (in AETERNITY, Aeternity campaign - Twitter search / Twitter).

AETERNITY, Non-fungible token example, https://github.com/aeternity/aepp-sophia-examples/tree/master/libraries/NonFungibleToken (accessed on 22 February 2021), (in AETERNITY, Non-fungible token example).

AETERNITY, The Sophia language, https://aeternity-sophia.readthedocs.io/en/latest (accessed on 22 February 2021), (in AETERNITY, The Sophia language).

AETERNITY, The Sophia Language, https://aeternity.com/documentation-hub/protocol/contracts/sophia (accessed on 12 February 2021), (in AETERNITY, The Sophia Language).

OFFICE OF JUSTICE OF THE PRINCIPALITY OF LIECHTENSTEIN, commercial register entry for ATERNITY ANSTALT, https://oera.li/cr-portal/auszug/auszug.xhtml?uid=FL-0002.528.358-1# (accessed on 28 February 2021), (in OFFICE OF JUSTICE OF THE PRINCIPALITY OF LIECHTENSTEIN, commercial register entry for ATERNITY ANSTALT).

OFFICE OF JUSTICE OF THE PRINCIPALITY OF LIECHTENSTEIN, Merkblatt zur Liberierung von Gesellschaftskapital mit einer Kryptowährung (Information Sheet on the Payment of Share Capital with a Cryptocurrency), https://www.llv.li/files/onlineschalter/Dokument-3306.pdf (accessed on 27 February 2021), (in OFFICE OF JUSTICE OF THE PRINCIPALITY OF LIECHTENSTEIN, Merkblatt zur Liberierung von Gesellschaftskapital mit einer Kryptowährung (Information Sheet on the Payment of Share Capital with a Cryptocurrency).

ARIANEE PROJECT, Arianee Certificate Schema, https://docs.arianee.org/docs/ArianeeProductCertificate-i18n (accessed on 16 February 2021), (in ARIANEE PROJECT, Arianee Certificate Schema).

ARIANEE PROJECT, Arianee Event Schema, https://docs.arianee.org/docs/ArianeeEvent-i18n (accessed on 20 February 2021), (in ARIANEE PROJECT, Arianee Event Schema).

ASHURST LLP, Ashurst press release (Ashurst advises Nomisma on Europe's first MiFID II license for a blockchain-based MTF), https://www.ashurst.com/en/news-and-insights/news-deals-and-awards/ashurst-advises-nomisma-on-europes-first-mifid-ii-license-for-a-blockchain-based-mtf (accessed on 26 April 2020), (in ASHURST LLP, Ashurst press release).

BITCOIN WIKI, Genesis block, https://en.bitcoin.it/wiki/Genesis_block, (in BITCOIN WIKI, Genesis block).

BITCOIN WIKI, Transaction, https://en.bitcoin.it/wiki/Transaction (accessed on 8 February 2021), (in BITCOIN WIKI, Transaction).

BLOCKAXS, Innovatives Vertragsmanagement der Zukunft (Innovative Contract Management of the Future), https://blockaxs.com/ (accessed on 25 February 2021), (in BLOCKAXS, Innovatives Vertragsmanagement der Zukunft (Innovative Contract Management of the Future)).

BLOCKCHAIN.INFO, Blockchain Explorer, https://www.blockchain.com/btc/tx/a5cbbb32c7f3e2508cd1edef8db817ee9c0fc94b46ee97d5e2f8dd981c4fef48 (accessed 17 May 2021), (in BLOCKCHAIN.INFO, Blockchain Explorer).

BLOCKCHAIN.INFO, currency statistics, https://blockchain.info/de/stats, (in BLOCKCHAIN.INFO, currency statistics).

BREITLING, Breitling press release (Breitling bietet als erste Luxusuhrenmanufaktur einen Blockchain-basierten digitalen Pass für alle neuen Uhren (Breitling is the First Luxury Goods Manufacturer to Offer a Blockchain-based Digital Pass for All New Watches)), https://www.breitling.com/de-de/press-lounge/press-release/33479 (accessed on 16 February 2021), (in BREITLING, Breitling press release).

BUNDESANSTALT FÜR FINANZDIENSTLEISTUNGSAUFSICHT (Federal Financial Supervisory Authority, or BAFIN), information sheet: Hinweise zum Tatbestand des Kryptoverwahrgeschäfts (Guidance notice concerning the statutory definition of crypto custody business), https://www.bafin.de/DE/Aufsicht/BankenFinanzdienstleister/Zulassung/Kryptoverwahrgeschaeft/kryptoverwahrgeschaeft_node.html (accessed on 19 April 2020), (in BAFIN, information sheet: Guidelines concerning the statutory definition of crypto custody business).

BUTERIN, Ethereum white paper, https://web.archive.org/web/20140206034718/http://www.ethereum.org/ethereum.html (accessed on 28 February 2021), (in BUTERIN, Ethereum white paper).

BUTERIN/VOGELSTELLER, ethereum/EIPs 20, https://github.com/ethereum/EIPs/blob/master/EIPS/eip-20.md (accessed on 2 February 2021), (in BUTERIN/VOGELSTELLER, ethereum/EIPs 20).

BUTERIN, On Settlement Finality, https://blog.ethereum.org/2016/05/09/on-settlement-finality (accessed on 19 January 2021), (in BUTERIN, On Settlement Finality).

CLAYTON, Statement on Cryptocurrencies and Initial Coin Offerings, https://www.sec.gov/news/public-statement/statement-clayton-2017-12-11 (accessed on 11 April 2020), (in CLAYTON, Statement on Cryptocurrencies and Initial Coin Offerings).

COINMARKETCAP, 24 Hour Volume Rankings (Currency), https://coinmarketcap.com/currencies/volume/24-hour (accessed on 14 April 2020), (in COINMARKETCAP, 24 Hour Volume Rankings (Currency)).

COINMARKETCAP, Aeternity price today, AE marketcap, chart, and info | CoinMarketCap, https://coinmarketcap.com/currencies/aeternity (accessed on 7 February 2021), (in COINMARKETCAP, Aeternity price today, AE marketcap, chart, and info | CoinMarketCap).

COINMARKETCAP, Bitcoin (BTC) Kurs, Grafiken, Marktkapitalisierung (Bitcoin (BTC) Price, Graphics, Market Capitalisation), https://coinmarketcap.com/de/currencies/bitcoin (accessed on 13 March 2021), (in COINMARKETCAP, Bitcoin (BTC) Kurs, Grafiken, Marktkapitalisierung) (CoinMarketCap, Bitcoin (BTC) Price, Graphics, Market Capitalisation).

CRYPTO51, Cost of a 51% Attack for Different Cryptocurrencies, https://www.crypto51.app/ (accessed on 7 February 2021), (in CRYPTO51, Cost of a 51% Attack for Different Cryptocurrencies).

DAPPER LABS INC., CryptoKitties (Collect and breed digital cats!), https://www.cryptokitties.co/catalogue/latest-cattributes (accessed on 12 February 2021), (in DAPPER LABS INC., CryptoKitties).

DEUTSCHE BUNDESBANK, Begriff und Aufgaben des Geldes (Money Terms and Functions), https://www.bundesbank.de/Redaktion/DE/Dossier/Service/schule_und_bildung_kapitel_1.html?notFirst=true&docId=153022#doc153022bodyText1, (in DEUTSCHE BUNDESBANK, Begriff und Aufgaben des Geldes (Money Terms and Functions)).

DEUTSCHE BUNDESBANK, Distributed-Ledger-Technologien im Zahlungsverkehr und in der Wertpapierabwicklung (Potenziale und Risiken) (Distributed Ledger Technologies in Payments and Securities Settlement (Potential and Risks)), https://www.bundesbank.de/resource/blob/665446/cfd6e8fbe0f2563b9fc1f48fabda8ca2/mL/2017-09-distributed-ledger-technologien-data.pdf (accessed on 19 January 2021), (in DEUTSCHE BUNDESBANK, Distributed-Ledger-

Technologien im Zahlungsverkehr und in der Wertpapierabwicklung (Distributed Ledger Technologies in Payments and Securities Settlement)).

DOSSA/RUIZ/VOGELSTELLER/GOSSELIN, ERC-1644: Controller Token Operation Standard · Issue #1644 · ethereum/EIPs, https://github.com/ethereum/EIPs/issues/1644 (accessed on 22 February 2021), (in DOSSA et al., ERC-1644: Controller Token Operation Standard · Issue #1644 · ethereum/EIPs).

SWISS FEDERAL TAX ADMINISTRATION, ICTax - Income & Capital Taxes, https://www.ictax.admin.ch/extern/de.html#/ratelist/2021 (accessed on 27 February 2021), (in SWISS FEDERAL TAX ADMINISTRATION, ICTax - Income & Capital Taxes).

ETHEREUM, ERC 1400: Security Token Standard · Issue #1411 · ethereum/EIPs, https://github.com/ethereum/eips/issues/1411 (accessed on 21 February 2021), (in ETHEREUM, ERC 1400: Security Token Standard · Issue #1411 · ethereum/EIPs).

ETHEREUM, ERC-20 Token Standard, https://ethereum.org/en/developers/docs/standards/tokens/erc-20 (accessed on 21 February 2021), (in ETHEREUM, ERC-20 Token Standard).

ETHEREUM, ERC-721 Non-Fungible Token Standard, https://ethereum.org/en/developers/docs/standards/tokens/erc-721 (accessed on 21 February 2021), (in ETHEREUM, ERC-721 Non-Fungible Token Standard).

ETHEREUM, Ethereum is a global, open-source platform for decentralized applications, https://ethereum.org/ (accessed on 14 April 2020), (in ETHEREUM, Ethereum is a global, open-source platform for decentralized applications).

ETHEREUM, ethereum/EIPs, https://github.com/ethereum/EIPs (accessed on 21 February 2021), (in ETHEREUM, ethereum/EIPs).

ETHEREUM, ethereum/EIPs Issue #16, https://github.com/ethereum/EIPs/issues/16 (accessed on 21 February 2021), (in ETHEREUM, ethereum/EIPs Issue #16 ·).

ETHEREUM, History of Ethereum, https://ethereum.org/en/history (accessed on 28 February 2021), (in ETHEREUM, History of Ethereum).

ETHEREUM, Solidity, https://github.com/ethereum/solidity (accessed on 12 February 2021), (in ETHEREUM, Solidity).

ETHERSCAN.IO, Aeternity (AE) Contract Address, https://etherscan.io/address/0x5ca9a71b1d01849c0a95490cc00559717fcf0d1d#code (accessed on 8 February 2021), (in ETHERSCAN.IO, Aeternity (AE) Contract Address).

ETHERSCAN.IO, Aeternity (AE) Token Tracker, https://etherscan.io/token/0x5ca9a71b1d01849c0a95490cc00559717fcf0d1d (accessed on 6 February 2021), (in ETHERSCAN.IO, Aeternity (AE) Token Tracker).

ETHERSCAN.IO, Aeternity (AE) Token Tracker - balances, https://etherscan.io/token/0x5ca9a71b1d01849c0a95490cc00559717fcf0d1d#balances (accessed on 6 February 2021), (in ETHERSCAN.IO, Aeternity (AE) Token Tracker - balances).

ETHERSCAN.IO, Ether Total Supply and Market Capitalization Chart, https://etherscan.io/stat/supply (accessed on 12 February 2021), (in ETHERSCAN.IO, Ether Total Supply and Market Capitalization Chart).

EUROPEAN COMMISSION, Proposal for a Regulation on Markets in Crypto-assets (MiCA), https://eur-lex.europa.eu/legal-content/EN/TXT/?uri=CELEX:52020PC0593 (accessed on 21 January

2021), (in EUROPEAN COMMISSION, Proposal for a Regulation on Markets in Crypto-assets (MiCa)).

FINANCIAL STABILITY, FINANCIAL SERVICES AND CAPITAL MARKETS UNION, Digital finance package, https://ec.europa.eu/info/publications/200924-digital-finance-proposals_en (accessed on 21 January 2021), (in FINANCIAL STABILITY, FINANCIAL SERVICES AND CAPITAL MARKETS UNION, Digital finance package).

LIECHTENSTEIN FINANCIAL MARKET AUTHORITY (FMA), FMA Communication 2019/1 (Ergänzende Pflichten bei der Ausgabe und Rücknahme sowie der Anteilsregisterführung bei Fondsanteils-Token) (Additional Obligations on Issue and Redemption and for Unit Register Maintenance for Fund Unit Tokens), https://www.fma-li.li/files/list/fma-mitteilung-2019-01.pdf (accessed on 11 April 2020), (in FMA, FMA Communication 2019/1).

LIECHTENSTEIN FINANCIAL MARKET AUTHORITY (FMA), FMA Communication 2019/2 (Pflichten für Emittenten von Wertpapieren und Security Token) (Obligations for Issuers of Securities and Security Tokens), https://www.fma-li.li/files/list/fma-mittteilung-2019-2-emittenten-wp-st.pdf (accessed on 24 March 2020), (in FMA, FMA Communication 2019/2).

LIECHTENSTEIN FINANCIAL MARKET AUTHORITY (FMA), Liste gebilligte Prospekte bis 20. Juli 2019 (List of Approved Prospectuses to 20 July 2019), register.fma-li.li/fileadmin/user_upload/dokumente/publikationen/Prospekte_nach_WPPG/Liste_geb_Prospekte_bis_20190720_6_20200103.pdf (accessed on 4 March 2020), (in FMA, Liste gebilligte Prospekte bis 20. Juli 2019) (List of Approved Prospectuses to 20 July 2019).

GITHUB, æternity, https://github.com/aeternity (accessed on 6 February 2021), (in GITHUB, æternity).

GITHUB, Fungible token example, https://github.com/aeternity/aepp-sophia-examples/tree/master/libraries/FungibleToken (accessed on 22 February 2021), (in GITHUB, Fungible token example).

HASLER, speech by Prime Minister Adrian Hasler on the occasion of the 4th Finance Forum Liechtenstein on 21 March 2018 in the Vaduzer Saal, https://www.regierung.li/media/medienarchiv/2018-03-21_Ansprache_Finance_Forum_2018_RC.pdf?t=637433298910799802 (accessed on 27 February 2021), (in HASLER, speech by Prime Minister Adrian Hasler on the occasion of the 4th Finance Forum Liechtenstein on 21 March 2018 in the Vaduzer Saal).

HUBER, Bitcoin 2020 – die Halbierung der Blockprämie (Bitcoin 2020 – Halving the Block Reward), https://www.bitcoinsuisse.com/de/outlook/bitcoin-in-2020-halving-the-block-reward-2 (accessed on 7 February 2021), (in HUBER, Bitcoin 2020 – die Halbierung der Blockprämie) (Bitcoin 2020 – Halving the Block Reward).

INTERNATIONAL ORGANIZATION FOR STANDARDIZATION (ISO), Information technology, https://www.iso.org/obp/ui/#iso:std:iso-iec:2382:ed-1:v1:en (accessed on 29 April 2021), (in ISO, Information technology).

MUZZY, What Is Proof of Stake? https://consensys.net/blog/blockchain-explained/what-is-proof-of-stake (accessed on 6 February 2021), (in MUZZY, What Is Proof of Stake?).

MYCRYPTOPEDIA, Bitcoin's UTXO Set Explained - Mycryptopedia, https://www.mycryptopedia.com/bitcoin-utxo-unspent-transaction-output-set-explained (accessed on 8 February 2021), (in MYCRYPTOPEDIA, Bitcoin's UTXO Set Explained - Mycryptopedia).

NÄGELE RECHTSANWÄLTE GMBH, on Twitter (We also accept cryptocurrencies like Bitcoin or Ethereum as payment for some of our services. Don't hesitate to contact us!), https://

twitter.com/NaegeleLAW/status/873156452482940930?s=20 (accessed on 23 January 2021), (in NÄGELE RECHTSANWÄLTE GMBH, on Twitter).

NÄGELE, MiCA — Markets in Crypto-assets Regulation and the DLT Pilot Regime — What impact might these proposed EU regulations have on Liechtenstein and the TVTG (aka Blockchain Act)? https://thomas-naegele.medium.com/mica-markets-in-crypto-assets-mica-and-dlt-pilot-regime-what-impacts-do-these-proposed-eu-fc3b85609dca, (in NÄGELE, MiCA — Markets in Crypto-assets Regulation and the DLT Pilot Regime — What impact might these proposed EU regulations have on Liechtenstein and the TVTG (aka Blockchain Act)?).

NÄGELE, Why Liechtenstein is an attractive location for the token economy, https://thomas-naegele.medium.com/why-liechtenstein-is-an-attractive-location-for-the-token-economy-91d23c8ab1b0, (in NÄGELE, Why Liechtenstein is an attractive location for the token economy).

NAKAMOTO, (PSEUDONYM), Bitcoin: A Peer-to-Peer Electronic Cash System (Bitcoin white paper), https://bitcoin.org/bitcoin.pdf (accessed on 11 April 2020), (in NAKAMOTO, Bitcoin: A Peer-to-Peer Electronic Cash System).

OPENDIME, World's First Bitcoin Credit Stick Wallet, https://opendime.com/ (accessed on 23 February 2021), (in OPENDIME, World's First Bitcoin Credit Stick Wallet).

PEERCOIN, The Pioneer of Proof of Stake, https://www.peercoin.net/ (accessed on 30 April 2021), (in PEERCOIN, The Pioneer of Proof of Stake).

POA SOKOL EXPLORER, ArianeeSmartAsset (0x512C1FCF40113368of373a386F3f752b98070BC5), https://blockscout.com/poa/sokol/address/0x512C1FCF40113368of373a386F3f752b98070BC5/contracts (accessed on 20 February 2021), (in POA SOKOL EXPLORER, ArianeeSmartAsset (0x512C1FCF40113368of373a386F3f752b98070BC5)).

REGIERUNG DES FÜRSTENTUMS LIECHTENSTEIN, Bericht und Antrag zum «Blockchain-Gesetz» verabschiedet (Report and Application on the "Blockchain Act" approved), https://www.regierung.li/de/mitteilungen/222667/?typ=news (accessed on 28 February 2021), (in GOVERNMENT OF THE PRINCIPALITY OF LIECHTENSTEIN, Report and Application for the "Blockchain Act" approved).

GOVERNMENT OF THE PRINCIPALITY OF LIECHTENSTEIN, Liechtensteins Blockchain-Gesetz stösst in der UNO auf grosses Interesse (Liechtenstein's Blockchain Act attracts wide interest at the UN), https://www.regierung.li/de/mitteilungen/223020/?typ=news (accessed on 28 February 2021), (in GOVERNMENT OF THE PRINCIPALITY OF LIECHTENSTEIN, Liechtensteins Blockchain-Gesetz stösst in der UNO auf grosses Interesse (Liechtenstein's Blockchain Act attracts wide interest at the UN)).

GOVERNMENT OF THE PRINCIPALITY OF LIECHTENSTEIN, Stellungnahme zum Token- und VT-Dienstleister-Gesetz («Blockchain-Gesetz») verabschiedet (Statement on the Token and TT Service Provider Act ("Blockchain Act"), approved), https://www.regierung.li/de/mitteilungen/222882 (accessed on 28 February 2021), (in GOVERNMENT OF THE PRINCIPALITY OF LIECHTENSTEIN, Stellungnahme zum Token- und VT-Dienstleister-Gesetz («Blockchain-Gesetz») verabschiedet (Statement on the Token and TT Service Provider Act ("Blockchain Act"), approved)).

GOVERNMENT OF THE PRINCIPALITY OF LIECHTENSTEIN, Vernehmlassung zum Blockchain-Gesetz gestartet (Consultation period on the Blockchain Act started), https://www.regierung.li/de/mitteilungen/212312/?typ=news (accessed on 28 February 2021), (in GOVERNMENT OF THE PRINCIPALITY OF LIECHTENSTEIN, Vernehmlassung zum Blockchain-Gesetz gestartet (Consultation period on the Blockchain Act started)).

RUGAARD, Towards a European token economy – driven by the EU Commission! (An interview with Dr Joachim Schwerin, Principal Economist at the European Commission), https://

thetokenizer.io/2021/01/10/towards-a-european-token-economy-driven-by-the-eu-commission (accessed on 23 January 2021), (in RUGAARD, Towards a European token economy – driven by the EU Commission!).

SATOSHI NAKAMOTO, Bitcoin P2P e-cash paper, http://www.metzdowd.com/pipermail/cryptography/2008-October/014810.html (accessed on 10 June 2017), (in SATOSHI NAKAMOTO, Bitcoin P2P e-cash paper).

SCHNABEL, Computertechnik-Fibel (Computer Technology Primer), https://www.elektronik-kompendium.de/shop/buecher/computertechnik-fibel, (in SCHNABEL, Computertechnik-Fibel[5] (Computer Technology Primer)).

THINKBLOCKTANK, Token Regulation Paper v1.0., (in THINKBLOCKTANK, Token Regulation Paper v1.0.).

UNIDROIT, Exploratory workshop on digital assets and private law, https://www.unidroit.org/89-news-and-events/2941-unidroit-exploratory-workshop-on-digital-assets-and-private-law (accessed on 15 February 2021), (in UNIDROIT, Exploratory workshop on digital assets and private law).

UNIVERSITY OF BASEL, Zertifikate basierend auf Blockchain-Technologie (Certificates Based on Blockchain Technology), https://cif.unibas.ch/de/blog/details/news/zertifikate-basierend-auf-blockchain-technologie (accessed on 21 February 2021), (in UNIVERSITY OF BASEL, Zertifikate basierend auf Blockchain-Technologie (Certificates Based on Blockchain Technology)).

UNIVERSITY OF LIECHTENSTEIN, Blockchain meets Liechtenstein, https://www.uni.li/de/universitaet/medienportal/medienmitteilungen/blockchain-meets-liechtenstein (accessed on 17 May 2021), (in UNIVERSITY OF LIECHTENSTEIN, Blockchain meets Liechtenstein).

VITTORIO MINACORI, Create ERC20 Token for FREE, https://vittominacori.github.io/erc20-generator (accessed on 21 February 2021), (in VITTORIO MINACORI, Create ERC20 Token for FREE).

VOGELSTELLER/BUTERIN, ERC-20 Token Standard, https://github.com/ethereum/EIPs/blob/master/EIPS/eip-20.md (21 February 2021), (in VOGELSTELLER/BUTERIN, ERC-20 Token Standard).

WIKIPEDIA, Byzantine fault, https://de.wikipedia.org/w/index.php?title=Byzantinischer_Fehler&oldid=206575177 (accessed on 17 January 2021), (in WIKIPEDIA, Byzantine fault).

WIKIPEDIA, Data storage, https://de.wikipedia.org/w/index.php?title=Datenspeicher&oldid=205970361 (accessed on 27 December 2020), (in WIKIPEDIA, Data storage).

WIKIPEDIA, European Article Number, https://de.wikipedia.org/w/index.php?title=European_Article_Number&oldid=208255311 (accessed on 18 February 2021), (in WIKIPEDIA, European Article Number).

WIKIPEDIA, Fiat money, https://de.wikipedia.org/w/index.php?title=Fiatgeld&oldid=206054572 (accessed on 23 January 2021), (in WIKIPEDIA, Fiat money).

WIKIPEDIA, Global Trade Item Number (GTIN), https://de.wikipedia.org/w/index.php?title=Global_Trade_Item_Number&oldid=208838895 (accessed on 18 February 2021), (in WIKIPEDIA, Global Trade Item Number (GTIN)).

WIKIPEDIA, List of highest-funded crowdfunding projects, https://en.wikipedia.org/w/index.php?title=List_of_highest-funded_crowdfunding_projects&oldid=1008322414 (accessed on 28 February 2021), (in WIKIPEDIA, List of highest-funded crowdfunding projects).

WIKIPEDIA, The DAO, https://en.wikipedia.org/w/index.php?title=The_DAO_(organization)&oldid=991306039 (accessed on 19 January 2021), (in WIKIPEDIA, The DAO).

6 Legislative materials

PARLIAMENT OF THE PRINCIPALITY OF LIECHTENSTEIN. Minutes of the public meeting of the Parliament from 2-3 October 2019, Part 2, p. 1893. (in minutes of the Parliament, 2-3 October 2019, Part 2).

PARLIAMENT OF THE PRINCIPALITY OF LIECHTENSTEIN. Minutes of the public meeting of the Parliament from 5-7 June 2019, Part 2, p. 956. (in minutes of the Parliament 5-7, June 2019, Part 2).

GOVERNMENT OF THE PRINCIPALITY OF LIECHTENSTEIN. Statement by the Government to the Parliament of the Principality of Liechtenstein on questions raised on the occasion of the first reading for the complete revision of the Act on the Register of Ultimate Beneficial Owners of Domestic Legal Entities as well as the amendment of the Due Diligence Act and the Complaints Commission Act. (in BuA No. 132/2020).

GOVERNMENT OF THE PRINCIPALITY OF LIECHTENSTEIN. Report and Application of the Government to the Parliament of the Principality of Liechtenstein on the amendment of Property Law (PL), the Jurisdiction Act (JA) and the Enforcement Act (EA). (in BuA No. 141/2007).

GOVERNMENT OF THE PRINCIPALITY OF LIECHTENSTEIN. Report and Application of the Government to the Parliament of the Principality of Liechtenstein on the Creation of a Law on Tokens and TT Service Providers (Token and TT Service Provider Act; TVTG) and the Amendment of Other Laws. (in BuA No. 54/2019).

GOVERNMENT OF THE PRINCIPALITY OF LIECHTENSTEIN. Report and Application of the Government to the Parliament of the Principality of Liechtenstein on the Amendment of the Persons and Companies Act (PGR) (review of the LLC law). (in BuA No. 68/2016).

GOVERNMENT OF THE PRINCIPALITY OF LIECHTENSTEIN. Report and Application of the Government to the Parliament of the Principality of Liechtenstein on the Amendment of the Persons and Companies Act (Immobilisation of Bearer Shares and Introduction of a Sanction Mechanism for the Maintenance of the Share Register for Registered Shares). (in BuA No. 69/2012).

GOVERNMENT OF THE PRINCIPALITY OF LIECHTENSTEIN. Statement by the Government to the Parliament of the Principality of Liechtenstein on the questions raised on the occasion of the first reading on the creation of a Law on Tokens and TT Service Providers (Token and TT Service Provider Act; TVTG) and the amendment of other laws. (in BuA No. 93/2019).

GOVERNMENT OF THE PRINCIPALITY OF LIECHTENSTEIN. Consultation report by the Government on the creation of a Law on Transaction Systems Based on Trustworthy-Technologies (TT) (Blockchain Act; TT Act; TTA) and the amendment of other laws (16 November 2018) (16 November 2018). (in Consultation report on the Blockchain Act).

7 Case law

SUPREME COURT OF THE PRINCIPALITY OF LIECHTENSTEIN (OGH) 9 CG.2000.137.

CONSTITUTIONAL COURT OF THE PRINCIPALITY OF LIECHTENSTEIN (StGH) StGH 1975/002 ElG 1973, 381, 383.

8 Laws and regulations

PUBLICATIONS OFFICE OF THE EUROPEAN UNION, Directive 96/9/EC of the European Parliament and the Council of 11 March 1996 on the legal protection of databases (Database Directive), Official Journal of the European Union (1996).

PUBLICATIONS OFFICE OF THE EUROPEAN UNION, Directive 98/26/EC of the European Parliament and of the Council of 19 May 1998 on settlement finality in payment and securities settlement systems (Finality Directive), Official Journal of the European Union (1998).

PUBLICATIONS OFFICE OF THE EUROPEAN UNION, Regulation (EU) 2016/679 of the European Parliament and of the Council of 27 April 2016 on the protection of natural persons with regard to the processing of personal data and on the free movement of such data, and repealing Directive 95/46/EC (General Data Protection Regulation) (text with EEA relevance) (GDPR), Official Journal of the European Union (2016).

PUBLICATIONS OFFICE OF THE EUROPEAN UNION, Regulation (EU) 2017/1129 of the European Parliament and of the Council of 14 June 2017 on the prospectus to be published when securities are offered to the public or admitted to trading on a regulated market, and repealing Directive 2003/71/EC (text with EEA relevance) (Prospectus Regulation), Official Journal of the European Union (2017).

FEDERAL ASSEMBLY OF THE SWISS CONFEDERATION, Swiss Federal Act on Copyright and Related Rights (Copyright Act) (URG), Federal Gazette (1992).

FEDERAL ASSEMBLY OF THE SWISS CONFEDERATION, Federal Act on Patents for Inventions (Patents Act) (PatA), Federal Gazette (1954).

FEDERAL ASSEMBLY OF THE SWISS CONFEDERATION, Swiss Civil Code (SCC), Federal Gazette (1907).

GERMAN BUNDESTAG (BT), Act on Banking (Banking Act) (KWG), Federal Gazette (1961).

PARLIAMENT OF THE PRINCIPALITY OF LIECHTENSTEIN, General Civil Code (ABGB), Liechtenstein Law Gazette (1 January 2020).

PARLIAMENT OF THE PRINCIPALITY OF LIECHTENSTEIN, Act of 11 September 2002 on the Protection of Design (Design Act) (DesG), Liechtenstein Law Gazette (2002).

PARLIAMENT OF THE PRINCIPALITY OF LIECHTENSTEIN, Act of 12 December 1996 on the Protection of Trademarks and Indications of Origin (Trademark Protection Act) (MSchG), Liechtenstein Law Gazette (1997).

PARLIAMENT OF THE PRINCIPALITY OF LIECHTENSTEIN, Act of 19 May 1999 on Copyright and Related Rights (Copyright Act) (URG), Liechtenstein Law Gazette (1999).

PARLIAMENT OF THE PRINCIPALITY OF LIECHTENSTEIN, Act of 19 May 1999 on the Protection of Topographies of Semiconductor Products (Topographies Act) (ToG), Liechtenstein Law Gazette (1999).

PARLIAMENT OF THE PRINCIPALITY OF LIECHTENSTEIN, Act of 26 May 1924 on the Introduction of the Swiss Franc (FrWG), Liechtenstein Law Gazette (1924).

PARLIAMENT OF THE PRINCIPALITY OF LIECHTENSTEIN, Act of 3 October 2019 on Token and TT Service Providers (TVTG), Liechtenstein Law Gazette (2019).

PARLIAMENT OF THE PRINCIPALITY OF LIECHTENSTEIN, Act of 6 December 2018 on the Register of Ultimate Beneficial Owners of Domestic Legal Entities (VwEG), Liechtenstein Law Gazette (2019).

PARLIAMENT OF THE PRINCIPALITY OF LIECHTENSTEIN, Persons and Companies Act (PGR), Liechtenstein Law Gazette (1926).

PARLIAMENT OF THE PRINCIPALITY OF LIECHTENSTEIN, Property Law of 31 December 1922 (PL), Liechtenstein Law Gazette (1923).

PARLIAMENT OF THE PRINCIPALITY OF LIECHTENSTEIN, Criminal Code (StGB), Liechtenstein Law Gazette (1988).

NATIONAL COUNCIL OF THE REPUBLIC OF AUSTRIA, Austrian General Civil Code for All the German Hereditary Provinces of the Austrian Monarchy (öABGB), Judicial Law Collection (1811).

GOVERNMENT OF THE PRINCIPALITY OF LIECHTENSTEIN, Ordinance of 11 February 2003 on the Commercial Register (Commercial Register Ordinance) (HRV), Liechtenstein Law Gazette (2003).

GOVERNMENT OF THE PRINCIPALITY OF LIECHTENSTEIN, Ordinance of 29 October 2002 on the Protection of Design (Design Ordinance) (DesV), Liechtenstein Law Gazette (2002).

Keyword-Index

Appendix 1 - Law of 3 October 2019 on Tokens and TT Service Providers (Token and TT Service Provider Act; TVTG)

Disclaimer

English is not an official language of the Principality of Liechtenstein. This translation is provided for information purposes only and has no legal force. The contents of the website https://www.regierung.li/law, where the latest version of translations may be found, have been compiled with the utmost care to reflect the current situation and the current state of knowledge. However, the Government of the Principality of Liechtenstein cannot accept any liability if any of its contents should be found to be inaccurate, incomplete or out of date.

Liechtenstein Legal Gazette

2019 No. 301 published on 2 December 2019

Law

of 03 October 2019

on Tokens and TT Service Providers (Token and TT Service Provider Act; TVTG)

I hereby grant my consent to the following resolution adopted by Parliament:[1]

I. General provisions

Art. 1

Object and Purpose

1) This law establishes the legal framework for all transaction systems based on Trustworthy Technology and in particular governs:

a) The basis in terms of civil law with regard to Tokens and the representation of rights through Tokens and their transfer;

b) The supervision and rights and obligations of TT Service Providers.

2) It aims:

a) to ensure trust in digital legal communication, in particular in the financial and economic sector and the protection of users in TT Systems;

b) to create excellent, innovation-friendly and technology-neutral framework conditions for rendering services concerning TT Systems.

1 Report and application, together with Comments from the Government No. 54/2019 and 93/2019

Art. 2

Definitions and designations

1) The following definitions are established for the purposes of this Act:

a) "Trustworthy Technology (TT)": Technologies through which the integrity of Tokens, the clear assignment of Tokens to TT Identifiers and the disposal over Tokens is ensured;

b) "TT Systems": Transaction systems which allow for the secure transfer and storage of Tokens and the rendering of services based on this by means of trustworthy technology;

c) "Token": a piece of information on a TT System which:

   1. can represent claims or rights of memberships against a person, rights to property or other absolute or relative rights; and
   2. is assigned to one or more TT Identifiers;

d) "TT Identifier": an identifier that allows for the clear assignment of Tokens;

e) "TT Keys": a key that allows for disposal over Tokens;

f) "Users": people who dispose over Tokens and/or use the TT Services;

g) "Token Issuance": the public offering of Tokens;

h) "Basic Information": Information about Tokens to be offered to the public, enabling the user to make a judgement about the rights and risks associated with the Tokens as well as the TT service providers involved;

i) "TT Service Provider": a person who exercises one or more functions under letters k to u;[2]

k) "Token Issuer": a person who publicly offers the Tokens in their own name or in the name of a client;

l) "Token Generator": a person who generates one or more Tokens;

m) "TT Key Depositary": a person who safeguards TT Keys for clients;

n) "TT Token Depositary": a person who safeguards Token in the name and on account of others;

o) "TT Protector": a person who holds Tokens on TT Systems in their own name on account for a third party;

2 Article 2(1) letter i amended by LGBl. 2021 no. 36.

p) "Physical Validator": a person who ensures the enforcement of rights in accordance with the agreement, in terms of property law, represented in Tokens on TT systems;

q) "TT Exchange Service Provider": a person, who exchanges legal tender against Tokens and vice versa and Tokens for Tokens;

r) "TT Verifying Authority": a person who verifies the legal capacity and the requirements for disposal over a Token;

s) "TT Price Service Provider": a person who provides TT System users with aggregated price information on the basis of purchase and sale offers or completed transactions;

t) "TT Identity Service Provider": a person who identifies the person in possession of the right of disposal related to a Token and records it in a directory.

u) "TT Agent": a person who distributes or provides TT Services in Liechtenstein on a professional basis in the name of and for the account of a foreign TT Service Provider.[3]

2) The designations used in this Act to denote persons and functions include persons of male and female gender.

II. Civil basis

Art. 3

Object and scope

1) This chapter governs the qualification of Tokens and their disposal on TT Systems under civil law.

2) It applies if:

a) Tokens are generated or issued by a TT Service Provider with headquarters or place of residence in Liechtenstein; or

b) Parties declare its provisions to expressly apply in a legal transaction over Tokens.

3) Articles 4 to 6 and 9 also apply correspondingly to Tokens that do not represent any rights.

3 Article 2(1) letter u inserted by LGBl. 2021 no. 36.

Art. 4

Qualification of Tokens

If Liechtenstein Law is applicable according to article 3, the Token is considered to be an asset located in Liechtenstein.

Art. 5

Power of Disposal and Right of Disposal

1) The TT Key holder has the power of disposal over the Token.

2) It is further assumed that the person possessing the power of disposal over a Token also has the right to dispose of the Token. For every previous holder of the power of disposal, it is presumed that he was the person possessing the right of disposal at the time of his ownership.

3) If someone is the holder of a power of disposal without wanting to be the person possessing the right of disposal, he can rely on the person from whom he received the Token in good faith is the person possessing the right of disposal.

Art. 6

Disposal over Tokens

1) Disposal is:

a) the transfer of the right of disposal to the Token; or

b) the justification of a securities or a right of usufruct to a Token.

2) Disposal over a Token requires that:

a) the transfer of the Token is concluded in line with the regulations of the TT System, where a restricted in rem right to a Token can also be ordered without transfer, if this is apparent to third parties and clearly establishes the time of ordering;

b) the transferring party and the recipient party unanimously declare that they are transferring the right of disposal to the Token or that they wish to justify a restricted in rem right; and

c) the transferring party is the person possessing the right of disposal pursuant to article 5; article 9 remains unaffected.

3) If a Token is disposed over without reason or a subsequent reason fails to exist, the revocation shall be accomplished in accordance with the provisions of the Enrichment Law (§§ 1431 et seq. ABGB).

Art. 7

Effects of Disposal

1) Disposal over the Token results in the disposal over the right represented by the Token.

2) If the legal effect under (1) does not come into force by law, the person obliged as a result of the disposal over the Token must ensure, through suitable measures, that:

a) the disposal over a Token directly or indirectly results in the disposal over the represented right, and

b) a competing disposal over the represented right is excluded.

3) The disposal over a Token is also legally binding in the event of enforcement proceedings against the transferor and effective vis-à-vis third parties, if the transfer:

a) was activated in the TT system prior to the commencement of the legal proceedings, or

b) was activated in the TT the system after the initiation of the legal proceedings and was executed on the day of the proceeding's openings, provided that the accepting party proves that he was without knowledge of the proceedings openings or would have remained without knowledge upon the exercise of due diligence.

Art. 8

Legitimacy and exemption

1) The person possessing the right of disposal reported by the TT System is considered the lawful holder of the right represented in the Token in respect of the Obligor.

2) By payment, the Obligor is withdrawn from his obligation against the person who has the power of disposal as reported by the TT system, unless he knew, or should have known with due care, that he is not the lawful owner of the right.

Art. 9

Acquisition in Good Faith

Those who receive Tokens in good faith, free of charge, for the purpose of acquiring the right of disposal or a restricted in rem right is to be protected in his acquisition, even if the transferring party was not entitled to the disposal over the Token unless the recipient party had been aware of the lack of right of disposal or should have been aware of such upon the exercise of due diligence.

Art. 10

Cancellation of Tokens

1) If a TT Key is unaccounted for or a Token is otherwise not functional, the person who possessed the right of disposal at the time of the loss or when the Token became non-functional can apply for the Token to be cancelled in non-contentious proceedings.

2) For this purpose, the applicant must convince the court of their right of disposal and the loss of the TT Key or the non-functionality of the Token.

3) The respondent is the person obliged from the right represented in the Token.

4) The declaration that a Token is non-functional shall be published without delay in the Official Journal and at the discretion of the District Court in any other appropriate manner.

5) The applicant may also assert their right without the Token upon cancellation or demand the generation of a new Token at their own expense.

III. Supervision of TT Service Providers

A. General

Art. 11

Object and scope

1) This chapter governs the registration and supervision of TT Service Providers with headquarters or place of residence in Liechtenstein and their rights and obligations.

2) It does not apply to the country, municipalities or municipal associations or public companies when acting as officials.

B. Registration of TT Service Providers

1. Obligation and requirements of registration

Art. 12

Registration obligation

1) Persons with headquarters or place of residence in Liechtenstein who wish to professionally act as TT Service Providers must apply to be entered into the TT Service Provider Register in writing (article 23) with the FMA before providing a service for the first time.

2) Token Issuers with headquarters or place of residence in Liechtenstein who issue Tokens in their own name or in the name of a client in a non-professional capacity must apply to be entered into the TT Service Provider Register in writing with the FMA before beginning their activity of Tokens in the amount of CHF 5 million or more will be issued within a period of twelve months.

3) Persons with headquarters or place of residence abroad who wish to provide TT Services using automatic teller machines in Liechtenstein must apply in writing to the FMA for entry in the TT Service Provider Register before the automatic teller machines are put into operation for the first time.[4]

4 Article 12(3) inserted by LGBl. 2021 no. 36.

Art. 13

Registration requirements

1) An entry in the TT Service Provider Register (article 23) requires the applicant to:

a) be capable of action;

b) be reliable (article 14);

c) be technically suitable (article 15);

d) have their headquarters or place of residence in Liechtenstein;

e) have the necessary minimum capital (article 16), where appropriate;

f) have a suitable organisational structure with defined areas of responsibility and a procedure to deal with conflicts of interest;

g) have written internal proceedings and control mechanisms that are appropriate in terms of the type, scope, complexity and risks of the TT Services provided, including ensuring sufficient documentation of these mechanisms;

e) have special internal control mechanisms (article 17), where appropriate;

i) have authorisation pursuant to the Trustees Act if they intend to act as a TT Protector; and

k) if they intend to conduct activity that is subject to an additional authorisation obligation in accordance with a law pursuant to article 5(1) of the Financial Market Supervision Act, for which the corresponding authorisation is available.

1a) (1) letters e to i do not apply to TT Agents.[5]

2) The government may rewrite the registration requirements in (1) subject to articles 14 to 17 in more detail by issuing an ordinance.

Art. 14

Reliability

1) A natural person is excluded from rendering a TT Service if:

a) they have not been convicted by a court for defrauding of creditors, detriment to third-party creditors, favouring of a creditor, or grossly negligent interference with creditor interests (§§ 156 to 159 of the

5 Article 13(1a) inserted by LGBl. 2021 no. 36.

Criminal Code, StGB), or have been sentenced for any other act to imprisonment of more than three years or a monetary penalty of more than 180 daily rates and the conviction has not been expunged; and[6]

b) they have not been convicted in the ten years prior to their application due to severe or repeated violations of the provisions of the Law on Unfair Competition, the Consumer Protection Act or a law pursuant to article 5(1) of the Financial Market Supervision Act;

c) they have been subject to a futile seizure in the five years prior to application;

d) bankruptcy proceedings were opened in respect of them in the five years prior to application or an application to open insolvency proceedings was rejected due to insufficient assets to cover the cost; or[7]

e) there is another reason which creates serious doubt concerning their reliability.

2) (1) letters a to d also applies for foreign decisions and proceedings if the underlying action is also a criminal offence pursuant to Liechtenstein law.

3) For legal persons, the requirements under (1) must be met by members of their bodies and shareholders, partners or holders who hold a qualified investment of 10 % or more in a legal person.

4) Upon request, the FMA may allow for exclusion under (1) and (2) if committing the same or similar offence when rendering the TT Service is not to be expected in consideration of the nature of the criminal offence and the personality of the person sentenced.

Art. 15

Technical suitability

Those who are sufficiently technically qualified due to their education or prior career for the task in question shall be considered technically suitable.

6 Article 14(1) letter a amended by LGBl. 2020 no. 414.

7 Article 14(1) letter d amended by LGBl. 2020 no. 414.

Art. 16

Minimum capital

1) Applicants who intend to act as TT Service Providers pursuant to article 2(1) letters l, n, o, p and r must have the appropriate minimum capital or a guarantee of the same value before starting their activity. Minimum capital is:

a) for Token Issuers pursuant to article 12(1):
   1. 50,000 Francs to the extent that Tokens with a total value of up to and including 5 million Francs are issued during one calendar year;
   2. 100,000 Francs, if Tokens with a total value of more than 5 million Francs up to and including 25 million Francs are issued within a period of twelve months;
   3. 250,000 Francs to the extent that Tokens with a total value of more than 25 million Francs are issued during one calendar year;

b) for TT Key Depositories: 100,000 Francs;

c) for TT Token Depositories: 100,000 Francs;

d) for TT Exchange Service Providers:
   1. 30,000 Francs, if transactions with a total value of more than 150,000 Francs up to and including 1 million Francs are carried out within a period of twelve months;
   2. 100,000 Francs, if transactions with a total value of more than 1 million Francs are carried out within a period of twelve months;

e) for Physical Validators:
   1. 125,000 Francs if the value of the property, the contractual enforcements of which are guaranteed by the Physical Validator, does not exceed 10 million Francs;
   2. 250,000 Francs if the value of the property, the contractual enforcements of which are guaranteed by the Physical Validator, exceeds 10 million Francs.

2) The minimum capital requirements under (1) must be adhered to at all times.

3) Applicants who intend to provide multiple TT Services shall meet the highest minimum capital requirement under (1).

Art. 17

Special internal control mechanisms

1) Applicants who intend to act as TT Service Providers pursuant to article 2(1) letters k to t must have suitable internal control mechanisms before starting their activity which ensure the following:

a) for Token Issuers:
   1. disclosure of basic information (articles 30 to 38) at any time during Token Issuance and for at least ten years afterwards;
   2. the prevention of abuse with regard to the option of Token recipients waiving basic information (article 31(1)(a));
   3. the execution of Token Issuance according to the conditions of the basic information;
   4. the maintenance of the provided services in the event of interruptions during the Token Issuance (business continuity management);

b) for Token Generators, the use of suitable measures which ensure that:
   1. the right in the Token is correctly represented during the Token's lifetime;
   2. that the disposal over a Token directly results in the disposal over the represented right;
   3. a competing disposal over the represented right are excluded both under the rules of the TT system and the provisions of applicable law.

c) for TT Key Depositories:
   1. establishing suitable security measures which in particular prevent the loss or abuse of TT Keys;
   2. the separate safekeeping of customers' TT Keys from the business assets of the TT Key Depositary; and
   3. the maintenance of the services in the event of interruptions (business continuity management);

d) for TT Token Depositories:
   1. establishing suitable security measures which in particular prevent the loss or abuse of TT Keys;
   2. the separate safekeeping of customers' Tokens from the business assets of the TT Token Depositary; and
   3. the clear assignment of Tokens to customers;

4. the execution of customers' orders in line with contracts;
5. the maintenance of the services in the event of interruptions (business continuity management);

e) for Physical Validators, their liability in the event that rights to property guaranteed by the Physical Validator cannot be enforced in accordance with the contract;

f) for TT Protectors:
   1. establishing suitable security measures which in particular prevent the loss or abuse of TT Keys;
   2 the separate safekeeping of customers' Tokens and business assets of the TT Protector; and
   3. the clear assignment of Tokens to customers;
   4. the execution of customers' orders in line with contracts;
   5. the maintenance of the services in the event of interruptions (business continuity management);

g) for TT Exchange Service Providers:
   1. the disclosure of comparable market prices of the traded Tokens;
   2. the disclosure of the purchase and sale prices of the traded Tokens;

h) for TT Verifying Authorities, the use of suitable measures which ensure that the verification services it offers are rendered reliably;

i) for TT Price Service Providers:
   1. the transparency of the published prices;
   2. the avoidance of conflicts of interest when setting prices;
   3. the disclosure of information to affected users regarding transactions concerning related parties.

k) for TT Identity Service Providers:
   1. the use of suitable measures that allow for the identity of the person possessing the right of disposal to be established; in doing so, it must be ensured that:
      aa) for natural persons or representatives of legal person present in person, their identity is determined based on official photo identification or by other evidence that has been or is to be document which is just as reliable; for representatives of legal persons, it must moreover be ensured that the necessary power of representation has been determined;

bb) for natural persons or legal persons not present in person, other identification methods are to be applied that allow for identification equivalent to under letter aa) to be determined;

2. the specific assignment of TT Identifiers to the lawful holder;
3. the secure storage of customer data.

2) The obligations arising from the internal control mechanisms under (1) must always be complied with.

2. Registration procedure

Art. 18

Registration application

1) The registration application pursuant to article 12 must include the following information and documents:

a) name or company and address of the applicant;
b) information about the intended TT Service;
c) information about the TT Systems to be used during the planned TT Service;
d) information about the legal nature of the applicant, in the event that the applicant is a legal entity;
e) evidence that the requirements pursuant to articles 13 to 17 have been met;
f) further information and documents at the request of the FMA if necessary to assess the registration application.

2) The registration application and the information and documents under (1) may be submitted in electronic form to the FMA. The FMA may demand certificates to be submitted in the original, or be notarised or apostilled.

3) Changes in the information and facts under (1) must be reported to the FMA without delay. This notification to the FMA must be made prior to any public announcement.

4)The FMA may waive the submission of certain information and documents under (1) if it already has access to them, in particular because:

a) the applicant already has authorisation according to the Financial Market Supervision Act;
b) the applicant is already registered to render another TT Service than the one he is applying for; or
c) the application has already been registered for the same TT Service.

5) The government shall regulate the registration application in more detail, in particular the evidence under (1)(e) by means of an ordinance.

Art. 19

Entry into the TT Service Provider Register

1) Based on the complete application and the information or documents submitted, the FMA must verify whether the registration requirements have been met.

2) The FMA must decide on the full application within three months.

3) If all registration requirements have been met, the FMA must enter the applicant into the TT Service Provider Register (article 23) and inform the applicant of the entry by sending an excerpt from the TT Service Provider Register. The FMA may carry out registration subject to conditions and obligations; the conditions and obligations must be available.

4) If the registration requirements are not met, the FMA must establish this within the period specified in (2), notwithstanding a procedure according to article 46 and prohibit the exercise of the TT Service in question.

5) The TT Service applied for may only be exercised for the first time after having been entered into the TT Service Provider Register.

3. Expiration and removal

Art. 20

Expiration of Registration

1) Registration in accordance with article 19 will expire if:
a) the business has not commenced within a year;
b) the business activity was not carried out for more than one year;

c) the registration is waived in writing;

d) bankruptcy proceedings have been opened in respect of the TT Service Provider with legal effect or an application to open insolvency proceedings was rejected due to insufficient assets to cover the cost; or[8]

e) the TT Service Provider's company has been deleted from the Commercial Register.

2) In justified circumstances the FMA may, upon application, extend the time-limits pursuant to (1) letters a and b.

3) The revocation of a registration must be communicated in writing to the TT Service Provider in question. After becoming legally effective the revocation must be published in the Official Journal at the expense of the TT Service Provider and must be noted in the TT Service Provider Register in accordance with article 23.

Art. 21

Removal of the registration

The FMA must remove a registration pursuant to article 19 if:

a) the registration requirements are no longer met;

b) the FMA was not aware of significant circumstances during registration;

c) the registration as a TT Service Provider expired due to false information or for other reasons;

d) a TT Service Provider systematically or seriously violates its legal obligations; or

e) a TT Service Provider does not comply with the FMA's requests to restore the lawful status in accordance with (2).

2) The FMA requests the affected TT Service Provider to restore the legal status in the cases according to (1) letters a and b, setting a time-limit of at least four weeks. If the request cannot be sent to the TT Service Provider due to a lack of delivery address or a lack of legal bodies, the invitation will be published once in the Official Journal.

3) The revocation of a registration must be communicated in writing to the TT Service Provider in question. After becoming legally effective, the revocation must be published in the Official Journal at the expense of

8 Article 20(1) letter d amended by LGBl. 2020 no. 414.

the TT Service Provider and must be noted in the TT Service Provider Register in accordance with (23).

Art. 22

Effect of the expiration and removal of the registration

1) With the expiration or removal of the registration pursuant to articles 20 and 21, the TT Service Provider must cease activity immediately.

2) The TT Service Provider must take the necessary precautions to ensure the interests of its clients are not impaired by the discontinuation of activities, and further, inform the FMA of these precautions immediately by providing a relevant description of the same.

3) If the FMA recognises that the precautions are insufficient, it must monitor implementation, and if necessary, commission an audit office to monitor implementation. The associated costs will be borne by the affected TT Service Provider.

4. TT Service Provider Register

Art. 23

Maintenance of the TT Service Provider Register

1) The FMA must maintain a publicly accessible register in which the following information must be entered:

a) the TT Service Providers registered in Liechtenstein, citing the date of registration;
b) the scope of the registered TT Services pursuant to article 12 including any possible requirements with the date of the entry of the TT Service in question;
c) the expiration or removal of the registration pursuant to articles 20 and 21.

2 The FMA must verify entries under (1) based on a notification pursuant to article 18(3) and update them immediately if necessary.

3) The FMA must make the TT Service Provider Register available free of charge on its website. In addition, the FMA must grant any person access to the TT Service Provider Register at its physical office location, so long as technically feasible.

5. Exercising of business activity

Art. 24

Designation Protection

1) Designations that indicate activity as a TT Service Provider, may only be used in the company, in the designation of the business purpose and in the company's advertising, by registered TT Service Providers.

2) The government can regulate the details of the designation protection by means of an ordinance.

Art. 25

Safeguarding Requirements

1) Tokens held on a fiduciary basis or in the name of the customer shall be deemed third-party assets in proceedings to secure rights or in the case of compulsory execution and insolvency proceedings of the TT Service Provider and shall be segregated in favour of the customer, subject to all claims of the TT Service Provider against the customer. The Tokens must be protected against claims of the TT Service Provider's other creditors, particularly in the event of bankruptcy proceedings, in the interest of the users. Tokens must be stored separately from the TT Service Provider's assets at all times.[9]

2) TT Keys which a TT Service Provider holds or keeps in safe custody for a customer in its own name or in the name of a third party shall be deemed third-party assets in proceedings to secure rights or in the case of compulsory execution and insolvency proceedings of the TT Service Provider and shall be segregated in favour of the customer, subject to all claims of the TT Service Provider against the customer. The TT Keys must be protected against claims of the TT Service Provider's other creditors, particularly in the event of bankruptcy proceedings, in the interest of the users.[10]

3) Upon request, during ongoing business operations, a TT Service Provider must present proof to the FMA showing that he has taken sufficient measures to comply with the requirements specified in (1). If the evidence is not provided or if the measures are insufficient, the FMA shall request that TT Service Provider furnish the necessary evidence or

9 Article 25(1) amended by LGBl. 2020 no. 414.

10 Article 25(2) amended by LGBl. 2020 no. 414.

take suitable and necessary precautions to remedy the existing defects. This must be carried out in accordance with an appropriate deadline set by the FMA. If the supporting documents are not submitted or precautions are not taken at all, or within the time frame stipulated by the FMA, the FMA may take further measures, in particular, those set out in article 43(5).

4) In the event of execution against the user's TT Service Provider, the user may raise an objection under public law (article 20 of the Execution Act) if the execution relates to the Tokens secured in accordance with (1) or the TT Keys secured in accordance with (2). Under the same conditions, in the event of bankruptcy proceedings in respect of the assets of the TT Service Provider, the user has the right to segregation (article 41 of the Insolvency Act).[11]

Art. 26

Storage of Records and Supporting Documents

1) TT Service Providers must keep relevant records and supporting documents for supervisory purposes for at least ten years.

2) More specific legal obligations remain unaffected.

Art. 27

Outsourcing Functions

1) The outsourcing of important operational functions is permitted if:

a) the quality of the internal control of the TT Service Provider is not significantly impacted;
b) the obligations of the TT Service Provider remain unchanged according to this Act; and
c) the registration requirements according to this Act are not undermined.

2) In this context, an operational function is particularly important if it, only partially fulfilled or neglected, would significantly affect the TT Service Provider's ongoing compliance with its obligations under this Act or its financial performance.

11 Article 25(4) amended by LGBl. 2020 no. 414.

3) A TT Service Provider outsourcing functions must take adequate precautions to ensure that the requirements of this Act are met.

4) Special statutory regulations on the outsourcing of functions remain reserved.

Art. 28

Reporting obligations

1) TT Service Providers must inform the FMA immediately of:

a) all changes with regard to the registration requirements;
b) the cessation of business activities;
c) the removal of the TT Service Provider from the Commercial Register;
d) the existence of another reason for cancellation pursuant to article 20.

2) TT Service Providers must inform the FMA of all information about its business activity required to exercise supervision.

3) The government shall regulate reporting obligations, in particular the frequency and content of the notifications under (2) in more detail by means of an ordinance.

Art. 29

Publication obligations

TT Service Providers must publish the following in a way that can be accessed by the public at any time:

a) information about the TT Systems it uses;
b) a declaration on the suitability of the TT Systems it uses for the application purposes in question; and
c) information about any possible change in a TT System, including a relevant justification.

6. Basic information for Token Issuance

Art. 30

Obligation to compile and publish basic information and to display the Token Issuance

Subject to (31), before issuing Tokens Token Issuers must:

a) prepare basic information according to the following provisions;

b) publish the basic information in an easily accessible way; and

c) report the Token Issuance to the FMA.

Art. 31

Exceptions

1) The obligations pursuant to article 30(a) and (b) shall not apply for public offerings of Tokens if:

a) all recipient parties demonstrably declare that they waive the basic information before acquiring the Token;

b) the offer is geared towards fewer than 150 users;

c) the sale price of the total issue does not exceed 5 million Francs or the corresponding equivalent in another currency; or

d) there is already an obligation to publish qualified information about the public offering of Tokens according to other laws.

2) No additional basic information needs to be published for any later public resale of Tokens if:

a) the basic information pursuant to article 30 has already been published; and

b) the issuer or the person responsible for preparing the basic information has approved its use in a written agreement.

Art. 32

Form and language of the basic information

1) Basic information must be prepared and published in a way that is easy to analyse and understand.

2) Basic information can be prepared and published in one or several documents.

3) If basic information consists of several documents, then the Token Issuer must prepare and publish a brief, easily understandable summary with information about the Token Issuer and the Tokens to be issued.

4) Basic information must be prepared and published in German or English.

Art. 33

Content of the basic information

1) Basic information must in particular include the following:

a) information about the Tokens to be issued and associated rights;
b) the name of the TT system used;
c) a description of the purpose and nature of the legal transaction underlying the Token Issuance;
d) a description of the purchase and transfer conditions for the Tokens;
e) information about the risks associated with purchasing the Tokens;
f) for the issuance of Tokens, the rights to property represent:
   1. evidence of a registered Physical Validator regarding ownership of the property; and
   2. a confirmation from a registered Physical Validator, that the rights registered in the issued Tokens are also enforceable in line with the basic information.

2) The basic information, moreover, includes a summary, which contains brief and generally understandable essential information in the language, in which the basic information was originally prepared. The summary must also include warnings that:

a) it is to be understood as an overview of the subsequent basic information;
b) the recipient party must read all of the basic information before purchasing; and
c) persons who have assumed responsibility for the summary, including its translation, or who prepare the summary or translation can only however be made liable in the event that the summary is misleading, incorrect or inconsistent if read together with other parts of the basic information.

3) The basic information must include the names and roles (and, for legal persons, the company and headquarters) of those who are responsible for the content. The basic information must include a declaration by these persons that the information is correct to the best of their knowledge and that no significant information has been left out.

4) The basic information must also include the names and roles (and, for legal persons, the company and headquarters) of those who are responsible for the technical and legal functionality of the Token.

5) The Token Issuer must put an issuance date on the basic information and ensure it cannot be amended through suitable measures.

6) The government may regulate the content of the basic information in more detail by means of an ordinance.

Art. 34

Addendum to the basic information

1) Every new material fact or every material error or inaccuracy with regard to the basic information that is determined after the basic information is first published must be named in an addendum to the basic information.

2) In addition, the summary and any translations of the summary must be supplemented by the information included in the addendum.

3) The government may regulate the addendum to the basic information in more detail by means of an ordinance.

Art. 35

Liability

1) If any facts in the basic information that is to be prepared according to this Act are incorrect or incomplete, or if the basic information in accordance with these provisions was not prepared, the persons responsible under articles 33(3) and (4) shall be liable to every user for damages that arise as a result, provided they do not demonstrate that they took the due care of a prudent businessman when preparing the basic information. Only damage directly suffered is considered to be damage, not also loss of profit.

2) The persons named in (1) shall also be liable for their vicarious agents and for the persons they employ, provided they do not demonstrate that the took the due care according to the circumstances in their selection, instruction and supervision.

3) Liability under (1) and (2) can be neither be excluded nor restricted in advance to the detriment of users in the event of intent or gross negligence.

4) Liability shall only be borne for information in the summary including its translations if they are misleading, incorrect or inconsistent in connection with other parts of the basic information or do not convey all material information. The summary must include a clear warning in this respect.

Art. 36

Severability

If several persons are liable to pay compensation for a damage, each of them shall be held jointly and severally liable with the others so long as the damage is personally attributable to their own negligence and circumstances.

Art. 37

Jurisdiction

The Court of Justice shall have jurisdiction for claims of the transferee of Token regarding the legal relationship with the Token Issuer with headquarters within the country.

Art. 38

Statute of limitations

Any claim for damages against the persons who are responsible in accordance with the above provisions will be barred by the statute of limitations one year from the date on which the cause of action accrues, the cause of action accruing on the date the injured party is both aware of the damage and the identity of the party liable for the damage, expiring regardless, ten years from the date of the harmful act.

C. Supervision

Art. 39

Jurisdiction

The Financial Markets Authority (FMA) is responsible for the supervision of TT Service Providers and the execution of the associated statutory provisions.

Art. 40

Official secrecy

1) The FMA, any other persons consulted by these authorities and bodies and all representatives of public authorities shall be subject to official secrecy without any time limits with respect to the confidential information that they gain knowledge of in the course of their official activities.

2) Confidential information within the scope (1) may be transmitted in accordance with this Act or special statutory provisions.

3) If bankruptcy proceedings have been opened or liquidation proceedings have been initiated in respect of a TT Service Provider by the decision of a court, confidential information which does not relate to third parties may be disclosed in civil law proceedings, provided this is necessary for the proceedings concerned.[12]

4) Without prejudice to cases covered by the requirements of criminal law, the FMA, all other administrative authorities, courts and bodies, natural persons or legal entities may only use confidential information that they receive in accordance with this Act only for purposes of fulfilling their responsibilities and tasks within the scope of this Act or for purposes for which the information was given, and/or in the case of administrative and judicial proceedings that specifically relate to the fulfilment of these tasks, provided this is required to do so. If the FMA, another administrative authority, court, body, or a person transmitting information, gives its consent; then the authority receiving the information may use it for other financial market supervision purposes.

12 Article 40(3) amended by LGBl. 2020 no. 414.

Art. 41

Cooperation Between National Authorities and Agencies

The FMA works with other competent national authorities and agencies provided this is required to fulfil its duties under this Act.

Art. 42

Processing and transferring personal data

1) The FMA and other competent national authorities and agencies may process personal data, including personal data regarding criminal sentences and offences of the persons subject to this Act, or have such processed, if this is necessary in order to fulfil its duties under this Act.

2) They may send personal data to each other or other competent authorities in other EEC member states if this is necessary in order to fulfil its duties under this Act.

3) They may send personal data to the competent authorities of third-party states if the data protection requirements under chapter V of Regulation (EU) 2016/679 have been met in addition to the requirements under (2).

Art. 43

FMA duties and authorisations

1) In the course of its supervision, the FMA monitors compliance with the provisions of this Act and its associated ordinances.

2) The FMA is responsible for the following duties in particular:

a) registering TT Service Providers and the removal of registrations;
b) issuing information about the application of this Act or another Act listed in article 5(1) FMAG (Financial Markets Supervision Act) for clearly determined facts in connection with Trustworthy Technology;
c) maintaining the TT Service Provider Register in accordance with article 23;
d) the prosecution of contraventions in accordance with article 47(2).

3) The FMA has all necessary authority to perform its duties and may, in particular:

a) require TT Service Providers to provide all information and documents required for the execution of this Act;
b) order or carry out extraordinary audits;
c) make decisions and ordinances;
d) issue legally binding decisions and rulings;
e) carry out on-site inspections of TT Service Providers; and
f) correct false information that has been published by naming the TT Service Provider involve and issue warnings;
g) temporarily prohibit the exercising of a TT Service.

4) If the FMA becomes aware of violations of this Act or of other deficits, it shall take the measures necessary to bring about a lawful state of affairs and to eliminate the deficits.

5) The FMA may assign an expert as its observer to a TT Service Provider if the interests of users or creditors appear to be acutely endangered by mismanagement. The external audit office appointed may be entrusted with this responsibility. The observer shall monitor the activities of the governing bodies, in particular the implementation of the measures ordered, and shall report to the FMA on an ongoing basis. The observer shall enjoy the unrestricted right to inspect the business activities and the books and files of the TT Service Provider. The cost of the supervisor must be borne by the TT Service Provider, insofar as a reasonable relationship exists between the work associated with the activity and its expenses.

6) If there is reason to assume that a person is rendering TT Services without authorisation pursuant to this Act, the FMA may demand information and documents from the person concerned if this person is a subordinate person. In urgent cases, the FMA may order the immediate cessation of the activity without prior warning and without imposing a deadline.

7) The costs incurred due to misconduct shall be borne by those responsible in accordance with article 26 of the Financial Market Supervision Act.

8) The government may regulate the details of the tasks and powers of the FMA by means of an ordinance.

Art. 44

Supervision taxes and fees

The Supervision taxes and fees are based on the Financial Market Supervision Act.

D. Proceedings and Legal Remedies

Art. 45

Proceedings

To the extent not otherwise specified in this Act, the provisions of the National Administration Act (LVG) shall apply to proceedings.

Art. 46

Legal remedy

1) Decisions and decrees of the FMA may be appealed within 14 days of service to the FMA Complaints Commission.

2) Decisions and decrees of the FMA Complaints Commission may be appealed within 14 days of service to the Administrative Court.

E. Penal Provisions

Art. 47

Offences and infractions

1) The following persons shall be penalised by the District Court for offences with up to one year imprisonment or a fine of up to 360 daily rates:

a) those who render TT Services requiring registration contrary to article 12;

b) those who use a designation contrary to article 24 which suggests activity as a TT Service Provider;

c) those whose registration as a TT Service Provider expired due to false information or other illegal matters; or

d) those who systematically violate their legal obligations in a serious manner as a TT Service Provider.

2) If the action does not constitute a criminal offence within the jurisdiction of the courts, TT Service Providers shall be fined by the FMA by up to 100,000 Francs due to an infraction, if:

a) they do not comply with the minimum capital requirements under article 16;

b) they do not have the internal control mechanisms listed in (17);

c) they violate the reporting obligations under article 18(3) and article 28;

d) they do not comply with the FMA requirements and conditions associated with registration pursuant to article 19(3);

a) they violate the security obligations pursuant to article 25;

f) they do not keep records, or keep insufficient records or do not store supporting documents contrary to article 26;

g) they outsource important operational functions without meeting the requirements pursuant to article 27;

a) they violate they publication obligations pursuant to article 29;

i) they violate their obligations in connection with the preparation and publication of basic information or the display of the Token Issuance pursuant to (30) ff.;

i) they fail to comply with a decree or order issued to them by the FMA with reference to the threat of punishment under this article.

3) The FMA must impose fines against legal persons if the infractions under (2) are committed in execution of the course of business of legal persons (offences) by persons who have either acted alone or as a member of the Administrative Board, Management Board or Supervisory Board of the legal person or another management position within the legal person, based on which they:

a) are authorised to outwardly represent the legal person;

b) exercise supervisory powers in a management position; or

c) otherwise exercise significant influence over the management of the legal person.

4) For infractions under (2) committed by the employees of the legal person, even if not culpably, the legal person is also responsible if the infraction is enabled or significantly facilitated as a result of the persons named in (3) failing to take the necessary and appropriate measures to prevent such offences.

5) The responsibility of the legal person for the offence and the punishability of the persons named in (3) or the employees named in (4) due to the same offence are not mutually exclusive. The FMA may refrain from pursuing a natural person if a fine has already been imposed on a legal person for the same violation and there are no other circumstances that oppose refraining from pursuing the natural person.

6) In the event of negligent conduct, the upper penalty limits in (1) and (2) above shall be halved.

Art. 48

Responsibility

Where violations are committed in the business operations of a legal person, the penal provisions shall apply to the members of management and other natural persons who acted or should have acted on its behalf. With all persons, including the legal entity, shall, however, be jointly and severally liable for monetary penalties, fines and costs.

Art. 49

Announcing sanctions; binding effect of convictions

1) The FMA may announce the imposition of lawful punishments at the expense of the party concerned if this fulfils the purpose of this Act and is proportionate.

2) A conviction under this Act shall not be binding for the civil court judge with regard to the assessment of guilt, unlawfulness and determination of damage.

IV. Transitional and final provisions

Art. 50

Transitional provisions

1) Persons who render a TT Service requiring registration pursuant to article 12 at the time that this Act comes into force undertake:

(a) to carry out their business in accordance with (25) to (38) in doing so, they may continue to use previous designations according to (24) until the expiry of the period according to letter b without registration; and

b) to apply for the entry into the TT Service Provider Register to the FMA within a period of twelve months after this Act comes into force; otherwise, the right to render TT Services under this Act shall expire.

2) The provisions regarding the basis for Tokens under civil law according to chapter II may also be applied by the parties for Tokens that were generated before this Act came into force according to article 3(2)(b).

3) The provisions on the basic information for Token Issuance according to articles 30 to 28 shall apply to Tokens that are publicly offered for the first time after this Act comes into force.

Art. 51

Entry into force

Provided that the referendum deadline expires unutilised this Act shall enter into force on 01 January 2020, otherwise on the day after the announcement.

Representing the Reigning Prince:
signed *Alois*
Hereditary Prince

signed *Adrian Hasler*
Prime Minister

Transitional provisions

950.6 Law on Tokens and TT Service Providers (Token and TT Service Provider Act; TVTG)

Liechtenstein Legal Gazette

2021 No. 36 published on 26 January 2021

Law

of 3 December 2020

amending the Token and TT Service Provider Act

...

II.

Transitional provision

Persons who at the time of entry into force[13] of this Act exercise an activity as a TT Agent subject to registration pursuant to article 12 must apply in writing to the FMA for entry in the TT Service Provider Register within a period of six months after entry into force of this Act; otherwise, the right to render TT Services as a TT Agent shall expire.

...

13 Entry into force: 1 April 2021.